Theory, Application, and Implementation of Monte Carlo Method in Science and Technology

Edited by Pooneh Saidi Bidokhti

Published in London, United Kingdom

IntechOpen

Supporting open minds since 2005

Theory, Application, and Implementation of Monte Carlo Method in Science and Technology
http://dx.doi.org/10.5772/intechopen.78141
Edited by Pooneh Saidi Bidokhti

Contributors
Hossam Donya, Baljeet Seniwal, Reem Darwesh, Telma Cristina Ferreira Fonseca, Sherif Sherif, Ivan Lima Jr., Pooneh Saidi Bidokhti, Mahdi Sadeghi, Artur Chrobak, Grzegorz Ziółkowska, Dariusz Chrobak, Fethi Khelfaoui, Oumelkheir Babahani, Bernt Leira, Sebastian Thons, Arifian Agusta, Gabriela Hoff, Bruno Golosio, Elaine Streck, Viviana Fanti

First published in London, United Kingdom, 2019 by IntechOpen
IntechOpen is the global imprint of INTECHOPEN LIMITED, registered in England and Wales, registration number: 11086078, 7th floor, 10 Lower Thames Street, London, EC3R 6AF, United Kingdom
Printed in Croatia

British Library Cataloguing-in-Publication Data
A catalogue record for this book is available from the British Library

Additional hard and PDF copies can be obtained from orders@intechopen.com

Theory, Application, and Implementation of Monte Carlo Method in Science and Technology
Edited by Pooneh Saidi Bidokhti
p. cm.
Print ISBN 978-1-78985-545-6
Online ISBN 978-1-78985-546-3
eBook (PDF) ISBN 978-1-83968-152-3

For EU product safety concerns:
IN TECH d.o.o., Prolaz Marije Krucifikse Kozulić 3, 51000 Rijeka, Croatia, info@intechopen.com or visit our website at intechopen.com.

Meet the editor

Dr. Pooneh Saidi earned her PhD in Nuclear Engineering from the Science and Research Branch of Azad University, Tehran. She also holds two MSc degrees, one in Nuclear Engineering and another in Construction Project Management, from Shahid Beheshti University, Tehran. She is a Project Management Professional certified by the Project Management Institute (PMI). Dr. Saidi is a member of the board of directors at Parsikan Iran Engineering & Management Consultants. She is a skilled project planner with more than 18 years of experience in design and research and development projects. She is the author of more than 30 scientific papers and conference communications, recipient of the 2012 ICTR-PHE best poster award, and the author of four book chapters published by IntechOpen.

Contents

Preface

The Monte Carlo method is a numerical technique to model the probability of all possible outcomes in a process that cannot easily be predicted due to the interference of random variables. It is a technique used to understand the impact of uncertainty, ambiguity, and risk in forecasting models. This technique, also known as the Stochastic Simulation Technique, is now an established method used routinely in a wide variety of disciplines such as industry, nuclear engineering, medicine, economics, and risk analysis. However, this technique is not without complications, one of which is the amount of computer time required to achieve sufficient precision in the simulations and evaluate their accuracy. This book is organized into three sections and presents the general principles of the Monte Carlo method with an emphasis on techniques to decrease simulation time and increase accuracy.

Section 1 discusses the major fields of application of the Monte Carlo method in medicine. It covers a variety of topics, including medical physics, dosimetry, radiation protection, diagnostic radiology, radiotherapy, and nuclear medicine.

Section 2 introduces the theory and application of the Monte Carlo method in material science. This method is now widely applied in the design of complex materials and has become a vital tool in the field.

Section 3 provides practical information needed to support simulation and analysis of structures by numerical models and introduces techniques to reduce the computation time for even larger and more complex models.

Each section is subdivided into chapters and the implementation of the Monte Carlo method in each section is illustrated in several examples.

Chapter 1 introduces sampling techniques for a standard Monte Carlo method that could enable fast simulation of signals from optical coherence tomography (OCT) imaging systems. The chapter presents a standard Monte Carlo method for simulating OCT signals and sampling implementations that reduce computational time.

Chapter 2 discusses the calculation of the dosimetric parameters of encapsulated radioactive materials. In this chapter, Monte Carlo simulations are performed to determine the dosimetric parameters of the Palladium-103 brachytherapy seed. It also investigates the dose distributions along the central axis of COMS eye plaques loaded with the seeds. The chapter also examines the effects of plaque backing and polymeric insert on dose distribution at critical ocular structures.

Chapter 3 reviews the physics of small radiation fields, cavity theory, and the methodology of small field dosimetry. Different types of commercial dosimeters used in small field dosimetry are introduced and the importance of accurate small field dosimetry is discussed. This chapter also focuses on the application and importance of Monte Carlo techniques used in the field and presents recommendations of the Code of Practice for dosimetry of small radiation fields.

Chapter 4 describes the general concepts and basis of Monte Carlo modeling, introduces some available codes, and discusses the validation and reliability of Monte Carlo codes. It also examines the limitations on cross-section library and random number generators. The chapter presents a comparison between two Monte Carlo codes, XRMC and Geant4, and examines the validation between them. Experimental data applied to mammography are also presented. Finally, the chapter discusses the considerations in choosing a Monte Carlo computer toolkit and raises important issues on validation and reliability tests.

Chapter 5 presents algorithms, techniques, and general rules for Monte Carlo simulation in the plasma-enhanced chemical vapor deposition method. This is currently the method of choice for producing hydrogenated amorphous silicon thin films, which are promising materials for flat panel display transistors, solar cells, and electronic devices. But the reactions during plasma deposition are complex and not possible to observe directly, hence Monte Carlo simulation is a powerful tool to study thermodynamic properties.

Chapter 6 introduces the application of local information entropy in cluster Monte Carlo algorithms. The cluster Monte Carlo methods are very efficient in analysis of critical phenomena, for example, transformation from a ferromagnetic to a paramagnetic phase. However, in some conditions below the Curie point, this method produces incorrect results. To solve this problem, the chapter introduces a new simulation procedure that is efficient, leading to physically reliable results, especially for multiphase magnetic composites.

Chapter 7 deals with the analysis of structures. In general, structure analysis involves large and complex numerical models that require extensive computation efforts. One way to avoid this problem is to introduce simplified numerical models. This chapter discusses various types of approximate models and illustrates application of response surface techniques for an offshore jacket structure in combination with the Monte Carlo technique.

This book is an excellent contribution of numerous scientists and researchers from all around the world. I hope it encourages readers, scientists, and researchers to look deeper into the Monte Carlo Method and opens up several possibilities for further novel development.

As an editor, I express heartfelt appreciation to each and every contributing author and technical reviewer because this book could not have been written without their effort.

I would like to give very special thanks to IntechOpen for their support in editing this book, especially Ms. Sara Bacvarova. Her help with the publication process and friendly and prompt responses to my queries motivated me to work hard during eight months of preparing this book.

Pooneh Saidi, Ph.D., PMP
Parsikan Iran Engineering and Management Consultants,
Tehran, IRAN

Section 1

Medicine

Chapter 1

Monte Carlo Methods for Simulation of Optical Coherence Tomography of Turbid Media

Ivan T. Lima Jr and Sherif S. Sherif

Abstract

We describe two importance sampling techniques for a standard Monte Carlo (MC) method that could enable fast simulation of signals from optical coherence tomography (OCT) imaging systems. These OCT signals are generated due to diffusive reflections from either multilayered or arbitrary shaped, turbid media, for example, tissue. Such signals typically consist of ballistic and quasi-ballistic components, of scattered photons inside the medium, in addition to photons that undergo multiple scattering. We show that MC simulation of these OCT signals using importance sampling reduces its computation time on a serial processor by up to three orders of magnitude compared to its corresponding standard implementation. Therefore, these importance sampling techniques enable practical simulation of OCT B-scans of turbid media, for example, tissue, using commonly available workstations.

Keywords: optical coherence tomography, Monte Carlo simulation, light transport in turbid media, importance sampling

1. Introduction

Optical coherence tomography (OCT) is a non-invasive sub-surface imaging technique that has experienced significant growth in biomedical applications [1, 2]. OCT systems could be implemented with a low-coherence light source and a mechanical scanning sub-system (time-domain OCT). More advanced systems use a low-coherence light source with a spectrometer or a wavelength-swept source (frequency-domain OCT). OCT has an imaging depth that could reach up to 3 mm, depending on the optical properties of the tissue, and it also has one to two orders of magnitude higher resolution than ultrasound imaging. OCT could also produce images inside the body when it is implemented using optical fiber probes. Unlike X-ray or gamma-ray imaging, OCT is safe for biological tissues because it utilizes non-ionizing radiation mainly in the infrared spectrum.

1.1 OCT signal simulation using a Monte Carlo method

The signal obtained by an OCT imaging system consists of ballistic and quasi-ballistic (Class I diffuse reflectance) photons, in addition to multiply scattered photons (Class II diffuse reflectance), that are reflected from tissue [3].

However, multiply scattered photons do not carry practically useful information about the imaged tissue; therefore, they result in a degradation of the OCT signal [4]. In addition, it has been shown that Class II diffuse reflectance represents a fundamental limit related to the imaging depth of OCT in tissue [5]. Therefore, it is important to account for both Class I and Class II diffusive reflectance in any practical simulation of OCT signals.

Since it is not practical to simulate light transport in turbid media, for example, tissue, using electromagnetic waves, especially due to diffusive scattering, a Monte Carlo (MC) method of simulating light transport in tissue has been typically used [6–9]. However, the computational cost of this MC-based simulation of OCT systems could be very high, as the probability of detecting diffusively reflected photons from tissue is very low [4, 5].

To reduce the computational cost, thereby accelerate, this MC simulation, importance sampling could be used to speed up simulations by orders of magnitude. Importance sampling has been applied earlier to optical communications [10, 11], confocal microscopy [12], atmospheric optics [13], and diffuse optical tomography [8].

To improve the computational efficiency of the MC-based simulation of OCT systems [6], Yao and Wang proposed the first importance sampling technique to simulate OCT signals from a multilayered turbid medium [3]. However, their method only enabled the simulation of OCT signals from a thin shallow layer in tissue, as the results obtained from deeper tissue regions were underestimated. In [14], we, the authors of this chapter, developed another more advanced importance sampling technique by implementing multiple biased scatterings per photon packet, and by developing a photon splitting procedure. Our advanced importance sampling resulted in more accurate and computationally efficient simulations of OCT signals due to ballistic and quasi-ballistic photons. However, it still underestimated OCT signals due to multiply scattered photons. To enable accurate simulation of OCT signals due to both Class I and Class II diffusive reflectances, we further developed our importance sampling technique to accurately and efficiently simulate diffusive reflectance due to photons that undergo multiple scattering [15]. In this method, additional biased scatterings were randomly applied, which enabled accurate simulation of both Class I and Class II diffusive reflectances, with a speed-up of three orders of magnitude compared to the standard MC method.

Our advanced importance sampling techniques above were implemented to simulate OCT of tissues with planar geometry [6]. To enable simulation of OCT of arbitrarily shaped turbid media, we used the mesh-based MC method of light transport in tissue proposed by Fang [16]. This method uses a Plücker coordinate system to efficiently calculate intersections between paths of light propagation with interfaces of the object regions that are modeled using tetrahedrons. We combined this mesh-based MC method with our importance sampling techniques to simulate OCT signals from tissue with arbitrarily shaped regions. However, since it was still computationally costly to simulate a full OCT B-scan using this method, we also developed a parallel implementation of this simulator that exploited the massively parallel computing capabilities of Graphics Processing Units (GPUs) to accelerate this simulator by two additional orders of magnitude [17, 18]. This GPU-based implementation enabled simulation of OCT B-scans of arbitrarily shaped turbid media in a few minutes using commonly available workstations.

In Section 2 of this chapter, we present a standard MC method for simulating OCT signals. In Section 3, we present our first importance sampling implementation that enables the simulation of OCT signals from higher depths inside turbid media. In Section 4, we present our more advanced importance sampling implementation that accurately calculates both Class I and Class II diffusive reflectances, and is three orders of magnitude faster than the standard MC simulation.

2. Standard MC method for simulating OCT signals

Our implementation of the MC method to simulate OCT signals is based on Monte Carlo simulation of light transport in multilayered tissues (MCML) [6]. MCML simulates an ensemble of photon packets that are launched as a steady-state pencil beam, normal to the top surface of the medium. Within the tissue, each such photon packet undergoes a random walk whose step size is determined by an exponentially distributed random variable that is parameterized by the *interaction coefficient* of this tissue. This interaction coefficient is equal to the sum of the absorption μ_a and the scattering μ_s coefficients of this tissue. The scattering events that take place at the end of the random steps are characterized by two random angles that determine the next direction of the photon packet. To account for the photon packet scattering, given an anisotropy factor, g, of the tissue, MCML uses the Henyey-Greenstein probability density function that is given by

$$f_{HG}(\cos(\theta_S)) = \frac{1-g^2}{2(1+g^2-2g\cdot\cos(\theta_S))^{3/2}}, \tag{1}$$

where θ_S is the angle between the propagation direction of the photon packet $\hat{\mathbf{u}}$ before the current scattering and $\hat{\mathbf{u}}'$ is the direction of the photon packet after the current scattering. The angle between the previous propagation direction and the new propagation direction is θ_S. Therefore, $\cos(\theta_S) = \hat{\mathbf{u}} \cdot \hat{\mathbf{u}}'$. To ensure that the new propagation direction is statistically correct, the provisional scattering direction $\hat{\mathbf{u}}'$ is rotated around $\hat{\mathbf{u}}$ by an angle ϕ, which is randomly selected from a uniform probability density function with a range from 0 to 2π to generate the propagation direction $\hat{\mathbf{u}}'$ after the current scattering. At the end of each scattering event, the photon packet weight W is reduced according to the step size and the local absorption coefficient μ_a. The weight W, which is initially set at 1, is proportional to the number of photons in the photon packet. The photon packet is either removed with probability $1/m$ or is allowed to continue propagating with probability $1-1/m$ and a new weight equal to $m\cdot W$ once the weight reaches $W_{\text{th}} = 10^{-4}$. We use the value $m = 10$ in this work. This procedure, denoted Russian roulette, is an unbiased technique to end simulation of photon packets that have a negligibly low contribution to the Monte Carlo simulation, so that a new photon packet can be initiated and simulated.

The Class I diffuse reflectance at depth equal to z is obtained by calculating the mean value of an indicator function I_1 that represents a spatial and temporal filter of Class I diffuse reflectance for all simulated photon packets. The indicator function I_1 of such spatial and temporal filter for the ith photon packet is defined as

$$I_1(z,i) = \begin{cases} 1, & r_i < d_{\max}, \;\; \theta_{z,i} < \theta_{\max}, \;\; |\Delta S_i - 2z| < l_c \\ 0, & \text{othwerise} \end{cases}, \tag{2}$$

where l_c is the optical source's coherence length; r_i is the distance to the origin of the ith reflected photon packet; $d_{\max}$ and $\theta_{\max}$ are the maximum photon packet collecting diameter and angle, respectively; $\theta_{z,i}$ is the angle with the z-axis (normal to the tissue interface); Δs_i is the optical path; and z is the photon packet's maximum depth.

At any depth, the diffuse reflectance R_1 is the expected value of I_1 at this depth, and its standard deviation $\sigma_{R,1}$ could be estimated by

$$R_1(z) = \frac{1}{N}\sum_{i=1}^{N} I_1(z,i)W(i) \tag{3}$$

and

$$\sigma^2_{R,1}(z) = \frac{1}{N(N-1)} \sum_{i=1}^{N} [I_1(z,i)W(i) - R_1]^2 \tag{4}$$

where N is the number of photons packets used in MC-based simulations.

3. Importance sampling for simulation of Class I OCT signal

Our first importance sampling technique to simulate OCT signals aimed at increasing the number of photons collected at the detector. This algorithm uses the same method described in Section 2, where we also use the same square time gating given by [3].

Since most tissues are highly forward-scattering, their anisotropy factor is close to 1. Therefore, there is a very small probability that a simulated photon packet at any given depth in the tissue would undergo scattering in the backward direction toward the OCT probe. The probability of collecting Class I photons drops rapidly with depth in the tissue from which the photon is scattered in the backward direction. To allow faster simulation of Class I photons, we designed an importance sampling method that biases the direction $\hat{\mathbf{u}}'$ of a scattered photon toward the tip of the light-collecting optical fiber, $\hat{\mathbf{v}}$, as the photon packet reaches the depth range of interest. By defining the origin of a Cartesian coordinate system at the center of the tip of the light-collecting optical fiber, the bias direction in which this fiber is located is defined as $\hat{\mathbf{v}} = -\boldsymbol{R}/|\boldsymbol{R}|$, where $\mathbf{R} = x\hat{\mathbf{x}} + y\hat{\mathbf{y}} + z\hat{\mathbf{z}}$ is the position vector of the scattering location in the tissue.

All photon packets propagating in a direction close to $\hat{\mathbf{v}}$ will contribute to the simulated Class I diffuse reflectance with a higher probability. Therefore, this bias direction is more efficient than biasing only in the backward direction, which may not be consistent with the direction of the light-collecting optical fiber. This choice of the bias direction is particularly effective for photon packets propagating deep in the tissue, where such photon packets experience one or more scattering events before they are diffusively reflected.

3.1 Scattering angle due to first event of backscattering

As the photon packet reaches the depth range targeted, the propagation direction $\hat{\mathbf{u}}'$ of the scattered photon packet is biased toward the bias direction $\hat{\mathbf{v}}$, as opposed to being most likely scattered close to the previous propagation direction $\hat{\mathbf{u}}$ as in the practical case with anisotropy g close to 1 and different from the bias toward $-\hat{\mathbf{u}}$, the opposite of the direction of propagation, as it is done in [3]. To randomly select the biased angle θ_B between the new scattering direction $\hat{\mathbf{u}}'$ and the biased direction $\hat{\mathbf{v}}$, we use the same probability density function in Eq. (1). However, the bias coefficient does not have to correspond to the anisotropy factor g. Therefore, the probability density function of the biased angle is given by

$$f_B(\cos(\theta_B)) = \frac{1-a^2}{2(1+a^2-2a\cdot\cos(\theta_B))^{3/2}}, \tag{5}$$

where a is a bias coefficient. After randomly sampling a biased angle θ_B away from the biased direction $\hat{\mathbf{v}}$, so that $\cos(\theta_B) = \hat{\mathbf{v}} \cdot \hat{\mathbf{u}}'$, the provisional scattering direction $\hat{\mathbf{u}}'$ is rotated around $\hat{\mathbf{v}}$ by an angle ϕ, which is randomly selected from a uniform probability density function with a range from 0 to 2π to generate the propagation direction $\hat{\mathbf{u}}'$ after the current scattering. This procedure ensures a more accurate model of the light scattering in tissue. The difference in the rotation by ϕ between the model with importance sampling and the standard model is that the rotation in the model with importance sampling is done around the biased direction $\hat{\mathbf{v}}$, while the rotation in the standard model in is done around the direction $\hat{\mathbf{u}}$ prior to the current scattering. After the first biased scattering, this procedure produces the new propagation direction $\hat{\mathbf{u}}'$ of the photon packet. Afterward, the scattered photon packet is associated with a likelihood ratio as discussed in other applications of this method [10, 11]. Using our biased angle's probability density function, the likelihood ratio of the photon packet, Eq. (5), is given by

$$L(\cos(\theta_B)) = \frac{f_{HG}(\cos(\theta_S))}{f_B(\cos(\theta_B))} = \frac{1-g^2}{1-a^2}\left(\frac{1+a^2-2a\cdot\cos(\theta_B)}{1+g^2-2g\cdot\cos(\theta_S)}\right)^{3/2}, \tag{6}$$

where $\cos(\theta_S) = \hat{\mathbf{u}} \cdot \hat{\mathbf{u}}'$ is determined, after the biased scattering, from the randomly sampled values of θ_B and ϕ. The ratio of the probability of the scattering angle appearing in the biased case with the standard case is the likelihood ratio that is shown in Eq. (6). In addition to depending on θ_B, the likelihood ratio also depends also on θ_S. **Figure 1** shows a schematic drawing of these vectors and the angles used in this direction biasing procedure. Note that the choice of bias distribution only affects the speed of convergence of the simulation. Therefore, other biased probability function could also be used to randomly generate the biased scattering toward the bias direction $\hat{v}$.

3.2 Scattering angles of additional events of backscattering

As a photon packet is biased toward the apparent position of the collecting optical fiber, at any given depth in the tissue, the photon packet becomes more likely to be collected at the tip of the fiber. However, the photon packet could be scattered several times after the first backscatter bias before reaching the optical collection system. These additional scatterings, according to Eq. (1), reduce the correlation between the biased direction and the event in which the photon packet is collected. We overcome this reduction in correlation by continuing to bias the

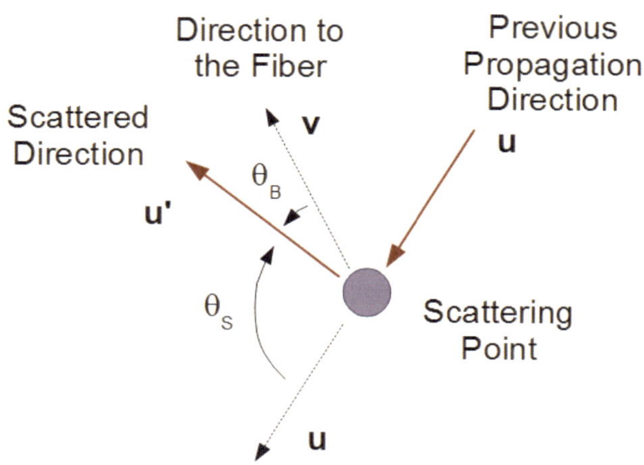

Figure 1.
Schematic representation of vectors and angles used in biasing the scattering direction. Reprinted with permission from [14] © The Optical Society of America.

scattering direction $\hat{\boldsymbol{u}}'$ toward the direction $\hat{\boldsymbol{v}}$, pointing to the apparent position of the optical collection system, at every scattering point until the photon packet is removed. These additional biases still use both Eqs. (7) and (8). Since the random values drawn for the angle between the scattering direction and the biased direction are independent of each other and are also independent of the previous scattering events, the overall likelihood ratio of a collected photon packet results from the multiplication of all the likelihood ratios of all the biased scattering in that particular simulation.

Once a photon packet experiences the first biased scattering, that photon packet is biased at all additional scattering points until it is removed from the simulation, which can occur when the photon packet is removed by Russian roulette, as described in Section 2, or it leaves the tissue. After simulating N launched photon packets using importance sampling, the diffuse reflectance R_1 and its standard deviation $\sigma_{R,1}$ could be calculated with

$$R_1(z) = \frac{1}{N}\sum_{i=1}^{N} I_1(z,i)L(i)W(i) \tag{7}$$

and

$$\sigma^2_{R,1}(z) = \frac{1}{N(N-1)}\sum_{i=1}^{N} [I_1(z,i)L(i)W(i) - R_1]^2. \tag{8}$$

Eqs. (7) and (8) are similar to Eqs. (3) and (4), except that the indicator function is multiplied by its corresponding likelihood ratio. Using this method, a significantly larger number of photon packets are scattered from a specific depth range toward the collecting optical system than the number obtained using a standard MCML implementation. At the end of this biased simulation, each photon packet is weighted by its likelihood ratio, which adjusts the contribution of each packet to the estimation of the Class I diffuse reflectance. The estimated diffuse reflectance converges toward its true value faster, by several orders of magnitude, when compared to the standard Monte Carlo method.

3.3 Importance sampling effectiveness and depth of tissue

One drawback of previously existing bias methods, for example, [3, 7, 8] is an underestimation of the diffuse reflectance beyond the targeted depth range. The application of the first backward bias reduces the probability that this photon packet would propagate beyond that portion of the tissue. This would lead to a statistical bias to this importance sampling method similar to that in the angle biasing procedure used in [3] and the method used in [7, 8], which limits the effectiveness of those methods to a thin target layer.

We make sure we obtain correct statistics by splitting the photon packet into two photon packets before the first biased scattering [14]. The first of these two photon packets is the one biased toward the collecting optical system. The second photon packet starts propagating from the location in which the biased backscattering occurred, where its initial direction calculated by applying the standard procedure to the previous direction $\hat{\boldsymbol{u}}$ as shown in Section 3.1. To ensure that there is no statistical bias associated with the forward-propagating photon packet that was split, it will be assigned a likelihood ratio $L'(i)$, which is a complement to the likelihood of the biased backward scattered photon packet $L(i)$ such that $L'(i) = 1 - L(i)$ to this second photon packet. This second photon packet, only generated if

$L(i) < 1$, also undergoes biased backscattering in the tissue at the end of the next step, which could result in another photon packet split, and successive additional biased scatterings toward the tip of the collecting optical fiber until the photon packet propagates beyond the simulation domain. In cases that we investigated, this procedure increased the computational time of each photon packet by five times when compared with a photon packet computed using the standard Monte Carlo method with the same number of launched photon packets N. The increase in the computational time of our importance sampling-based implementation, compared to the standard method with the same number of launched photon packets, depends on the average value of the mean free path, and on the width of the target depth range. We note that in our importance sampling implementation, we do not count split photon packets as additional photon packets when determining the value of N in Eqs. (7) and (8), as the use of their corresponding likelihood ratios will generate the correct result. As a photon packet propagates beyond the target region, the packet will propagate using the standard scattering procedure until it is terminated. Once this photon packet is terminated, a new photon packet will be simulated from the OCT probe, as it is the case in the standard MCML. Even though the splitting procedure implies that the cost of simulating a launched photon with this importance sampling method is higher than the computational cost of simulating launched photos using the standard MCML, the computation cost of the Class I diffuse reflectance in our Monte Carlo simulations with importance sampling required as little as one-thousandth of the computational cost required by the standard Monte Carlo method to achieve the same accuracy in the calculated diffuse reflectance.

3.4 Numerical results

We validate our importance sampling technique for simulation of OCT signals from multilayered tissue, with different refractive indices and scattering properties, by comparing its results with those obtained by the standard Monte Carlo method. As shown in **Figure 2**, light is emitted by an optical fiber probe that is reflected by a prism.

The shown optical system has a focusing lens with a numerical aperture (NA) that allows collecting light at an angle of up to 4° and a diameter of 0.5 mm. Similar to the setups in [5, 10, 11], we assume a point source that emits in the vertical direction. Air is present between the center of the probe and the first layer of tissue, which is placed 2.12 mm from the center of the fiber. We simulate a three-layer turbid medium with refractive-index mismatch at its interfaces. The first layer, extending from 2.12 to 2.22 mm from the tip of the fiber, has absorption coefficient $\mu_a = 1.5\ \text{cm}^{-1}$, scattering coefficient $\mu_s = 60\ \text{cm}^{-1}$, and refractive index $n = 1$.

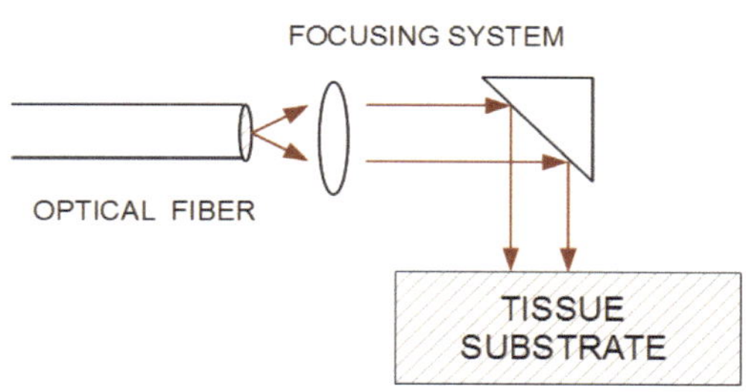

Figure 2.
Schematic representation of a setup to simulate OCT signals. Reprinted with permission from [14]
© The Optical Society of America.

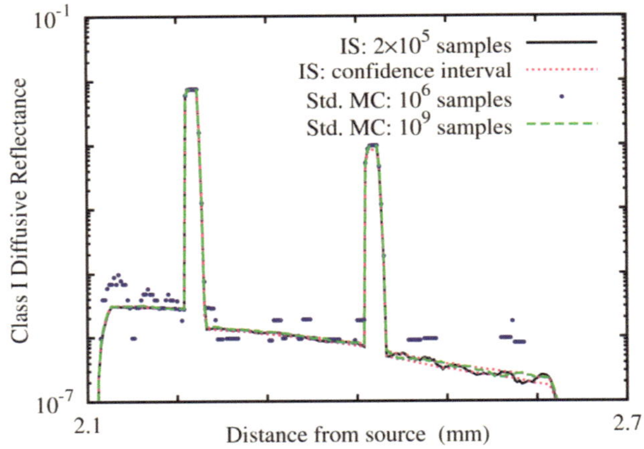

Figure 3.
Class I diffuse reflectance dependence on the distance from the center of the optical fiber for the simulation whose schematic is shown in ***Figure 4****. The solid black line represents the result obtained with* 2×10^5 *photon packets using the importance sampling technique presented in Section 3. The green long dashed line is the result obtained with* 10^9 *photon packets using standard MCML. The blue dots represent results obtained with* 10^6 *photon packets using MCML. The pink short dashed lines show the confidence interval of the importance sampling simulations with* 2×10^5 *photon packets that were estimated using a much larger ensemble of* 64×10^5 *simulations. Reprinted with permission from [14] © The Optical Society of America.*

The second layer, extending from 2.32 to 2.42 mm from the tip of the fiber, has the same absorption and scattering coefficients as the first layer, but its refractive index is $n = 1.33$. The third layer, extending from 2.42 to 2.62 mm from the tip of the fiber, has the following parameters: $\mu_a = 1.5\ \text{cm}^{-1}$, $\mu_s = 30\ \text{cm}^{-1}$, and $n = 1$. After the third layer, the medium was assumed to be air: $\mu_a = 0\ \text{cm}^{-1}$, $\mu_s = 0\ \text{cm}^{-1}$, and $n = 1$. The anisotropy factor was assumed $g = 0.9$ for the three diffusive layers.

From **Figure 3**, we note an excellent correspondence between results obtained with our new importance sampling method and results obtained using MCML, that is, standard Monte Carlo simulations. However, our results were obtained in one-thousandth of the time required by the standard method.

4. Importance sampling for simulation of Class I and Class II OCT signals

In this section, we further improve the importance sampling technique that was described in Section 3, so we can simulate Class II OCT signals more accurately and more efficiently [19].

4.1 Scattering angle of first backscattering event

In the MC simulation described in Section 3, we note that the bias function in (5) produces large values of the likelihood ratio (>>1) when photon packets are scattered in the then unlikely forward direction. These photon packets contributed to a slow decrease in the relative variation, which corresponds to relative error, with the increase in the number of photon packets launched for the calculation of the OCT signal. Referring to **Figure 1**, we could reduce this relative variation by choosing a distribution function for the scattering angle that limits it to the backward direction. This modified distribution is given by:

$$f_B(\cos(\theta_B)) = \begin{cases} \left(1 - \frac{1-a}{\sqrt{a^2+1}}\right)^{-1} \dfrac{a(1-a)}{(1+a^2-2a\cos(\theta_B))^{3/2}}, \cos(\theta_B) \in [0,1] \\ 0, \text{ otherwise} \end{cases}, \quad (9)$$

where a is the bias coefficient that can be selected between 0 and 1. Once a biased angle θ_B is randomly selected, away from the direction of the center of the OCT probe $\hat{\boldsymbol{v}}$, where $\cos(\theta_B) = \hat{\boldsymbol{v}} \cdot \hat{\boldsymbol{u}}'$, the provisional biased scattering direction $\hat{\boldsymbol{u}}'$ is rotated around $\hat{\boldsymbol{v}}$ by an angle ϕ randomly sampled from a uniform distribution in the range from 0 to 2π. These parameters are defined in the same manner as those used in the biased distribution presented in Section 3. The only difference is that the domain of $\cos(\theta_B)$ is restricted to a maximum deviation from the biased angle by 90°. This ensures that there would not be packets with very large likelihood ratio that could reduce the efficiency of our importance sampling. The likelihood ratio of the photon packet that uses the biased probability density function in Eq. (9) is given by

$$L(\cos(\theta_B)) = \frac{f_{HG}(\cos(\theta_S))}{f_B(\cos(\theta_B))} = \frac{1-g^2}{2a(1-a)} \left(1 - \frac{1-a}{\sqrt{a^2+1}}\right) \left(\frac{1+a^2-2a\cos(\theta_B)}{1+g^2-2g\cos(\theta_S)}\right)^{3/2}, \quad (10)$$

where $\cos(\theta_S) = \hat{\boldsymbol{u}} \cdot \hat{\boldsymbol{u}}'$. We note that $\cos(\theta_B)$ is obtained using the probability density function in Eq. (9), where it is used to obtain the new propagation direction $\hat{\boldsymbol{u}}'$.

To sample angles according to the biased probability density function in (8), one could use any uniform pseudo-random number generator that would be typically available in scientific software libraries. For example, if u_i is a random number distributed uniformly between 0 and 1, a random value for $\cos(\theta_B)$ that satisfies Eq. (9) with bias coefficient a could be generated with the following conversion formula

$$\cos\theta_{B,i} = \frac{1}{2a}\left\{a^2 + 1 - \left[u_i\left(\frac{1}{1-a} - \frac{1}{\sqrt{a^2+1}}\right) + \frac{1}{\sqrt{a^2+1}}\right]^2\right\}. \quad (11)$$

This conversion formula was derived using probability theory [20].

4.2 Scattering angles of additional biased backscatterings

A second enhancement that could be made to the importance sampling technique, described in Section 3, is to bias the additional scatterings toward the center of the OCT probe $\hat{\boldsymbol{v}}$ with probability $0 \leq p \leq 1$. That contrasts with the technique presented in Section 3, in which $p = 1$ (all the additional scatterings were biased). An unbiased scattering is performed in case a bias scattering is not applied in a given point where scattering takes place. The likelihood ratio associated with this scattering is calculated according to the formula

$$L(\cos\theta_B) = \frac{f_{HG}(\cos\theta_B)}{p \cdot f_{HG}(\cos\theta_B) + (1-p) \cdot f_{HG}(\cos\theta_S)}. \quad (12)$$

If the biased function $f_B(\cos(\theta_B))$ is selected to sample a random value of $\cos(\theta_S)$, which is an event with probability p, $\cos(\theta_S) = \hat{\boldsymbol{u}} \cdot \hat{\boldsymbol{u}}'$ is a function of $\cos(\theta_B)$ that is statistically sampled from the probability density function in Eq. (9).

Otherwise, in the case of the complementary event with probability $1 - p$, the unbiased function $f_{HG}(\cos(\theta_S))$ is used to sample a random value of $\cos(\theta_S)$ and $\cos(\theta_B) = \hat{\boldsymbol{v}} \cdot \hat{\boldsymbol{u}}'$ depends on the value of $\cos(\theta_S)$. Since the two random angles associated to each scattering do not depend on the random angles selected in the previous scatterings, the likelihood ratio of each collected photon packet results from the multiplication of all the likelihood ratios of all the biased scatterings in that simulated photon packet.

4.3 Numerical results

We validate our importance sampling technique for simulation of OCT signals from multilayered tissue, with different refractive indices and scattering properties, by comparing its results with those obtained by the standard Monte Carlo method. We consider a tissue model that consists of multiple layers that could be imaged with an OCT system, as shown schematically in **Figure 4**. The modeled tissue extends from 0 to 1 mm, and consists primarily of a turbid layer with absorption coefficient μ_a = 1.5 cm^{-1} and a scattering coefficient μ_s = 60 cm^{-1}, and also contains five thin layers with absorption coefficient μ_a = 3 cm^{-1} and a scattering coefficient μ_s = 120 cm^{-1}. These five thin layers with higher scattering coefficient are located from 200 to 215 μm, from 365 to 395 μm, from 645 to 660 μm, from 760 to 775 μm, and from 900 to 915 μm. We assume that this tissue has the same refractive index n = 1 and an anisotropy factor g = 0.9. We note that our method is robust in the presence of refractive index mismatch along layer boundaries of the tissue [19]. We simulate an OCT system where the light is delivered/collected by the tip of an

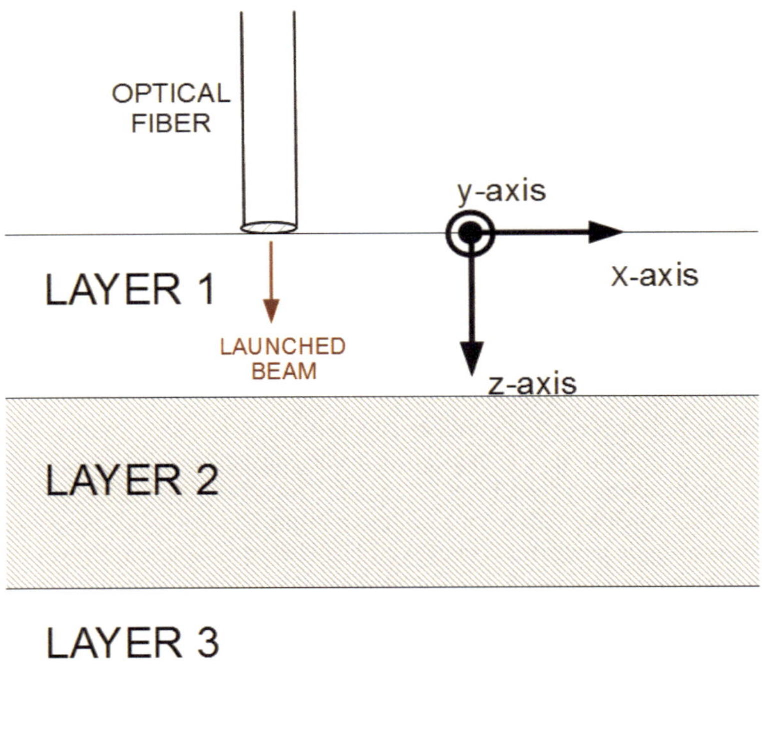

Figure 4.
Schematic representation of a setup to simulate OCT signals similar to one in Ref. [3]. Reprinted with permission from [15] © The Optical Society of America.

optical fiber having a radius of 10 μm and an acceptance angle of 5°. For simplicity, the light source is assumed to be a one-dimensional light beam propagating along the vertical direction as in [3, 8], since the purpose of this example is to validate and demonstrate the effectiveness of our second importance sampling technique when it is applied to the standard MC simulation.

In **Figures 5** and **6**, we show results obtained with 10^8 Monte Carlo photon packets with importance sampling, which has a computational cost of simulating about 9×10^8 photon packets using standard Monte Carlo. The computational cost of applying this importance sampling technique depends on the target depth range, and on the average photon mean free path in the given tissue. The target depths in the shown simulations were set from 0 to 1 mm. Therefore, every single photon scattering that occurs in the depth range from 0 to 1 mm would be biased. We used a bias coefficient $a = 0.925$, and an additional bias probability $p = 0.5$, to run the Monte Carlo simulations with importance sampling. The results shown in

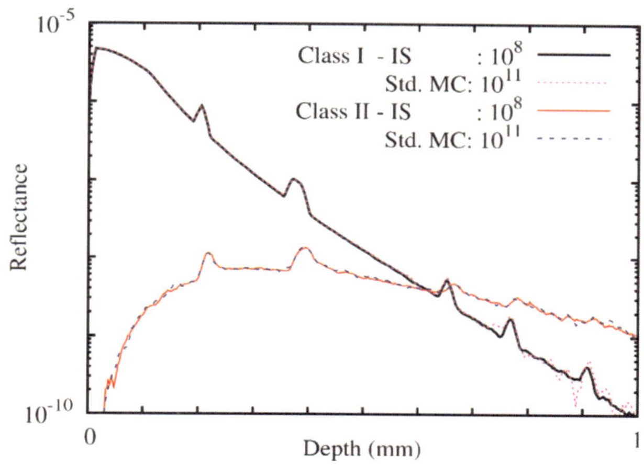

Figure 5.
The Class I diffusive reflectance (thick solid black curve) and the Class II reflectance (thin solid red curve), as a function of the tissue depth using the importance sampling technique presented in Section 4 with 10^8 photon packets. The pink short dashed and the blue long dashed curves are results of simulating Class I reflectance and the Class II reflectance using standard Monte Carlo with 10^{11} photon packets, respectively. Reprinted with permission from [15] © The Optical Society of America.

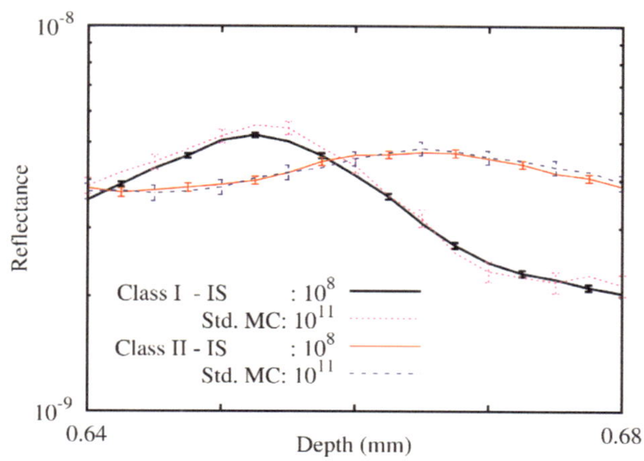

Figure 6.
*Details of reflectance results shown in **Figure 5** for depths between 640 and 680 μm. The error bars shown were estimated by the same ensemble of simulations. Reprinted with permission from [15] © The Optical Society of America.*

Figures 5 and **6** show that our new importance sampling technique reduces the computational cost for obtaining the Class I diffuse reflectance by approximately three orders of magnitude when compared to the standard Monte Carlo method. This algorithm is optimum when the additional bias probability is equal to $p = 0.5$. Since only half of the back-scatterings are biased, this choice contributes toward enabling an optimum number of Class II photons to be collected by the tip of the optical fiber.

We note that the results obtained with the MCML have confidence intervals that are noticeably larger than those of the results obtained with importance sampling shown in **Figure 6**, even though the standard Monte Carlo simulations have a computational cost 113 times larger than those obtained with importance sampling. In **Figure 6**, we also note that our importance sampling technique reduces the computational cost of calculating the Class II reflectance by more than two orders of magnitude.

In **Figure 7** we show the relationship between the relative error in calculating Class I and the Class II reflectances at two different depths: 400 and 670 μm and the bias coefficient a for $p = 0.5$. The depths at 400 and 670 μm correspond to tissue regions near the second and third regions with high local reflectance due to the higher local scattering coefficient. The relative variation in the results is the ratio between the square root of the variance, shown in Eq. (4), and the reflectance in Eq. (3).

We note that Class I reflectance has a minimum relative error at 400 μm with $a = 0.925$, but the minimum error at 670 μm occurs at $a = 0.95$ μm at 670 μm. The deeper the tissue region, the stronger the required bias because of the increase in the number of scatterings with the depth. However, as the bias coefficient is increased toward 1, larger variations in the likelihood ratio lead to an increase in the relative error. We also note that Class II reflectance has its minimum relative error at 400 μm with $a = 0.91$, while its minimum relative error at 670 μm increased to only about $a = 0.925$ μm. The optimum amount of bias required by the Classs II diffusive reflectance in both wavelengths is lower than the optimum bias coefficient observed in the Class I reflectance because the number of ballistic and quasi-ballistic photons increases with the bias, which leads to a decrease in the number of collected photon packets that undergo multiple scatterings. **Figure 7** also shows that there is a range for the bias parameter a between 0.9 and 0.95 that enables fast calculation of

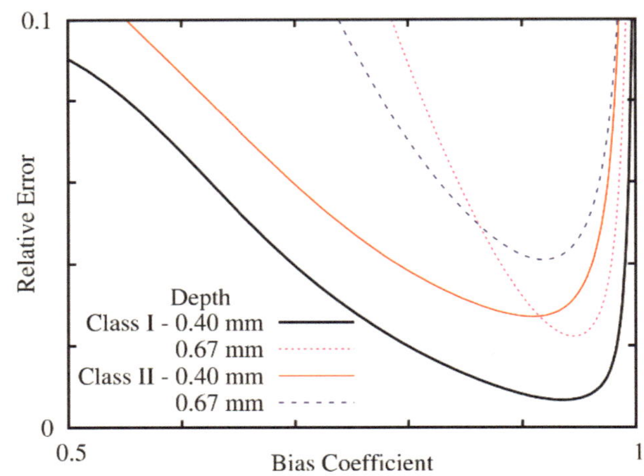

Figure 7.
The relative error in calculated reflectance using importance sampling as a function of bias coefficient a*. Reprinted with permission from [15] © The Optical Society of America.*

both Class I and Class II reflectances using our importance sampling-based implementation.

5. Conclusions

We described two importance sampling techniques for a standard Monte Carlo (MC) method that could enable fast simulation of signals from optical coherence tomography (OCT) imaging systems. These OCT signals are generated due to diffusive reflections from either multilayered or arbitrarily shaped, turbid media, for example, tissue. Such signals typically consist of ballistic and quasi-ballistic components, of scattered photons inside the medium, in addition to photons that undergo multiple scattering. We showed that MC simulation of these OCT signals using our importance sampling reduced its computation time on a serial processor by up to three orders of magnitude compared to its corresponding standard implementation. Therefore, our importance sampling techniques enable practical simulation of OCT B-scans of turbid media, for example, tissue, using commonly available workstations.

Conflict of interest

The authors declare no conflict of interest.

Author details

Ivan T. Lima Jr[1] and Sherif S. Sherif[2]*

1 Department of Electrical and Computer Engineering, North Dakota State University, Fargo, North Dakota, USA

2 Department of Electrical and Computer Engineering, University of Manitoba, Winnipeg, Manitoba, Canada

*Address all correspondence to: sherif.sherif@umanitoba.ca

References

[1] Brezinski M, Fujimoto J. Optical coherence tomography: High-resolution imaging in non transparent tissue. IEEE Journal of Selected Topics in Quantum Electronics. 1999;**5**:1185-1192

[2] Drexler W, Fujimoto JG. Optical coherence tomography technology and applications. Berlin, Heidelberg: Springer; 2008. DOI: 10.1108/02640470510611517

[3] Yao G, Wang LV. Monte Carlo simulation of an optical coherence tomography signal in homogeneous turbid media. Physics in Medicine and Biology. 1999;**44**:2307-2320

[4] Sherif SS, Rosa CC, Flueraru C, et al. Statistics of the depth-scan photocurrent in time-domain optical coherence tomography. Journal of the Optical Society of America. A. 2008;**25**: 16-20

[5] Yadlowsky MJ, Schmitt JM, Bonner RF. Multiple scattering in optical coherence microscopy. Applied Optics. 1995;**34**:5699-5707

[6] Jacques SL, Wang L. Monte Carlo modeling of light transport in tissues. Optical-Thermal Response of Laser-Irradiated Tissue. 2013;**2607**:73-100

[7] Chen NG, Bai J. Estimation of quasi-straightforward propagating light in tissues. Physics in Medicine and Biology. 1999;**44**:1669-1676

[8] Chen N. Controlled Monte Carlo method for light propagation in tissue of semi-infinite geometry. Applied Optics. 2007;**46**:1597

[9] Wilson BC, Adam G. A Monte Carlo model for the absorption and flux distributions of light in tissue. Medical Physics. 1983;**10**:824-830

[10] Biondini G, Kath WL, Menyuk CR. Importance sampling for polarization-mode dispersion. IEEE Photonics Technology Letters; 2002;**14**(3):310-312

[11] Lima IT et al. Efficient computation of outage probabilities due to polarization effects in a WDM system using a reduced stokes model and importance sampling. IEEE Photonics Technology Letters. 2003;**15**(1):45-47

[12] Schmitt JM, Ben.-Letaief K. Efficient Monte Carlo simulation of confocal microscopy in biological tissue. Journal of the Optical Society of America. A. 1996;**13**:952-961

[13] Iwabuchi H. Efficient Monte Carlo method for radiative transfer modeling. Journal of the Atmospheric Sciences. 2006;**63**:2324-2339

[14] Lima IT Jr, Kalra A, Sherif SS. Improved importance sampling for Monte Carlo simulation of time-domain optical coherence tomography. Biomedical Optics Express. 2011;**2**(5): 1069-1081. DOI: 10.1364/BOE.2001069

[15] Lima IT, Kalra A, Hernández-Figueroa HE, Sherif SS. Fast calculation of multipath diffusive reflectance in optical coherence tomography. Biomedical Optics Express. 2012;**3**: 692-700

[16] Fang Q. Mesh-based Monte Carlo method using fast ray-tracing in Plücker coordinates. Biomedical Optics Express. 2010;**1**:165-175

[17] Malektaji S, Lima IT Jr, Sherif SS. Monte Carlo simulation of optical coherence tomography for turbid media with arbitrary spatial distributions. Journal of Biomedical Optics. 2 April 2014;**19**(4):046001. DOI: 10.1117/1.JBO.19.4.046001

[18] Malektaji S, Lima IT, Escobar I, et al. Massively parallel simulator of optical coherence tomography of

inhomogeneous turbid media. Computer Methods and Programs in Biomedicine. 2017;**150**:97-105

[19] Lima IT, Kalra A, Hernández-Figueroa HE, et al. Fast calculation of multipath diffusive reflectance in optical coherence tomography. Biomedical Optics Express. 2012;**3**:692

[20] Papoulis A. Probability, Random Variables, and Stochastic Processes. New York, NY: McGraw-Hill; 1984

Chapter 2

Modelling, Simulation and Dosimetry of ^{103}-Pd Eye Plaque Brachytherapy

Pooneh Saidi and Mahdi Sadeghi

Abstract

In this study, the dose distribution has been calculated for the Collaborative Ocular Melanoma Study (COMS) eye plaques at various diameters 10–22 mm, loaded with the ^{103}-Pd brachytherapy seeds (Model IR06-^{103}Pd). Several Monte Carlo (MC) simulations have been employed to carry out the gold backing and Silastic insert effect on dose distribution around the eye plaque. Version 5 of the Monte Carlo N-particle (MCNP) code has been used to carry out the simulations. The new palladium seed was modelled in three geometric orientations (ideal, vertical and diagonal). Results are compared with the calculated data for COMS eye plaque loaded with Theragenics model 200 and Best model 2335 palladium-103 seeds and model 6711 iodine-125 seeds. The calculated dose rate constant of the IR06-^{103}Pd seed was found to be 0.692 ± 0.020 cGy h^{-1} U^{-1}. The air kerma strength to deliver 85 Gy to tumour apex in a water medium was found to be 4.10 U/seed. The dosimetric parameters calculated in this work for the new palladium seed indicate the IR06-^{103}Pd seed is suitable for use in brachytherapy. In COMS plaques, the dose distribution to points of interest was compared for three ^{103}-Pd seed models. With the exception of sclera dose and for a given prescription dose, the IR06 seed delivers lower dose ocular points of interest.

Keywords: eye plaque, palladium-103, brachytherapy, dosimetry

1. Introduction

The most common primary intraocular malignancy in adults is choroidal melanoma, accounting for 5% of all melanomas, originating within the pigmented cells of the choroid. More common in Caucasians, the Collaborative Ocular Melanoma Study (COMS) found the mean age at diagnosis to be 60 years. Generally, they are located posterior to the ciliary body and often found during ophthalmic examination [1, 2].

The plaque is temporarily sutured to the sclera overlying the tumour, left in place for 5–7 days and then surgically removed. Temporary placement of an episcleral plaque containing radioactive material has gained acceptance as a treatment for choroidal melanoma. Compared to enucleation, eye plaque brachytherapy provides better outcomes for uveal melanoma [3]. The choice of the treatment method is depending on the size and location of the tumour [4, 5]. One of the most common primary intraocular malignancies is the choroidal. Patients with a medium-sized choroidal melanoma (between 2.5 and 10 mm in height and <16 mm basal diameter) are candidates for episcleral plaques [6]. It offers good chances of conserving the eye, often with at least some useful vision [7, 8]. Compared to charged particle radiation, the collimating effects of an eye plaque provides better conformality than possible with protons and essentially zero dose to the brain and orbit behind the plaque. Different types of eye plaque are used for the treatment of intraocular tumours, which are most often round, made of gold, silver, or stainless steel and come in several diameters depending on the tumour size. The Collaborative Ocular Melanoma Study group provided the first standardized methods for administering ocular brachytherapy treatments for uveal melanoma in 1985, by the eye plaques, and for the brachytherapy seeds, the dose was calculated using a point source approximation, and no corrections were made for source anisotropy, the plaque or insert materials of the plaques and also photon backscatter or fluorescence photons from the plaque backing. In the early 1990s, the begging of the investigation of the effect of the plaque backing and material insert (such as Silastic) on dose distribution and the recommended dosimetry protocol for eye plaques was issued by the Task Group (TG) 129 report. This report includes the correction factors/formula for heterogeneous plaque materials (backing and insert material) [9–12]. Common isotopes used in ocular brachytherapy are ^{125}I, ^{103}-Pd and 106-Ru. Iodine−125 is currently the most commonly used and well documented in the literature. Some few centers use palladium-103, observing that the low gamma emission of ^{103}-Pd, 20 keV, presents less radiation exposure hazard to personnel [13]. But due to the low energy of the photons from ^{103}-Pd, the effect of backscatter from plaque backing on dose distribution is expected to be significant. Many reports are available concerning the effect of the gold plaque backing on dose rate [14, 15]. They reported a dose enhancement near the seed due to the backscatter photons from the gold backing. Chiu-Tsao et al. [16], Thomson et al. [17] and de la Zerda et al. [12] reported that dose at small distances from the seed was reduced due to the presence of gold backing. In this work, the Monte Carlo technique is used to study dose rate distributions around the COMS gold eye plaques having diameters from 10 to 22 mm and fully loaded with a palladium seed. The seeds were distributed into Silastic insert inside the 10–22 mm diameter COMS eye plaques. As reported by the American Association of Physicists in Medicine (AAPM), TG-43U1 recommendations, before using each new source, the dosimetric characteristics of the source need to be determined to provide reliable data for use in treatment planning calculations [18]. As stated by TG-43U1 guidelines, we have calculated the dosimetric parameters of the IR06-^{103}Pd source. As the internal components of the seed are free to move within the titanium capsule, their location can vary with seed orientations. In our Monte Carlo calculations, three geometric models of the seed (ideal, vertical and diagonal) were also developed. Since the tumour control rate for plaque brachytherapy is high, the most important issue is the side effects in healthy structures (points of interest) in the eye region. Doses at points of interest were calculated for selected plaque positions on the surface of an eye. Further Monte Carlo simulations have been employed to investigate the effect of plaque gold backing and Silastic inserts on dose distributions along the central axis of the eye plaque and at critical points in the eye region. To investigate the effect of the plaque backing and Silastic insert on dose distributions, four different configurations of plaque were simulated for the IR06-palladium seed model, namely:

1. Silastic insert with gold backing

2. Silastic insert with water replacing gold backing

3. Liquid water replacing Silastic, with gold

4. Liquid water replacing Silastic and gold (seeds alone in water)

Finally, dose along the plaque's central axis and at the critical points are compared with 125-I (6711 model) and ^{103}-Pd (Theragenics model 200) seeds loaded in COMS eye plaque [17].

2. Materials and methods

In this work, the Monte Carlo calculations have been performed to calculate the dose distribution around the eye plaque. The Monte Carlo method is a numerical technique using random numbers and probability to solve problems. It performs an effort to model nature through direct simulation for any possible results, by a probability distribution, for any cause that has inherent uncertainty. The name of this method comes from the casino name in Monaco, because of roulette, a simple random number generator. Clinical dose calculations are generally carried out with the patient treated as water equivalent and a dose of 85 Gy prescribed to the tumour apex. In the calculation the effects from the presence of the plaque backing, insert and intraocular media are considered [19]. In this work, the dose distributions were simulated using the MCNP5 Monte Carlo (MC) radiation transport code published by the Los Alamos National Laboratory, and the MCPLIB04 photon cross-section library is based on the ENDF/B-VI data [20]. The ^{103}-Pd photon spectrum used in these simulations was obtained from TG-43U1 table XIII [18]. To calculate absorbed dose and kerma, the particle fluence and cell-heating tallies, F4 and F6, have been used, respectively.

2.1 ^{103}-Pd source description

The source used in this study is the palladium-103 source model IR06-^{103}Pd seed which is designed and fabricated in Agricultural, Medical and Industrial Research School (AMIRS). The production of ^{103}-Pd is carried out via the $^{103}Rh(p,n)^{103}Pd$ reaction which is well suited to low-energy cyclotrons. 103-Rh target was irradiated via cyclotron (IBA-Cyclone30, Belgium) at the AMIRS. The solid targetry system in this cyclotron is made up of a pure copper backing on which the target materials are electrodeposited. The target that undergoes bombardments by the proton beam at the cyclotron production consists of three layers as follows: (I) rhodium layer, (II) copper layer and (III) copper layer without induced proton beam [21]. All irradiation of the electroplated Rh targets were performed at 200 μA beam current. The rhodium targets were prepared by the electrodeposition technique. Thus, the electrodeposition experiments were performed in acidic sulphate media using $RhCl_3.3H_2O$, $Rh_2(SO_4)_3$. The radiochemical processing of the irradiation targets involved (a) dissolution, (b) radiochemical separation of ^{103}-Pd from the Rh target solution and (c) recovery of ^{103}-Pd as the final product from the organic phases [22]. After the chemical separation process, ^{103}-Pd radioactive material is absorbed uniformly in the resin Amberlite IR-93 resin (20–50 mesh) bead to encapsulate inside the titanium capsule. The seed contains five resin beads, each in diameter of 0.6 mm with the compositions of (by weight percent) C, 90%; H, 8%; Pd, 1%; Cl, 0.7%; and N, 0.3%, with the density equal to 1.14 g/cm^3. The resin beads are packed inside a titanium capsule of 4.7 mm length; 0.7 and 0.8 mm internal and external diameters, respectively; and 0.6 mm thick end caps and with an effective length of 3 mm. ^{103}-Pd radioactive material is absorbed uniformly in the resin bead volume [23]. **Figure 1** shows a schematic diagram of the IR06-^{103}Pd seed. As the resin beads are free to move within the titanium capsule, their location can vary with seed orientations. Following the TG-43U1 recommendation for "good practice for Monte Carlo calculations" [18], mechanical mobility of the internal component of the seed has been considered in the simulations, and three geometric models (ideal, vertical and diagonal) of the seed were developed as shown in **Figure 1a–c**.

2.2 Seed Monte Carlo dosimetry

The IR06-^{103}Pd brachytherapy seed has been simulated in the center of a spherical water phantom in 15 cm radius with an array of 1 mm thick detector rings. Detectors were defined at distances of r = 0.25, 0.5, 0.75, 1, 2, 3, 4, 5 and 7 cm, away from the palladium-103 seed and at polar angles relative to the seed longitudinal axis from 0 to 90°. The rings were also bounded with two cones (10°) bisecting the phantom sphere corresponding to points in two-dimensional TG-43U1 dose formalism for ideal orientation and from 0 to 180° for vertical and diagonal orientations, with 10° increment. A cross section of the detector arrangement is shown in **Figure 2**.

To calculate the dosimetric parameters of the seed, TG43-U1 formalism has been used, which are briefly described by Sadeghi et al. [24].

According to TG43-U1 recommendation, the proposed formula for two-dimensional dose rate is

$$\dot{D}(r,\theta) = S_K \Lambda \frac{G(r,\theta)}{G(r_0,\theta_0)} g(r) F(r,\theta) \tag{1}$$

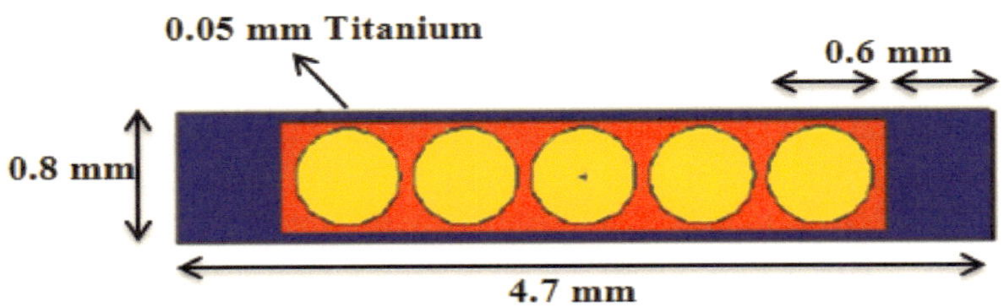

(a)

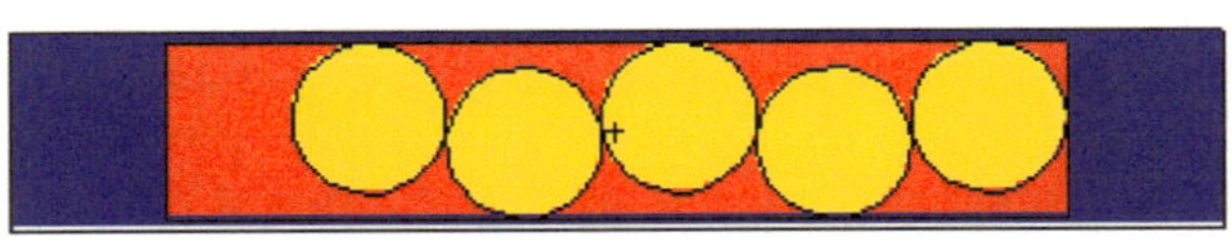

(b)

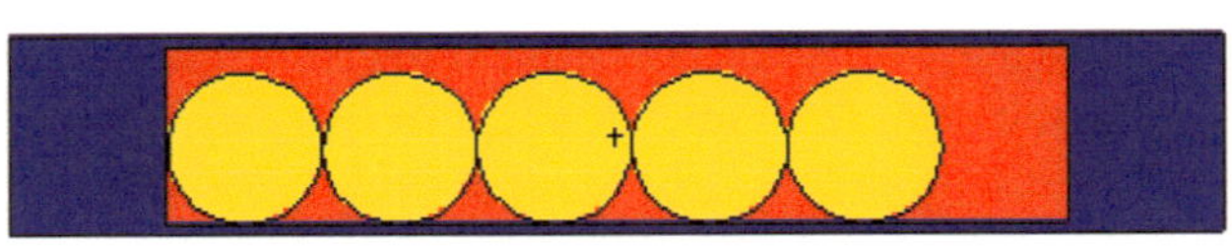

(c)

Figure 1.
Schematic diagram of the IR06-^{103}Pd seed in (a) ideal, (b) diagonal and (c) vertical orientation.

Figure 2.
Cross section of the detector arrangement for Monte Carlo calculations.

where:

$\dot{D}(r,\theta)$ is the dose rate in the water at the distance r in cm from the source.
θ is the polar angle specifying the point of interest.
S_K is the air kerma strength and the unit is $U = cGy\ cm^2h^{-1}$.
Λ is the dose rate constant with the unit of $cGy\ h^{-1}U^{-1}$.
$\frac{G(r,\theta)}{G(r_0,\theta_0)}$ is the geometry factor; $r_0 = 1\,cm$ and $\theta_0 = 90^0$ (reference position).
$g(r)$ and $F(r,\theta)$ are the radial dose function and the anisotropy function, respectively.

The dose rate constant, Λ, for the seed was calculated as the ratio of the dose to water at 1 cm from the seed along the transverse axis to the source's air kerma strength, S_K, at distance r from the source center. The air kerma strength was calculated using the following equation [18]:

$$S_K = \dot{K}_\delta(r)r^2 \tag{2}$$

As the energy of the photons from ^{103}-Pd are low, in the Monte Carlo calculations, all the generated electrons from the photon collisions are absorbed locally, so it was expected that dose is equal to kerma at all points of interest. The air kerma rate, $\dot{K}_\delta(r)$, of the seed was determined by calculating the dose in 1 mm thick air-filled rings in a vacuum. The rings were bounded by 86 and 94° conics and defined with a radial increment of 5–150 cm along the transverse axis of the source to find the SK that is independent to distance [14]. The dose distributions were calculated from the energy deposition averaged over a cell tally F6 in MeV/g/source photon. For the calculations, the titanium characteristic X-ray production was suppressed with δ = 5 keV (δ is the energy cut-off) [25]. The radial dose function expresses the effect of tissue attenuation on photons emitted from seed and defines the dose fall-off along the seed transverse axis due to the attenuation and scattering of the photon. g(r) was calculated by the following equation:

$$g_X(r) = \frac{\dot{D}(r,\theta_0)}{\dot{D}(r_0,\theta_0)}\frac{G_L(r_0,\theta_0)}{G_L(r,\theta_0)} \tag{3}$$

Dose variations, as the distribution of seed radioactivity, oblique filtration, and self-absorption in the encapsulating material, are defined by the 2D anisotropy function as follows:

$$F(r,\theta) = \frac{\dot{D}(r,\theta)}{\dot{D}(r,\theta_0)} \frac{G_L(r,\theta_0)}{G_L(r,\theta)} \tag{4}$$

The simulations were performed in water with 1 × 109 histories giving statistical uncertainties of 2.5 and 3.5% at 1 and 5 cm along the long axis and 0.05–0.1% at 1 and 5 cm on the transverse plane. The statistical uncertainty in the air was 1% with 7 × 107 histories. In this study, the Monte Carlo simulation was benchmarked with the brachytherapy seed model Theragenics 200 [18, 26].

2.3 Eye plaque simulation

To determine the dose rate around the eye plaque, eyeball and eye plaque, which are loaded with the seeds, are modelled in the center of 20 × 20 × 15 cm^3 water phantom. The seeds were distributed in the Silastic insert. The longitudinal axes of the seeds are perpendicular to the eye phantom central plane.

The total dose is calculated by the following equation [14]:

$$\dot{d}(x,y,z) = {}_{SP}\dot{d}(x,y,z)\left[{}_{source}S_K\left(\frac{SK}{A}\right)^{-1}K\right].n \tag{5}$$

where $\dot{d}(x,y,z)$ is the dose rate at (x, y, z) position, S_k is the air kerma strength per history calculated by using Monte Carlo methods, A is the activity (mCi), K is the photons emitted per unit activity (photons mCi^{-1}) and n is the number of seeds which are loaded in the eye plaque. The COMS eye plaques which are used in this study are composed of two parts with diameters ranging from 10 to 22 mm in 2 mm increments:

a. The gold backing, with the composition of (by weight) 77% gold, 14% silver, 8% 159 copper and 1% palladium and a density of 15.8 g/cm^3 [27]

b. The Silastic insert as a seed career with the composition of (by weight) 6.3% hydrogen, 24.9% carbon, 28.9% oxygen, 39.9% silicon and 0.005% platinum and a density of 1.12 g/cm^3 [15]

*The plaque assumed a standard eye diameter of 24.6 mm by considering lens and homogenized eye materials according to ICRU 46 [28]. The position of the points is followed by Thomson et al. [17] (**Figure 3**). The lens is modelled in the homogenized eye, and to obtain the dose rate, the plaque and eye ball are then modelled at the center of the spherical water phantom with 30 cm diameter. The plaque backing and Silastic insert effect on dose rate is obtained by replacing water with gold and Silastic insert. Central axis depth dose to water was determined using the F6 tally of MCNP for 0.05 mm radius and 0.01 mm thick cylindrical voxels from the outer sclera (−1 mm) to 11 mm inside the eye in 0.5 mm steps [2]. For the comparison doses to interest points (center of the eye, macula, optic disk, proximal sclera, tumour apex, lacrimal gland and retina opposite the apex) have been determined. The total dose is calculated following Melhus and Rivard [14] and Thomson et al. [17] verbatim: "The Monte Carlo simulations provide the dose in a voxel per history. The dose rate is calculated by dividing this number by the air kerma strength per history for the relevant seed type and multiplying by the number of seeds and the air kerma strength per seed. The air kerma strength per seed is chosen in order to obtain a prescription dose of 85Gy at the tumour apex (5 mm on the central axis) in 168 hours for ^{103}-Pd. The total dose delivered during treatment is then*

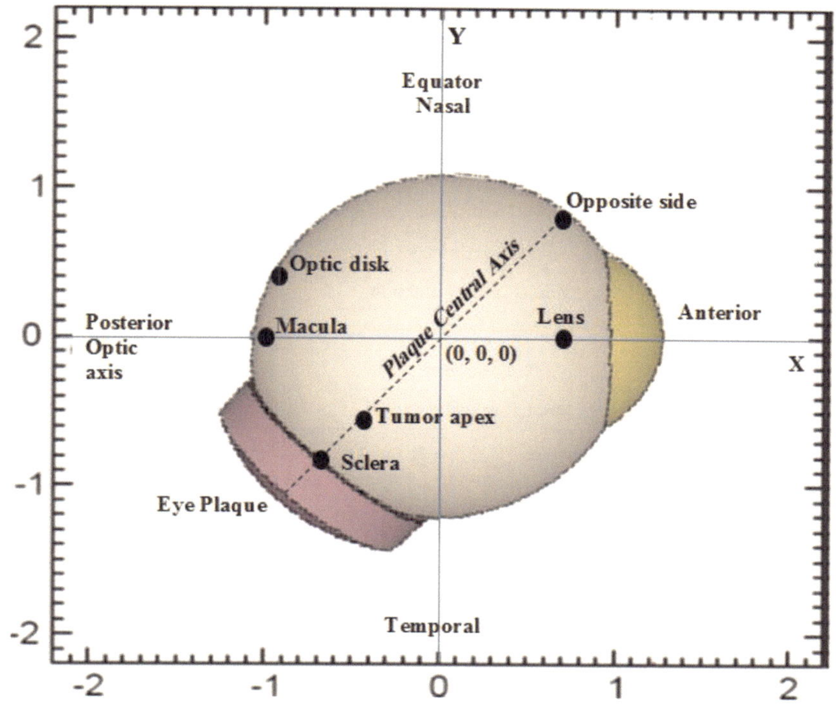

Figure 3.
Points of interest for eye plaque dosimetry, given in the center of eye reference frame (scale in centimeters) for a right eye [17]. In the figure a plaque midway between the posterior pole and equator temporal is shown. All points of interest are indicated (with the exception of the lacrimal gland, which does not lie in the plane shown).

determined by integrating over the treatment time, taking into account the exponential decay of the source". Also, the photoelectric absorption, fluorescent emission and Rayleigh and Compton scattering, of characteristic K- and L-shell X-rays, are all simulated. For variance reduction, the electron and photon transport energy cut-off in all calculations was selected at 1 and 5 keV, respectively [29]. In the simulation 3.8 × 10⁸ photon histories were simulated, and the statistical uncertainties at 5 and 11 mm (tumour apex) depth of central axis were obtained at 0.7 and 1.1%, respectively. Statistical uncertainties at the opposite side of the eye exceeded 4% which has the greatest uncertainty among the points on interest.

3. Results and discussions

3.1 Seed dosimetry benchmarking

In this work, the Monte Carlo simulation was benchmarked with the Theragenics model 200 source. The comparison between the calculated value of Λ for the model 200 in this study, 0.685 cGy h^{-1} U^{-1}, and the previously published data for the seed [18], 0.686 cGy h^{-1} U^{-1} (~0.1% difference), shows the accuracy of our simulation method. The result has been presented in **Table 1**. Based on the calculations, the dose rate constant for the IR06-^{103}Pd source in ideal orientation is estimated to be 0.692 ± 0.020 cGy·h^{-1}·U^{-1} which is comparable with the other two commercial sources. Calculated S_K per contained activity for model 200 in this work was 0.722 U mCi^{-1}. The result was compared to 0.721 U mCi^{-1} for Williamson's WAFAC simulation, [26] and Melhus et al. [14] calculations. The values of Λ in three seed orientations ranged from 0.689 to 0.697 cGy h^{-1} U^{-1}, with a 0.34%

Source type	Method	Medium	Λ (cGy h^{-1} U^{-1})
IR06-^{103}Pd	Monte Carlo simulation (ideal)[a]	Liquid water	0.692 ± 0.021
	Monte Carlo simulation (diagonal)[a]	Liquid water	0.697 ± 0.021
	Monte Carlo simulation (vertical)[a]	Liquid water	0.689 ± 0.021
MED3633	TLD dosimetry[b]	Solid water	0.688 ± 0.05
	Monte Carlo simulation[c]	Liquid water	0.677 ± 0.02
Theragenics model 200	TLD dosimetry[d]	Solid water	0.650 ± 0.08
	Monte Carlo simulation[e]	Liquid water	0.686 ± 0.03
	Monte Carlo simulation[a]	Liquid water	0.685 ± 0.02
Best model 2335	TLD dosimetry[f]	Solid water	0.69 ± 0.08
	Monte Carlo simulation[f]	Liquid water	0.67 ± 0.02

[a] *Present work.*
[b] *Ref. [33].*
[c] *Ref. [34].*
[d] *Ref. [32].*
[e] *Ref. [26].*
[f] *Ref. [27].*

Table 1.
Monte Carlo calculated dose rate constant, Λ, of the IR06-^{103}Pd and model 200 seeds in comparison with the measured and calculated values of model MED3633, model 200 and model 2335 seeds.

uncertainty. According to TG-43U1, a standard uncertainty of 3% is acceptable for Monte Carlo studies. The dose rate constant can be calculated by normalizing to the S_K of the vertical orientation and the source geometry during the NIST calibration. The values, in this case, are 0.680 ± 0.020 cGy h^{-1} U^{-1}, ~1.7% lower than the value in the ideal orientation. This result obtained in this study is comparable with Λ values obtained for other ^{103}-Pd sources which are presented in TG-43U1 report. **Table 1** shows the calculated dose rate constant for the IR06-^{103}Pd seed and the measured and calculated values of Λ, for NASI model MED3633, Theragenics model 200 and Best model sources.

The calculated line radial dose function $g_L(r)$, of the IR06-^{103}Pd for ideal orientation, was fit to a fifth-order polynomial function yielding the following relationship:

$$g_L(r) = a_0 + a_1 r + a_2 r^2 + a_3 r^3 + a_4 r^4 + a_5 r^5 \quad (6)$$

where:

a_0 = 1.785, a_1 = −1.064, a_2 = 3.385 × 10^{-1}, a_3 = −7.062 × 10^{-2}, a_4 = 8.469 × 10^{-3} and a_5 = −4.173 × 10^{-4} define R^2 = 9.999 × 10^{-1}.

Figure 4 presents the radial dos—e function, $g(r)$, for IR06-^{103}Pd seed and three other commercial sources. **Table 2** shows the differences between the results of this study and AAPM TG-43U1 reference data for model 200. As the differences are <3%, the agreement between these data sets is acceptable. The radial dose function values for two other geometric models, vertical and diagonal, were also calculated, and the disagreement between them varied from <2%. The anisotropy function, $F(r,\theta)$, of the IR06-^{103}Pd seed was calculated in the phantom of water, at radial distances of r = 0.25, 0.5, 0.75, 1, 1.5, 2, 3, 4, 5 and 7 cm relative to the seed center and polar angle, θ, ranging from 0 to 180° for vertical and diagonal orientations and 0–90° for ideal orientation, in 10° increment with respect to the seed long axis. The results are shown in **Table 3**.

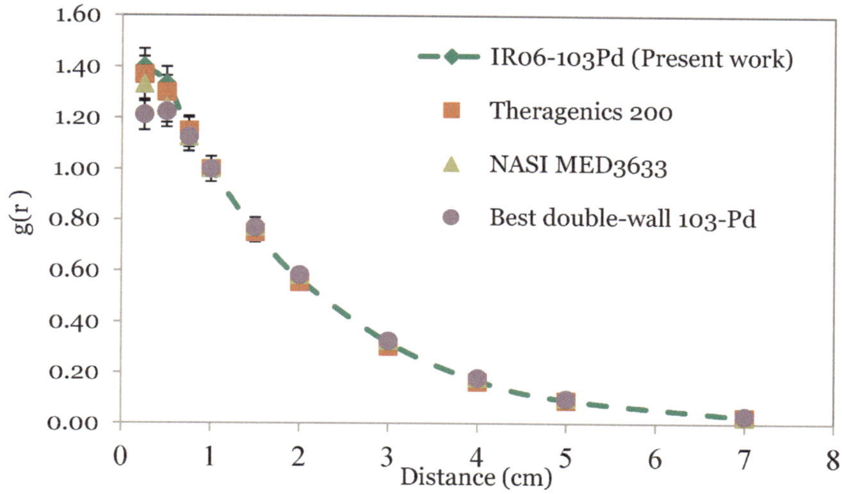

Figure 4.
Comparison of the calculated radial dose function of IR06-^{103}Pd seeds in water versus other available sources [18, 30].

r (cm)	$g_L(r)$			
	Theragenics 200		Percent difference (%)	IR06-^{103}Pd
	Ref. [26]	Present work		
0.5	1.300	1.330	−2	1.333
0.75	1.150	1.170	−2	1.144
1	1.000	1.000	0	1.000
1.5	0.749	0.755	−1	0.756
2	0.555	0.567	−2	0.566
3	0.302	0.305	−1	0.318
4	0.163	0.168	−3	0.168
5	0.089	0.091	−3	0.091
7	0.026	0.027	−2	0.026

Table 2.
Monte Carlo calculations for radial dose function, $g_L(r)$, for IR06-^{103}Pd and model 200 seeds compared to reference Monte Carlo data.

Figure 5 shows a comparison between the calculated anisotropy function of the IR06-^{103}Pd seeds at a distance of 2 cm from the source center in water with the other published data (in ideal orientation). The values of the anisotropy function for the new ^{103}-Pd sources agreed with those for the model MED3633, Theragenics model 200 and Best® double-wall ^{103}-Pd sources [18, 26, 30] are found in 4% in angles >20°. Due to the thick end caps of the IR06-^{103}Pd source, the differences in smaller angles can be as large as up to 17%.

3.2 Plaque Monte Carlo simulations

Table 4 shows the calculated central depth dose distribution for COMS eye plaques loaded with IR06-^{103}Pd seeds in the Silastic insert.

The depth dose distribution has been calculated in 0.5 mm steps between the outer sclera (−1 mm) to 3 mm and in 1 mm steps from 4 to 10 mm. The dose distribution is also calculated in water medium to obtain the effect of the Silastic insert and the plaque backing on central axis dose distribution. In this study, the

a. 2-D anisotropy function, F(r,θ), in ideal seed orientation

r (cm)	Θ=									
	0°	10°	20°	30°	40°	50°	60°	70°	80°	90°
0.25	0.053	0.074	0.616	0.854	0.924	0.959	0.979	0.992	0.998	1.000
0.5	0.132	0.165	0.472	0.701	0.845	0.927	0.964	0.985	0.996	1.000
0.75	0.169	0.211	0.480	0.686	0.823	0.912	0.960	0.985	0.997	1.000
1	0.190	0.242	0.491	0.686	0.816	0.903	0.956	0.982	0.996	1.000
1.5	0.229	0.281	0.512	0.692	0.813	0.899	0.952	0.982	0.995	1.000
2	0.265	0.309	0.526	0.696	0.814	0.896	0.950	0.982	0.996	1.000
3	0.294	0.345	0.545	0.705	0.815	0.897	0.949	0.981	0.997	1.000
4	0.319	0.369	0.558	0.709	0.818	0.895	0.948	0.979	0.995	1.000
5	0.337	0.392	0.568	0.715	0.820	0.900	0.948	0.981	0.995	1.000
7	0.405	0.428	0.601	0.730	0.831	0.900	0.948	0.982	1.004	1.000

b. 2-D anisotropy function, F(r,θ), in vertical seed orientation

r (cm)	Θ=									
	0°	10°	20°	30°	40°	50°	60°	70°	80°	90°
0.25	1.155	0.471	0.526	0.591	0.568	0.504	0.426	0.351	0.308	1.000
0.5	0.958	0.436	0.485	0.597	0.650	0.672	0.682	0.695	0.720	1.000
0.75	0.931	0.453	0.508	0.631	0.702	0.743	0.775	0.806	0.840	1.000
1	0.907	0.471	0.531	0.656	0.733	0.784	0.823	0.856	0.895	1.000
1.5	0.900	0.497	0.560	0.685	0.767	0.824	0.868	0.905	0.945	1.000
2	0.880	0.514	0.579	0.704	0.786	0.845	0.888	0.928	0.967	1.000
3	0.859	0.541	0.606	0.724	0.810	0.867	0.912	0.952	0.992	1.000
4	0.851	0.557	0.623	0.737	0.817	0.875	0.924	0.961	1.004	1.000
5	0.810	0.577	0.637	0.747	0.826	0.883	0.927	0.968	1.009	1.000
7	0.889	0.610	0.668	0.769	0.846	0.901	0.946	0.977	1.024	1.000
r (cm)	**100°**	**110°**	**120°**	**130°**	**140°**	**150°**	**160°**	**170°**	**180°**	
0.25	0.945	0.682	0.877	0.942	0.975	0.993	1.003	1.005	1.002	
0.5	0.918	0.652	0.741	0.855	0.933	0.974	0.994	1.003	1.002	
0.75	0.887	0.661	0.739	0.837	0.916	0.964	0.989	1.000	1.001	
1	0.874	0.673	0.743	0.835	0.908	0.960	0.988	1.000	1.001	
1.5	0.856	0.685	0.753	0.837	0.906	0.956	0.985	0.999	1.001	
2	0.851	0.696	0.758	0.840	0.905	0.954	0.984	0.998	1.001	
3	0.845	0.712	0.768	0.845	0.907	0.954	0.984	0.998	1.001	
4	0.842	0.722	0.778	0.848	0.907	0.953	0.983	0.997	1.000	
5	0.839	0.733	0.785	0.853	0.909	0.953	0.983	0.996	1.000	
7	0.852	0.757	0.805	0.869	0.919	0.963	0.988	1.003	1.004	

c. 2-D anisotropy function, F(r,θ), in diagonal seed orientation										
r (cm)	**Θ=**									
	0°	**10°**	**20°**	**30°**	**40°**	**50°**	**60°**	**70°**	**80°**	**90°**
0.25	1.155	0.471	0.525	0.591	0.567	0.502	0.424	0.352	0.310	1.000
0.5	0.969	0.438	0.485	0.597	0.651	0.673	0.682	0.696	0.723	1.000
0.75	0.941	0.453	0.508	0.631	0.701	0.744	0.775	0.805	0.842	1.000
1	0.918	0.471	0.530	0.657	0.734	0.783	0.822	0.857	0.897	1.000
1.5	0.907	0.497	0.560	0.686	0.767	0.824	0.866	0.906	0.947	1.000
2	0.881	0.515	0.579	0.704	0.786	0.845	0.889	0.930	0.972	1.000
3	0.857	0.540	0.607	0.724	0.806	0.865	0.910	0.953	0.995	1.000
4	0.852	0.556	0.623	0.738	0.817	0.873	0.921	0.962	1.003	1.000
5	0.810	0.577	0.637	0.746	0.825	0.883	0.928	0.969	1.012	1.000
7	0.888	0.610	0.669	0.769	0.846	0.902	0.946	0.979	1.027	1.000
r (cm)	**100°**	**110°**	**120°**	**130°**	**140°**	**150°**	**160°**	**170°**	**180°**	
0.25	0.945	0.684	0.879	0.943	0.974	0.993	1.002	1.003	1.004	
0.5	0.921	0.652	0.741	0.856	0.935	0.975	0.994	1.002	1.003	
0.75	0.889	0.663	0.739	0.837	0.915	0.964	0.989	1.001	1.002	
1	0.876	0.673	0.744	0.836	0.910	0.961	0.989	1.000	1.002	
1.5	0.860	0.686	0.752	0.837	0.905	0.956	0.985	0.999	1.001	
2	0.852	0.697	0.758	0.841	0.905	0.955	0.984	0.999	1.001	
3	0.847	0.713	0.769	0.845	0.906	0.954	0.984	0.998	1.002	
4	0.843	0.723	0.778	0.848	0.907	0.954	0.983	0.997	1.001	
5	0.842	0.733	0.785	0.853	0.908	0.953	0.983	0.996	1.000	
7	0.856	0.759	0.806	0.868	0.919	0.963	0.988	1.003	1.005	

Table 3.
2-D anisotropy functions for the IR06-^{103}Pd seed calculated by Monte Carlo method for the (a) ideal orientation, (b) vertical orientation and (c) diagonal orientation.

required air kerma strength per seed (S_K) is calculated to deliver prescription dose (85 Gy) to the apex of the tumour (5 mm depth) for 168 hours of implant. In addition, to investigate the effect of different materials constituting the COMS plaque on dose distributions near the plaque, the ratio of dose in three media (discussed above) relative to dose in water medium is shown in **Figure 6**.

3.3 Effect of the gold backing

The effect of 20 mm gold plaque backing on dose distribution along the central axis is shown in **Figure 7**, which provides central axis depth dose curve for full loaded IR06-^{103}Pd, Theragenics 200 and model 2335 seeds with water replacing the Silastic. This figure demonstrates dose is increased near the plaque; now this well-known effect is due to L-shell fluorescence photons emitted by atoms in the plaque backing [27]. Emission photons from palladium seeds with an average energy of about 21 keV excite the L-shell in gold and silver [31] which are the composition of the plaque backing. The excitation of these shells results in the emission of fluorescence photons, so this event explains why dose increases near the plaque. About

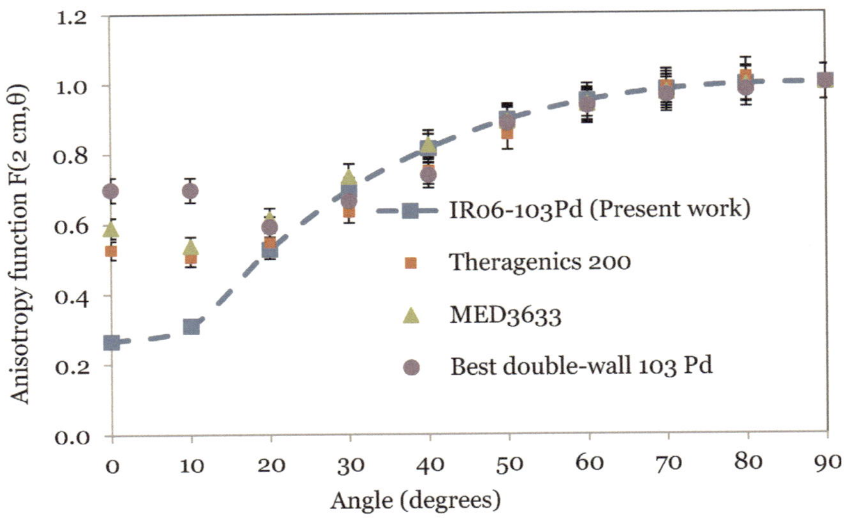

Figure 5.
Comparison of the calculated anisotropy function of the IR06-^{103}Pd seed versus other available sources at 2 cm [18, 30].

0.7% dose enhancement is observed near the plaque which is loaded with IR06-^{103}Pd seeds, but as the fluorescence photons are absorbed (mean free path is about 2 mm), after a few millimeters, the dose decreases in the order of 6.5%. In Thomson et al. [17] work, a dose decrease of about 6–6.3% at the opposite side of the eye for ^{103}-Pd (Theragenics model 200) seed in gold backing (no Silastic) was reported. Chiu-Tsao et al. reported a dose decrease of about 10% for ^{125}I (model 6711) seed with 20 mm gold plaque (no Silastic) at 7.6 mm. Since the emitted photons from the ^{125}I seed have higher energy than those emitted by ^{103}-Pd seed, more fluorescence photons are observed when ^{125}I source is used. Due to the emission of fluorescence photons from the plaque backing for all seed and backing models without any polymer insert, there is a small dose enhancement near the plaque. The spectrum of fluorescence photons depends on the energy of photons emitted by the seed and its active length and also depends on the composition of plaque backing.

3.4 Effect of silastic insert

The central axis doses for the IR06-^{103}Pd seeds in Silastic insert with plaque backing are shown in **Figure 8** relative to the doses for the same seeds in the water medium. Silastic with an effective atomic number of ~10.7 has a greater attenuating effect than water with an effective atomic number of Zeff (~7.4) [17]. The average variation in dose distribution due to Silastic insert relative to water is about 17%. Thomson et al. [27] reported 17% dose reduction for Theragenics model 200^{103}-Pd seed at a distance of 1 cm in COMS plaque due to the presence of Silastic insert. Chiu-Tsao et al. [16] calculated a 10% dose reduction at 1 cm for Silastic insert only, in 20 mm COMS eye plaque for 125I, and 16% for ^{103}-Pd (without gold backing) relative to water along the central axis; according to their study also, they presented that the effect of gold+ Silastic combination is comparable with the effect of Silastic insert only. The reduction of dose for 125I source in Silastic insert is more than ^{103}-Pd source due to its higher energy of emitted photons. The dose reduction for the gold + Silastic combination relative to water medium as shown in **Figures 6** and **8** is

Central axis depth (mm)	a. Gold backing + Silastic						
	IR06-^{103}Pd seeds						
	COMS eye plaque diameter (mm)						
	10	12	14	16	18	20	22
−1	582.3	462.1	411.1	325.7	309.1	297.4	300.3
−0.5	474.1	401.5	375.2	305.5	296.3	232.3	298.5
0	380.7	325.8	302.1	271.5	264.3	212.8	254.7
0.5	312.5	300.0	267.4	250.7	220.2	202.8	222.8
1	302.7	248.6	220.2	243.9	189.2	176.4	196.8
1.5	254.8	220.1	215.3	214.4	180.5	167.8	178.7
2	198.4	190.5	170.0	188.9	168.7	159.8	168.2
2.5	180.8	183.7	162.5	164.3	152.4	140.6	154.6
3	148.9	150.3	130.8	148.2	132.8	122.7	155.2
4	120.3	105.1	110.2	120.4	108.7	100.2	104.5
5 (Apex)	85.0	85.0	85.0	85.0	85.0	85.0	85.0
6	63.7	64.1	72.5	80.0	78.2	69.5	72.4
7	50.0	50.0	52.4	69.2	60.5	58.4	60.1
8	32.4	35.2	35.3	55.4	48.9	55.1	51.2
9	28.4	29.8	34.8	40.5	41.5	38	40.5
10	22.5	24.6	28.9	28.8	33.1	35.5	34.4
$S_K(U)$	*10.88*	*7.11*	*5.1*	*5.23*	*3.52*	*3.33*	*3.61*
Central axis depth (mm)	**b. Gold backing + Silastic**						
	^{103}Pd model 200 seeds [14]						
	COMS eye plaque diameter (mm)						
	10	**12**	**14**	**16**	**18**	**20**	**22**
−1	640.1	479.9	406.9	279.0	306.2	272.0	310.3
−0.5	547.0	423.8	368.7	277.7	281.2	252.7	278.1
0	452.4	366.5	322.4	259.1	250.6	227.6	242.1
0.5	376.3	313.1	278.8	234.2	221.7	204.6	213.0
1	313.8	268.0	241.9	210.4	198.5	183.8	187.9
1.5	260.6	230.2	211.9	189.1	177.8	166.5	166.2
2	218.2	199.1	185.4	169.0	160.7	151.3	150.4
2.5	183.8	171.0	162.0	151.3	143.9	137.2	136.7
3	155.5	147.1	142.5	134.1	129.9	124.9	123.6
4	113.4	111.0	109.6	107.2	105.5	102.9	102.4
5 (Apex)	85.0	85.0	85.0	85.0	85.0	85.0	85.0
6	64.7	65.8	67.2	68.1	69.8	70.2	70.8
7	49.7	51.8	53.4	54.3	56.8	57.8	58.6
8	39.3	41.3	42.7	44.1	46.6	48.3	48.7
9	31.2	32.7	34.4	36.1	38.1	40.0	40.9
10	25.2	26.1	28.1	29.4	31.9	33.1	34.6
$S_K(U)$	*11.057*	*7.299*	*4.809*	*5.062*	*3.405*	*3.139*	*3.738*

Central axis depth (mm)	c. Gold backing + Silastic/water medium						
	IR06-^{103}Pd seeds						
	COMS eye plaque diameter (mm)						
	10	12	14	16	18	20	22
−1	0.74	0.72	0.71	0.65	0.68	0.66	0.71
−0.5	0.75	0.75	0.73	0.72	0.73	0.72	0.73
0	0.76	0.76	0.76	0.73	0.76	0.73	0.76
0.5	0.78	0.78	0.78	0.77	0.77	0.76	0.77
1	0.80	0.80	0.79	0.79	0.79	0.79	0.78
1.5	0.81	0.81	0.81	0.81	0.8	0.79	0.78
2	0.81	0.81	0.81	0.81	0.81	0.80	0.78
2.5	0.81	0.81	0.81	0.81	0.81	0.80	0.79
3	0.81	0.81	0.81	0.81	0.82	0.80	0.81
4	0.81	0.81	0.81	0.81	0.82	0.80	0.81
5 (Apex)	0.81	0.81	0.81	0.81	0.82	0.81	0.81
6	0.80	0.80	0.81	0.8	0.82	0.81	0.81
7	0.80	0.80	0.81	0.8	0.82	0.81	0.81
8	0.80	0.80	0.81	0.8	0.82	0.81	0.81
9	0.80	0.80	0.81	0.81	0.81	0.83	0.80
10	0.80	0.80	0.81	0.81	0.81	0.83	0.80
$S_K(U)$	*8.87*	*6.12*	*4*	*4.13*	*2.75*	*2.45*	*3.07*

Table 4.
Central axis dose distributions: (a) in 10–22 mm diameter COMS eye plaques (gold backing + Silastic insert) loaded with IR06-^{103}Pd seeds, (b) gold backing + Silastic insert loaded with ^{103}Pd model 200 seeds [14] and (c) the ratio of the central axis dose of the 10–22 mm COMS plaque (gold backing + silastic) to the central axis dose in water medium loaded with IR06-^{103}Pd seeds.

about 19% at 1 cm and 17% and at 0.5 cm, and the average dose reduction due to the presence of gold backing + Silastic insert along the COMS central axis loaded with the new palladium seeds is about 18%. Thomson et al. have obtained a reduction of the dose relative to water of 20% for ^{103}-Pd seed at 1 cm in the COMS plaque central axis; the main reduction is due to the Silastic insert. The comparison shows that the dose reduction with IR06-^{103}Pd seeds is lower along the central axis of the plaque with the exception of sclera than the other two palladium seed models, Theragenics 200 and model 2335 loaded in COMS plaque.

3.5 Dose comparison at points of interest

To determine the effect of plaque backing and Silastic insert on dose rate at points of interest, more Monte Carlo simulations were employed by replacing the plaque backing and Silastic inserts with water. **Table 5** presents the dose (in Gy) at points of interest for different plaque materials of 20 and 16 mm COMS plaque fully loaded with IR06-^{103}Pd seeds. To obtain the dose at the points of interest in a water

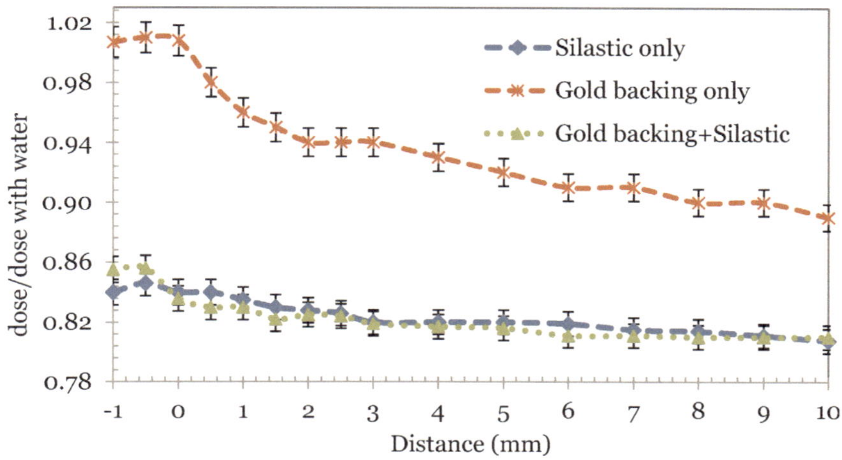

Figure 6.
Ratio of the doses along the plaque's central axis for 20 mm COMS plaque fully loaded with IR06-^{103}Pd to the doses in water medium.

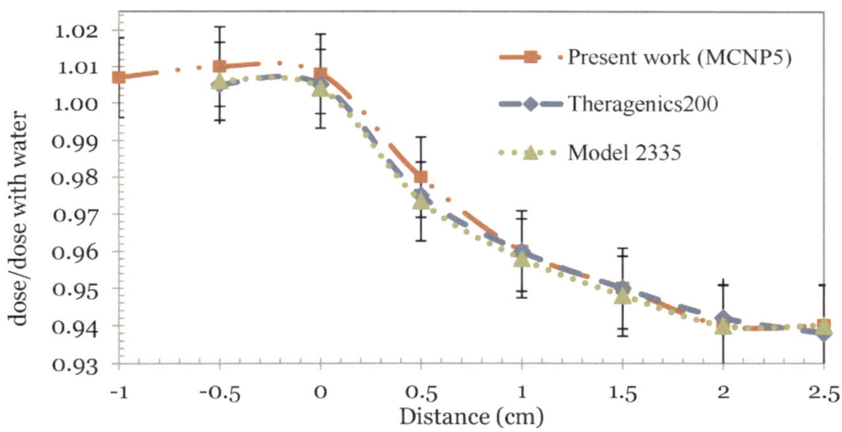

Figure 7.
Ratio of the doses along the plaque's central axis for 20 mm COMS plaque (no Silastic insert) loaded with IR06-^{103}Pd, model 200 and model 2335 seeds to the doses in water medium.

medium, the air kerma strength for each seed, (SK), is required to deliver 85 Gy to the tumour apex in 168 hours. All of the results have been renormalized to deliver the same dose (85 Gy) to the apex of the tumour. The results are compared with the dose at the same points when COMS plaque is loaded with Theragenics model 200 and 6711-125I seeds. According to **Table 5**, dose decreases at the optic disk by ~40% when moving a plaque from nasal to temporal equatorial centers. This is due to the fact that the optic disk is not centered on the eye anterior-posterior (AP) axis and is nearer the nasal plaque. For the plaque position between the posterior pole and equator temporal to the eyeball, the decrease in dose is due to the gold backing, and Silastic insert related to water medium is about 14% for IR06-^{103}Pd seed and 21% for the model 200 at the opposite side of the eye [17]. When compared to identical plaques loaded with model 6711 125I sources, the doses at points of interest are consistently lower in plaque loaded with any of the ^{103}-Pd models in this study.

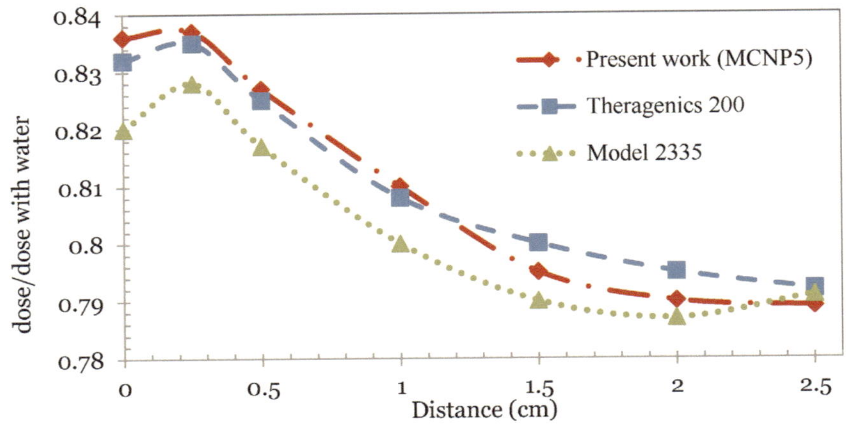

Figure 8.
Ratio of the doses along the plaque's central axis for 20 mm COMS plaque (gold backing + Silastic insert) fully loaded with IR06-^{103}Pd, model 200 and model 2335 seeds [17] to the doses in water medium.

Points of interest	**a. 20 mm COMS**			
	IR06-^{103}Pd[a]			
	Water medium	**Silastic insert only**	**Gold backing only**	**Gold backing + Silastic**
Centre of eye	29.08	34.31	30.82	34.37
Macula (equator and p.p)	15.57	17.22	16.55	18.29
Optic disk (temporal)	7.52	8.81	7.98	8.85
Optic disk (nasal)	18.29	21.47	19.42	21.44
Centre of lens (equator and p.p)	16.21	18.98	17.23	19.00
Sclera	351.81	367.38	374.68	383.73
Apex	85.00	85.00	85.00	85.00
Lacrimal gland (nasal)	4.82	5.59	5.12	5.62
Opposite side	3.39	3.94	3.59	3.95

	b. 16 mm COMS				
	Water medium		**Gold backing + Silastic**		
	IR06-^{103}Pd[a]	**Theragenics 200[b]**	**IR06-^{103}Pd[a]**	**Theragenics 200[b]**	**6711-^{125}I[c]**
Centre of eye	22.52	22.75	17.8	18.3	23.79
Macula (equator and p.p)	10.61	11.43	9.8	8.089	12.82
Optic disk (temporal)	6.32	7.193	5.12	5.35	8.98
Optic disk (nasal)	19.63	21.65	13.67	14.13	21.02
Centre of lens (equator and p.p)	15.63	16.34	11.83	12.5	17.58
Sclera	297.41	287.92	261.4	211	222.9
Apex	85.00	85.00	68.23	68.7	74.43
Lacrimal gland (nasal)	3.72	—	2.75	3.03	—
Opposite side	3.63	3.77	2.22	2.94	5.55

[a]*Present work.*
[b]*Ref. [17].*
[c]*Ref. [27].*

Table 5.
Doses in grey at points of interest for (a) 20 mm (b) 16 mm COMS eye plaque loaded with IR06-^{103}Pd seeds compared with the doses at the same points for model 200 (^{103}Pd) and model 6711 (^{125}I), in 16 mm COMS eye plaque. Eye plaque centerd in the midway of equator and posterior pole (equator and p.p) and centerd on equator temporal and nasal.

4. Conclusion

In this study, the dosimetry of a new design brachytherapy seed IR06-^{103}Pd was determined by Monte Carlo using MCNP (version 5). Simulations were considered in three seed orientations with the result that there are no significant statistical differences among the orientations (i.e., ideal, vertical and diagonal). The dosimetric parameters of the new seed are presented in TG-43U1 format. These parameters are in acceptable agreement with those of other commercially available seed models. Thus, the IR06-^{103}Pd seed is dosimetrically suitable for use in routine brachytherapy where the other similar seeds are employed. Also in this study, the dosimetry of IR06-^{103}Pd seed was evaluated in COMS eye plaques and compared to results for commercially available ^{103}-Pd and 125I seeds in the same plaque geometries.

The COMS Silastic insert has a significant effect in reducing dose along the plaque central axis. The presence of gold backing enhances the dose near the plaque gold surfaces. This effect is due to secondary fluorescence photons arising from the backing material. Due to the energy of these emissions, the effect is significantly attenuated at a distance >2 mm. The dose decrease depends on the composition of the plaque backing material and therefore on the emitted photon spectrum of the seeds and the fluorescence of the backing material.

The combination of gold backing with the Silastic insert decreases the dose relative to water by 19% at 1 cm along the plaque central axis.

This study shows that this 19% effect is lower than for either model 200 or 2335 ^{103}-Pd seeds. Doses to interest points including the macula, optic disk, lens, sclera and lacrimal gland have been determined; and also the effects of plaque backing material and Silastic insert have also been studied at these points. The study affirms that dose and dose rate at these points of interest in COMS plaques are routinely lower when using ^{103}-Pd rather than 125-I seeds. The dose to the proximal sclera, underlying the plaque, is greater using ^{103}-Pd seeds due to lessened penetration than 125-I seeds.

Author details

Pooneh Saidi[1*] and Mahdi Sadeghi[2]

1 Parsikan Iran Engineering and Management Consultants, Tehran, Iran

2 Medical Physics Department, School of Medicine, Iran University of Medical Sciences, Tehran, Iran

*Address all correspondence to: poonehsaidi@gmail.com

References

[1] Maheshwari A, Finger PT. Cancers of the eye. Cancer and Metastasis Reviews. 2018;**37**(4):677-690. DOI: 10.1007/s10555-018-9762-9

[2] Saidi P, Sadeghi M, Shirazi A, Tenreiro C. ROPES eye plaque brachytherapy dosimetry for two models of ^{103}-Pd seeds. Australasian Physical & Engineering Sciences in Medicine. 2011;**34**:223-231. DOI: 10.1007/s13246-011-0069-1

[3] Rivard MJ, Melhus CS, Sioshansi S, Morr J. The impact of prescription depth, dose rate, plaque size, and source loading on the central axis using ^{103}-Pd, 125I, and 131Cs. Brachytherapy. 2008;7:327-335. DOI: 10.1016/j.brachy.2008.05.002

[4] Robertson DM. Changing concepts in the management of choroidal melanoma. American Journal of Ophthalmology. 2003;**136**:161-170. DOI: 10.1016/S0002-9394(03)00265-4

[5] Finger PT. Radiation therapy for choroidal melanoma. Survey of Ophthalmology. 1997;**42**:215-232

[6] Nag S, Quivey J, Earle J, Followill D, Fontanesi J, Finger PT. The American brachytherapy society recommendations for brachytherapy of uveal melanomas. International Journal of Radiation Oncology, Biology, Physics. 2003;**56**:544-555. DOI: 10.1016/S0360-3016(03)00006-3

[7] Char DH, Kroll S, Quivey JM, Castro J. Long term visual outcome of radiated uveal melanomas in eyes eligible for randomisation to enucleation versus brachytherapy. The British Journal of Ophthalmology. 1996;**80**(2):117-124. DOI: 10.1136/bjo.80.2.117.

[8] Melia BM, Abramson DH, Albert DM, Boldt HC, Earle JD, Hanson WF, et al. Collaborative ocular melanoma study (COMS) randomized trial of 125I brachytherapy for medium choroidal melanoma, I. Visual acuity after 3 years: COMS report no. 16. Ophthalmology. 2001;**108**:348-366. DOI: 10.1016/S0161-6420(00)00526-1

[9] Collaborative Ocular Melanoma Study Group. COMS Manual of Procedures PB95-179693. Ch 12. Springfield, VA: National Technical Information Service; 1995

[10] Mourtada F, Chiu-Tsao S, Astrahan M, Finger P, Followill D, Meigooni A, et al. WE-D-BRB-01: Eye plaque dosimetry: Report of the AAPM therapy physics committee task group no. 129. Medical Physics. 2009;**36**(6):2771-2772. DOI: 10.1118/1.3182515

[11] Morrison H, Menon G, Larocque MP, van Veelen B, Niatsetski Y, Weis E, et al. Initial evaluation of advanced collapsed cone engine dose calculations in water medium for I-125 seeds and COMS eye plaques. Medical Physics. 2018;**45**(3):1276-1286. DOI: 10.1002/mp.12776

[12] de la Zerda A, Chiu-Tsao S, Lin J, Boulay LL, Kanna I, Tsao H. 125I plaque dose distribution including penumbra characteristics. Medical Physics. 1996;**23**:407-418. DOI: 10.1118/1.597803

[13] Saidi P, Sadeghi M, Shirazi A, Tenreiro C. Monte Carlo calculation of dosimetry parameters for the IR08-^{103}Pd brachytherapy source. Medical Physics. 2010;**37**:2509-2515. DOI: 10.1118/1.3416922

[14] Melhus CS, Rivard MJ. COMS eye plaque brachytherapy dosimetry simulations for ^{103}-Pd, 125I, and 131Cs. Medical Physics. 2008;**35**:3364-3371. DOI: 10.1118/1.2940604

[15] Saidi P, Sadeghi M, Tenreiro C. Experimental measurements and Monte

Carlo calculations for ^{103}-Pd dosimetry of the 12 mm COMS eye plaque. Physica Medica. 2013;**29**:286-294. DOI: 10.1016/j.ejmp.2012.04.002

[16] Chiu-Tsao ST, Astrahan MA, Finger PT, Followill DS, Meigooni AS, Melhus CS, et al. Dosimetry of 125I and ^{103}-Pd COMS eye plaques for intraocular tumors: Report of task group 129 by the AAPM and ABS. Medical Physics. 2012; **39**:6161-6184. DOI: 10.1118/1.4749933

[17] Thomson RM, Rogers DWO. Monte Carlo dosimetry for 125I and ^{103}-Pd eye plaque brachytherapy with various seed models. Medical Physics. 2010;**37**: 368-376. DOI: 10.1118/1.3271104

[18] Rivard MJ, Coursey BM, DeWerd LA, Hanson WF, Huq MS, Ibbott GS, et al. Update of AAPM task group no. 43 report: A revised AAPM protocol for brachytherapy dose calculations. Medical Physics. 2004;**31**:633-674. DOI: 10.1118/1.1646040

[19] Lesperance M, Inglis-Whalen M, Thomson RM. Model-based dose calculations for COMS eye plaque brachytherapy using an anatomically realistic eye phantom. Medical Physics. 2014;**41**(2):021717. DOI: 10.1118/1.4861715

[20] Monte Carlo Team. MCNP-A General Monte Carlo N-Particle Transport Code-Version 5. Los Alamos National Laboratory; Available from: http://mcnp-green.lanl.gov/index.html [Accessed: 29 January 2004]

[21] Sadeghi M, Tenreiro C, van den Winkel P. Study of heat transfer parameters on rhodium target for ^{103}-Pd production. Nukleonika. 2009;**54**:169-173

[22] Saidi P, Sadeghi M, Enferadi M, Aslani GH. Investigation of palladium-103 production and IR07-^{103}Pd brachytherapy seed preparation. Annals of Nuclear Energy. 2011;**38**:2168-2173. DOI: 10.1016/j.anucene.2011.06.018

[23] Saidi P, Sadeghi M, Hosseini SH. Thermoluminescent dosimetry of the IR06-^{103}-Pd brachytherapy source. Journal of Applied Clinical Medical Physics. 2011;**12**(4):286-295. DOI: 10.1120/jacmp.v12i4.3581

[24] Sadeghi M, Saidi P, Tenreiro C. Dosimetric characteristics of the brachytherapy sources based on Monte Carlo method. In: Mode CJ, editor. Applications of Monte Carlo Methods in Biology, Medicine and Other Fields of Science. Intech; 2011. pp. 155-176. DOI: 10.5772/15884

[25] Sadeghi M, Farshadi A, Saidi P, Hosseini SH, Jafari A. Monte Carlo dosimetry for 125-I eye plaque brachytherapy. Journal of Nuclear Medicine and Radiation Therapy. 2018; **9**(4):1000367. DOI: 10.4172/2155-9619.1000367.

[26] Williamson JF. Monte Carlo modeling of the transverse-axis dose distribution of the model 200 ^{103}Pd interstitial brachytherapy source. Medical Physics. 2000;27:643–654

[27] Thomson RM, Taylor REP, Rogers DWO. Monte Carlo dosimetry for 125I and ^{103}-Pd eye plaque brachytherapy. Medical Physics. 2008;**35**:5530-5543. DOI: 10.1118/1.3002412

[28] ICRU. Photon, Electron, Photon and Neutron Interaction Data for Body Tissues. ICRU Report 46; Washington D.C.: ICRU; 1992

[29] Saidi P, Sadeghi M, Tenreiro C. Theory and applications of Monte Carlo simulations. In: Chan WKV, editor. Variance Reduction of Monte Carlo Simulation in Nuclear Engineering Field. Intech; 2013. pp. 153-172. DOI: 10.5772/53384., 2013

[30] Meigooni AS, Bharucha Z, Yoe-Sein M, Sowards K. Dosimetric characteristic of the best double-wall ^{103}-Pd brachytherapy source. Medical Physics.

2001;**28**:2568-2575. DOI: 10.1118/1.1414007

[31] Bearden JA, Burr AF. Reevaluation of X-ray atomic energy levels. Medical Physics. 1967;**39**:125-142. DOI: 10.1103

[32] Nath R, Yue N, Shahnazi K, Bongiorni PJ. Measurement of dose-rate constant for ^{103}-Pd seeds with air kerma strength calibration based upon a primary national standard. Medical Physics. 2000;**27**:655-658. DOI: 10.1118/1.598925

[33] Wallace RE, Fan JJ. Dosimetric characterization of a new design 103-palladium brachytherapy source. Medical Physics. 1999;**26**:2465-2470. DOI: 10.1118/1.598765

[34] Li Z, Palta JR, Fan JJ. Monte Carlo calculations and experimental measurements of dosimetry parameters of a new ^{103}-Pd source. Medical Physics. 2000;**27**:1108-1112. DOI: 10.1118/1.598975

Chapter 3

Prospective Monte Carlo Simulation for Choosing High Efficient Detectors for Small-Field Dosimetry

Hossam Donya, Baljeet Seniwal, Reem Darwesh and Telma C.F. Fonseca

Abstract

In this chapter, a detailed study on physics and methodology of small field dosimetry are reported. It introduces talking about how small radiation fields came into existence and the importance of accurate small-field dosimetry. In addition, it discusses small and long cavity theories for evaluating accurate dose response. It sheds the spot on pencil beam algorithms for evaluating dose response and uses Monte Carlo (MC) simulation in categorizing primary and scattering components of the radiotherapeutic photon beam. Moreover, it summarizes all commercial dosimeters used in small-field dosimetry. It gives good knowledge about detectors and equipment like ionization chambers for reference dosimetry in small and non-reference fields and different types of solid-state detector. The importance and applications of Monte Carlo techniques in small-field dosimetry and radio-therapeutic treatment methods based on small field are reported. For this purpose, different commonly used Monte Carlo codes are handled like Electron Gamma Shower (EGSnrc), Geant4, PENELOPE, and Monte Carlo N-Particle (MCNP). A review on the recent studies of using Monte Carlo simulation particularly on the small-field dosimetric studies is also reported. This chapter also discusses the recommendations of the code of practices (COPs) for dosimetry of small radiation fields. It mentions all recommendations provided by TRS-483 for accurate beam data collection and accurate dosimetric measurements. It gives good knowledge to the user for selecting a suitable dosimeter in small-field dosimetry through investigation of different practical methods and Monte Carlo simulations.

Keywords: Monte Carlo simulation, radiotherapy physics, small-field dosimetry, machine-specific reference field, cavity theory, output factors

1. Introduction

In the current state of external photon beam radiation therapy, the "small fields" are generated by collimating the photon beam, flattened or unflattened. This is done with the help of collimating system available on medical electron linear accelerators (linacs), which includes secondary jaws, multi-leaf collimators (MLCs), tertiary collimators, etc. [1]. The small photon beams differ from traditionally used radiation fields (4 cm × 4 cm up to 40 cm × 40 cm) in terms of their size. Due to their small size, the penumbra region generated from the edges of the fields overlap, resulting in apparent field widening of the fields [2]. As a result the traditional detectors used for dosimetry become large relative to the size of the field, and this may lead to unintended errors while performing measurements for small field [3].

The widely accepted Code of Practices (COPs) reported in the Technical Reports Series No.398 of IAEA have procedures to determine absorbed dose to water from measurements made with an ionization chamber in photon, electron, proton, and heavy-ion beams [4–7]. The ionization chambers are used to perform the measurement using the calibration coefficients obtained from primary standard dosimetry laboratories (PSDL) in terms of absorbed dose to water under reference conditions. However, these COPs do not consider the conditions deviating from reference conditions in detail [8].

As a result of technological improvements and introduction to new radiation therapy techniques, the small static radiation beams are rapidly used, which is achieved by using standard or add-on MLCs or by the design of the radiation equipment. Consequently, the uncertainties related to the clinical dosimetry based on traditionally used COPs have been considerably increasing, and errors related to dosimetry have been growing larger. The main causes of this increase in the size of dosimetric errors are that it is not possible to achieve the reference conditions as recommended by traditional COPs on some radiation equipment and non-standardization of dose measurement procedures in small and composite radiation fields. Hence, many accidents have been reported that have occurred due to the use of recommendations of traditional COPs in dosimetry of small fields [8, 9].

The dosimetry of small fields is quite important. The beam data once configured during commissioning will be used for treatment in the future, so there should be high accuracy in the dosimetry of these small fields. To achieve high accuracy in beam data measurement in small fields and to be able to measure the dose in small fields with high precision, it is quite important to understand the physical aspects of the small fields. The measurement of output factors, beam profiles, and depth dose data is highly influenced by the beam energy, scattering, and field dimensions at the level of detector. The knowledge of the important characteristics of small fields is required to measure the dose parameters and to collect data for treatment. Hence, in 2017 a joint working group from the International Atomic Energy Agency (IAEA) and American Association of Physicists in Medicine (AAPM) proposed a new COP, Technical Report Series (TRS) No. 483 (Dosimetry of Small Static Fields Used in External Beam Radiotherapy). [9] This COP provides recommendations related to the relative and reference dosimetry of small and composite fields. Hence, this chapter discusses the concepts related to the dosimetry of small and composite field sizes.

2. Field size definition

In general, two types of field sizes have been defined by the International Electrotechnical Commission. The first is called the *geometric field size*; it is defined as two-dimensional projection by the source of radiation of the collimator opening on a plane orthogonal to the central axis of the primary photon beam. The second is called the *irradiation field size*; it is defined as the two-dimensional area bounded by specific isodose lines in a plane orthogonal to the central axis of the radiation beam. An alternative way to define irradiation field size is by using full width at half maximum (FWHM) of radiation beam profiles obtained along the lateral direction (in-line or crossline profiles) at isocenter depth. This FWHM is equal to the opening of the collimating jaws at the isocenter. Therefore, at isocenter the geometrical and irradiation fields are in consonance with each other. Hence, this agreement can be verified by FWHM measurement of the beam profile along the lateral direction. However, in the small beam condition due to the partial blockage of primary source of photon and reduction in the head scatter along the central axis, the output of radiation is reduced. As a consequence the condition of lateral charged particle equilibrium (LCPE) is not fulfilled. Hence, due to the reduction in the radiation output along the central axis, the value of maximum dose also gets reduced, and agreement between the geometrical and irradiation fields is lost. **Figure 1** illustrates the overlapping of penumbra region with decrease in field size, as it leads to decrease in output and increase in penumbra width. Hence, the parameters like FWHM breaks down for small-field sizes [3, 10]. In case of small beams due to the overlap of penumbra region, the FWHM of the profile gets broader relative to the collimator settings, and this effect is called apparent field widening.

2.1 Conditions of small beam

2.1.1 Definition of small field

Any radiation beam which fulfills at least one of the following conditions can be named as small field:

i. The absence of LCPE along the central axis of the radiation field (see **Figure 1**).

ii. The partial blockage of the radiation source by the collimating devices along the central axis (see **Figure 2**).

iii. The detector size is equal to or larger than the size of the radiation beam (see **Figure 3**).

Conditions I and II are related to the size of the radiation beam, whereas condition III refers to the size of the detector. If all the above mentioned conditions are fulfilled, then the penumbra region overlaps with the volume of the detector.

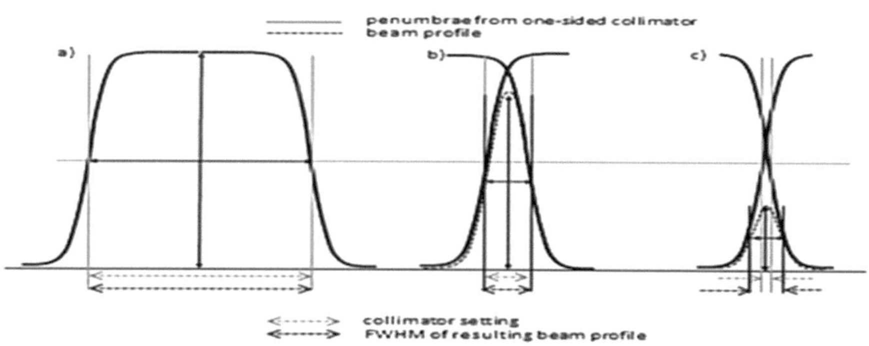

Figure 1.
Schematic illustration of the definition of geometrical and irradiation field size using the concept of geometrical projection and FWHM of radiation beam profile for both broad and small beam conditions: (a) for large field sizes, where condition of LCPE is fulfilled and radiation source is not blocked, the full width at half maximum (FWHM) of the lateral dose profiles is equal to the opening of the collimating jaws at the isocenter. Hence, for large field sizes at isocenter, geometrical field size and irradiation field size are in agreement with each other; (b) for the field sizes of the order of the range of secondary charged particles, the penumbra region of opposite jaws. It results in small error in determining the field size from the FWHM of lateral beam profiles; (c) however, for small field sizes due to the reduction in the radiation output along the central axis, the value of maximum dose is reduced. Hence, the FWHM of lateral beam profile is pushed outward and agreement between the geometrical and irradiation fields is lost.

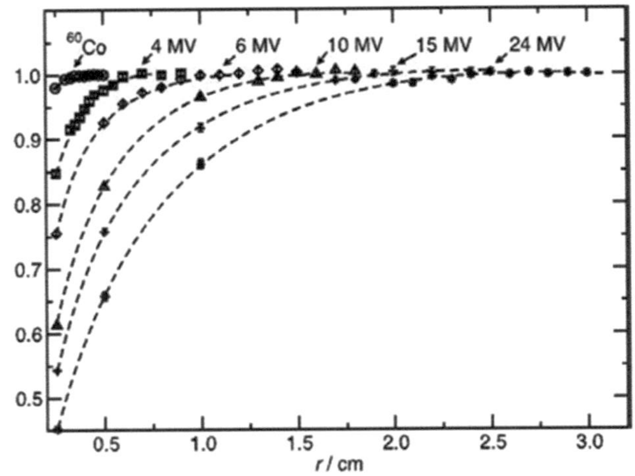

Figure 2.
The ratio of collisional kerma in water and absorbed dose in water at a depth of 5 cm. Source to surface distance (SSD) of 80 cm is used for Co^{60} and SSD of 100 cm was used for photon beam. X axis represents the radius of the beam and the Y axis represents the ratio of the quantities.

2.1.1.1 Conditions based on field size

For the radiation beams with FWHM lesser than the maximum range of the secondary electrons, the LCPE is absent. The absence of LCPE makes it difficult to perform measurements for absorbed dose to water for detectors made of non-water equivalent material. In order to find a relation between the size of the beam and the size of the detector for which the LCPE exists, LCPE range (r_{LCPE}) has been proposed. r_{LCPE} can be defined as the minimum radius of circular photon field for which the ratio of collisional kerma in water and dose deposited in water is equal to 1 at the center of the beam. **Figure 2** illustrates the concept of LCPE, where the ratio of collisional kerma in water and dose deposited in water are calculated using Monte Carlo simulations at a depth of 5 cm along the central axis of the radiation beam [11].

r_{LCPE} (in cm) can be manifested as a function of beam quality of photon beam, Tissue Phantom Ratio (TPR), $TPR_{20,10}(10)$:

$$r_{LCPE} = 8.369 \times TPR_{20,10}(10) - 4.382 \quad (1)$$

In the case of beam quality defined in terms of percentage depth dose at a depth of 10 cm, $\%dd(10,10)_x$, r_{LCPE} can be calculated using the correspondence between $\%dd(10,10)_x$ and $TPR_{20,10}(10)$ [12]:

$$r_{LCPE} = 77.97 \times 10^{-3} \times \%\,dd(10,10)_x - 4.382 \quad (2)$$

The second condition related to the partial blockage of the primary radiation source is illustrated in **Figure 3**. It is based on the finite size of the extended focal spot, which can be determined by FWHM measurement of bremsstrahlung spectrum emitted by the radiation source. The partial shielding of the radiation source by the beam modifier, used for the definition of small beam, results in decrement of radiation output along the central axis of the radiation beam relative to the unshielded condition. The radiation beams with size equal to or less than the FWHM of the emission spectra emitted from the source, the effect of partial occlusion of radiation source becomes more dominant. Since the source size is generally less than 5 mm, as it can be observed from **Figure 2**, the loss of LCPE also starts for radiation beams with a radius of 5 mm. Therefore, the partial blockage of radiation source starts when loss of charge equilibrium starts [1]. The partial blockage of radiation source results in a decrease in the beam output. Hence, result in the sharp dose gradient, as a consequence of which the response of the detector is affected.

Therefore, the absence of LCPE and partial blockage of small beams of photon radiation source is the main cause of the decrease in the radiation output along the beam axis. This effect gets more dominant with increase in the energy of the radiation beam and decrease in the density of the medium.

2.1.1.2 Conditions related to detector size

The last condition is related to the size of the detector relative to the size of the radiation beam. The signal produced by the detector on irradiation is directly proportional to the average of the deposited dose within the detector's sensitive volume. The signal obtained from the detector is responsive to the uniformity of deposited radiation dose over the sensitive volume of the detector, also known as volume averaging as illustrated in **Figure 4** [13]. Hence, in order to obtain dose

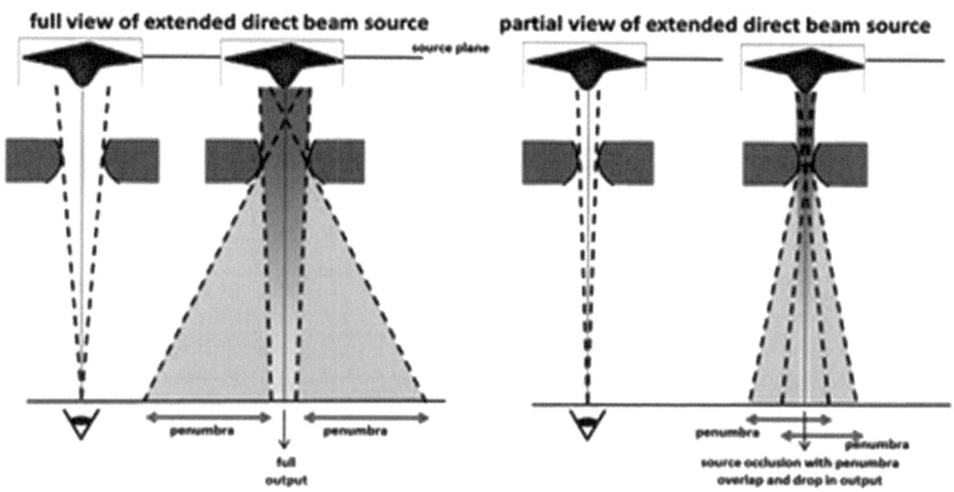

Figure 3.
A schematic illustration of the source occlusion effect.

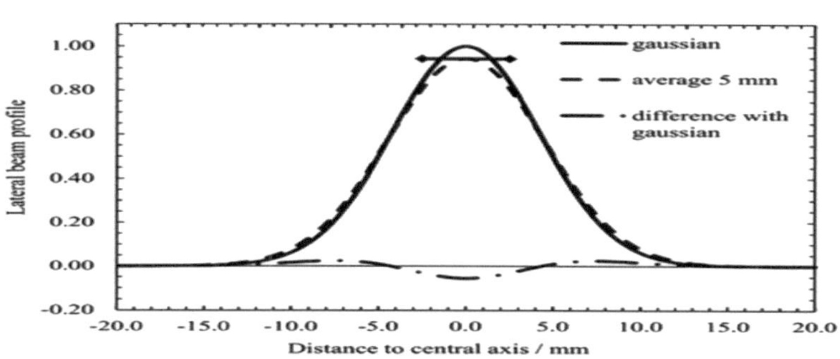

Figure 4.
A schematic representation of volume averaging effect along the central axis of the beam. The Gaussian curve in black represents the actual beam profile; the measured profile obtained using the detector (5 mm long) is given represented by dashed line; the dimensions of the detector along the scanning axis is represented by double arrow; the variation between the measured profile and Gaussian curve is given by dash-dotted line.

deposited to the water from the signal produced by the detector, the correction factor must be used for the volume averaging. It can be defined as a ratio of dose deposited in water at the point of reference in the nonexistence of the detector to the average of the dose deposited over the detection volume of the detector in the nonexistence of the detector. It can be acquired by integrating the three-dimensional distribution of dose over the detector's sensitive volume [14–19].

The general expression that can be used in calculation of correction factor for averaging of the signal over the detector's sensitive volume is:

$$k_{vol} = \frac{\iint_A w(x,y)\, dxdy}{\iint_A w(x,y)\, OAR(x,y)\, dxdy} \tag{3}$$

where (x,y) are the positions of the points on the axis orthogonal to the beam axis, A is the projected area of the detector's sensitive volume in a plane perpendicular to the central axis of the beam, OAR (x,y) gives the off-axis ratio at position (x,y), and w(x) is the weighting function that represents extension of cavity of the air-filled detector along the central axis (z) of the beam in relation to the lateral coordinates of the beam (x and y).

The volume averaging effect and the disturbance caused by the existence of detector to the fluence of the charged particles are two main effects observed in small beam dose measurement. As discussed above, due to the presence of dose gradients and absence of LCPE, the perturbation effect becomes dominant and cannot be modeled easily. Along with this, the errors related to the averaging of the detector signal along its volume become larger. Consequently, the dose gradients and nonexistence of LCPE make it difficult to perform dosimetric measurements for small beams.

The radiation fields, having the distance between the edges of the field and outer surface of the detector volume less than the r_{LCPE} within a medium, satisfy the small beam condition. In order to prevent such condition and perform dosimetric measurements accurately, the FWHM or the radius of the photon beam must be equal to the sum of r_{LCPE} and half of the detector's outer volume.

2.2 The machine-specific reference field (f_{msr})

For radiotherapy radiation emitters, where the reference beam size (f_{ref}) of 10 cm × 10 cm cannot be obtained, a new concept of machine-specific reference (msr) field size has been proposed. The dimensions of the msr field (f_{msr}) should be as close as possible to that of f_{ref} and must be at least equal to the sum of r_{LCPE} and half of the detector's outer volume.

3. Detectors and equipment

3.1 Ionization chambers for reference dosimetry in small and non-reference fields

An ideal air-filled detector to be used for measurement of dose deposited in water must be equivalent to the water and not perturb the charged particle fluence; its response must not be affected by dose rate or directional dependence; it must show good sensitivity, in terms of signal to noise ratio and time taken to obtain the signal; the detector signal must be beam energy independent and directly proportional to the dose deposited in water; and it must show minimum fluctuations, leakage, and no effect of cable irradiation.

The detector size must be such that it fulfills r_{LCPE} criteria. The positioning of the air-filled detector must be such that the charged particle fluence remains approximately uniform over the sensitive volume of the detector.

3.1.1 The square equivalent msr field (f_{msr}) greater than 6 cm × 6 cm

Modern radiotherapy linear accelerators are available in two general models, that is, with flattening filter (WFF) and flattening filter free (FFF). For WFF radiation emitters, air-filled detectors with sensitive volume range between 0.3 and 1 cm^3, since these detectors are often water resistant and easy to use for in-phantom measurements have negligible leakage effect and good signal to noise ratio [20]. In the case of FFF radiation emitters, air-filled detectors with sensitive volume lying in the range of 0.1–0.3 cm^3 are preferred over the commonly used Farmer type air-filled detectors [21]. In case the Farmer type air-filled detectors is used in FFF beam, then the beam profiles must be corrected for their non-uniformity; the factor for correction can be 1.5% for FFF photon beam of 6 MV [22, 23].

3.1.2 The square equivalent msr field (f_{msr}) less than 6 cm × 6 cm

A comparative study was performed by Le Roy et al. [24] using 24 small volume air-filled detectors of 8 different types, to study the probability of their use in high-energy photon beams for reference dosimetry, with beam size ranging down to 2 cm × 2 cm. The authors reported that out of eight different types of air-filled detectors only three types of chambers were found suitable for small beam dosimetry, which includes CC04, CC01 models from IBA, and AISL from Exradin.

In case of very small circular msr fields as that of Gamma Knife machine having the diameter of the radiation beam 1.6 or 1.8 cm. It is found that these fields exhibit LCPE, r_{LCPE} was found to be 0.6 cm for ^{60}Co [25]. The chambers fulfilling the condition of r_{LCPE} in msr fields are suitable for use in these very small circular fields for reference dosimetry.

The air-filled detectors with sensitive volume less than 0.3 cm^3 and air cavity length of 7 mm are preferred for dosimetric measurements for f_{msr} less than 6 cm × 6 cm. The criteria used for selection of detector volume and air cavity length can be demonstrated by relating it with the size of the radiation beam and beam energy. The detector with air cavity of 7 mm satisfies r_{LCPE} condition for field sizes down to 4 cm in 10 MV beam, down to 3 cm in 6 MV beam, and down to 2 cm for Co^{60} radiation beam.

3.2 Different types of detectors for relative dosimetry in small radiation beams

The concept of relative dosimetry is based on the determination of various dosimetric beam parameters, such as measurement of dose distribution with depth along central axis of the beam, lateral beam profiles, etc. as a function of the size of the radiation beam and its shape. The choice of appropriate detector is based on the specific type of parameter being measured. Hence, two or more suitable detectors of different kinds can be used to perform the same measurement to be sure about the accuracy of measurements.

For the measurements of output factor, volume averaging effect, dependence on the: size of the radiation beam; beam energy; dose rate; equivalence to water and overall perturbation are the deciding factors to find the suitable detector for measurements. However, in case of beam profile measurements, the detectors with high spatial resolution, direction-independent response, dose-rate independence, and suitable volume are preferred. Since the selection of detector with suitable volume makes it possible to measure penumbra region accurately, uniformity in directional response may result in accurate measurement of beam profiles; dose rate independence is also important for accurate measurement of beam profiles. Otherwise, correction factors are required for each of these effects for accurate measurement. As in the case of dose-rate dependence, correction factor needs to be applied in case of FFF beams, as these beams have high dose rate per pulse in the center of the beam in comparison to the edges. Otherwise it may lead to overestimation in the region of beam with high dose rate.

There is no ideal detector available for relative dosimetry of small beams. A number of detectors that can be used for relative dosimetry have been described in literature, and each of these detectors has been discussed briefly below:

- *Small air-vented ionization chambers*: These detectors are also known as minichambers or pinpoint chambers. The sensitive volume of these detectors ranges from 0.001 to 0.3 cm^3. These can be used for measurements in radiation beams with size down to 2 cm $\times$ 2 cm [24, 26]. These detectors are dose-rate independent and have uniform response in all directions and appropriate response for photons of low energy.

- *Micro-ionization chambers*: Also known as microchambers. The sensitive volume of these detectors ranges from 0.002 to 0.01 cm^3. These detectors have small volume averaging effect, and sensitivity is also reduced due to small sensitive volume.

- *Liquid ionization chambers (LICs)*: These chambers are filled with dielectric liquids, which results in higher chamber signal per detector volume than air-filled ionization chambers, due to the higher density of liquid than air. The chambers are almost water equivalent; hence the chamber perturbation effect is reduced. However, the chambers are dose-rate dependent because of its large recombination effect.

- *Silicon diodes*: The sensitive volume of these detectors is less than 0.2 mm^3. These detectors exhibit angular dependency because of its construction and material composition and small volume averaging effect. The axis of symmetry of these detectors must be placed on the central axis of the beam. These detectors exhibit over-response in the case of low-energy photons due to the non-water equivalence. For small beam measurement, the use of unshielded diodes is preferred over the use of shielded diodes, and for field sizes below 1 cm, output correction factors are needed to be applied [26–30]. For very small beam size measurements, stereotactic diodes can be utilized. The sensitivity of these detectors depends on the accumulated dose, and they have limited lifetime. Therefore, time-to-time checking for constancy of relative response must be performed.

- *Diamond detectors*: These detectors exhibit high sensitivity, energy independence, and uniform response in all directions [31]. However, having dose-rate dependence and substantial pre-irradiation are required. The natural diamond detectors have been replaced by the artificial chemical vapor deposition (CVD) diamonds [32–34]. The bias voltage is not required for these detectors while using them for dosimetric measurements [35, 36]. However, due to the difference in mass density relative to water, output correction factors are required when these detectors are used in field sizes below 1 cm [37].

- *Plastic and organic scintillators*: In these detectors light is produced in the scintillator when it is exposed to radiation. These detectors are almost energy independent, equivalent to water in terms of mass energy coefficient and electron density, and exhibit linear response for measurement of dose deposition in water [14, 19, 38–40]. Hence, these detectors can be directly used to determine the dose deposited. The corrections are needed to be applied for the production of Cerenkov light in optical fiber, which is used to transport the signals outside the treatment room. Different methods such as the use of hollow core fibers or the use of spectral filtration had been proposed to correct it [41]. Exradin W1 was found to be the only commercially available plastic scintillator.

- *Radiochromic film dosimetry*: Radiochromic films are the detectors with superior dimensional resolution. These are self-developing films and do not need chemical processing for development [42]. In case of high-energy photon beams, the radiochromic films are almost equivalent to tissue, resistant to water, and nearly energy independent [42, 43]. These films can be read with the help of suitable flatbed scanner. Before reading the films, it must be calibrated in terms of dose deposited in water, the spatial non-uniformity in the response of film must be carefully considered, and the response of the scanner and effect of orientation of film on the signal must be considered and should be corrected [44]. The radiochromic film can be used for measurements of lateral beam profiles, penumbra region, and field output factors.

- *Thermoluminescent dosimeters (TLDs)*: TLDs are available in the form of powder, chips, microchips, rods, and ribbon. The most commonly used TLD material is LiF:Mg,Ti. In order to determine the dose deposited in water from the reading of thermoluminescence response, correction factors must be applied for non-linear relationship with the signal and dose deposited and also fading of the signal and energy correction. In order to accurately perform measurements in small beams of photon, careful handling and control of procedures are required to obtain measurement uncertainty within 2% or better [19].

- *Optically stimulated luminescence detectors (OSLDs)*: The linearity in response, dependence on beam energy, and dependence on dose rate are similar to that of TLDs. OSLDs are generally composed of Al_2O_3:C and are available in the form of rods, chips, and nano-dots. The principle used in measurement of dose is similar to that of TLDs. In OSLD system, laser light is used to eject the energy trapped as luminescence. They can be used both as passive dosimeters and online readout system by connecting them with laser-based readout system and optical fiber.

- *Radiophotoluminescent (RPL) dosimeters*: These are solid-state dosimeters (SSD) based on the principle of radiophotoluminescence. They are accumulation type dosimeters and use silver activated phosphate glass for the measurement to absorbed dose. RPL dosimeters are generally available in the form of glass rods. When this silver-activated glass rod is exposed to radiation, it resulted in formation of stable luminescence centers in silver ions. They can be read using the technique of pulsed ultraviolet laser excitation. RPL dosimeters exhibit linear response, flat energy response in the energy range of keV and MeV, good reproducibility, good spatial resolution, and negligible fading of signal [45, 46].

- *Alanine:* Its macroscopic interaction coefficients and density are close to that of water. The exhibit volume averaging effect because of its large size, low sensitivity, and high doses of radiation is needed to be delivered to obtain reproducibility of less than 0.5%.

3.3 Solid-state dosimeters and dose response compensation in external radiotherapy

This section shed light on describing the dosimetric response of solid-state dosimeters that are used for the dose measurement of external radiotherapy. Two approaches are presented for this purpose. The first approach, implementation of empirical method approach that considers the radiation beam, is separated into two components: primary and scattered beams. The spectral variation of radiotherapeutic beam is evaluated by their contribution in the dose to the medium that contains the region of interest. Solid-state dosimeters of high-density materials have an over-response issue that is commonly used in large and small fields. Hence, compensation factor should be calculated based on beam parameters such as energy, field size, depth, and other irradiation parameters. Dealing with over-response issue is not an easy task; however, it generates a significant improvement in accuracy in dose measurements over non-compensated measurements.

The second approach is to implement a compensation method based on a modified cavity theory. In this method, dose response of solid-state dosimeter is described considering the local spectrum and monoenergetic response. The local spectrum could be obtained by convolution method of pencil beam kernels using a pre-evaluated database that considers different separated types of particles according to their history of interaction (primary photon and electron and secondary photons and electrons). On the other hand, monoenergetic response of solid-state dosimeter could be calculated using the Monte Carlo simulation using different codes like PENELOPE [47, 48]. The accuracy of compensation methods should be evaluated by comparing simulated data with the corresponding measurements. This approach could be applied in situations where there is no lateral electron equilibrium compared to the previous method of compensation. Since the compensation accuracy depends on the local reconstructed spectrum, it is possible to implement this process in more complex irradiation conditions such as small fields. However, this method requires specific information such as the field size, beam quality, and detector position. Yet using two dosimeters whose materials in the sensitive volume are different can be instead used without considering beam information and enough to evaluate over-response correction.

3.3.1 The first approach: primer-released contribution separation

Cunningham [49] proposed a method for separation of primary beam component out of beam spectrum through dose calculation technique for irregular fields. He assumed that dosimeter placement does not introduce any local spectral disturbance in the volume of interest and the difference of dose response between solid-state dosimeter and water depends on the material difference and the ionization spectrum. The primary component of the spectrum photon beam is dependent on the design of the collimation system, for example, the primary collimator and flattening filter [50]. Accordingly, the difference between dosimetric response of solid-state dosimeter and water is due to the primary component of the beam that remains almost invariant for the given beam quality and does not depend on the volume. On the other hand, the scattered component of the photon beam depends largely on the volume surrounding it; therefore, it depends on dosimeter depth, irradiated field size, etc. Hence, it is convenient to calculate the difference of the response caused by these two components separately and additively combine the two parts at the end of the calculation. To quantify the response rate provided by the primary and scattered components, a scattered factor (*SF*) could be introduced, defined as follows:

$$SF_w = \frac{D_w^{sc}}{D_w^{pr}} \tag{4}$$

$$SF_{SSD} = \frac{D_{SSD}^{sc}}{D_{SSD}^{pr}} \tag{5}$$

where D_w^{sc} and D_w^{pr} correspond to the dose contributions in water by primary and scattered components of photon beam, respectively. A scattered factor of solid-state dosimeter may be defined in the same manner, as shown in Eq. (5). The scattered factor is dependent on the field size and depth position of the dosimeter.

The total dose of water (D_w) or SSD (D_{SSD}) is the sum of the two components, primary and scattered. This can be expressed in terms of scatter factor as follows:

$$D_w = D_w^{pr}(1 + SF_w) \tag{6}$$

$$D_{SSD} = D_{SSD}^{pr}(1 + SF_{SSD}) \tag{7}$$

The response factor (RF) of SSD dose to water ratio is defined as:

$$RF_w^{SSD} = \frac{D_{SSD}}{D_w} \tag{8}$$

Therefore, the dose response of SSD could be corrected and applied to all SSD measurement by the evaluation of RF_w^{SSD} before the measurement implementation. Eq. (8) can also be expressed in terms of scattered factor, combining Eqs. (6) and (7):

$$RF_w^{SSD} = \frac{D_{SSD}^{pr}(1 + SF_{SSD})}{D_w^{pr}(1 + SF_w)} \tag{9}$$

In this way, expressing the response factor to fulfill the following objectives: The ratio between the primary dose of SSD to the dose of water (D_{SSD}^{pr}/D_w^{pr}) can be considered relatively stable, because once the charged-particle equilibrium (CPE) is established, the local spectra of the primary electrons and photons remain invariant which are independent of irradiation condition variations. Therefore, the RF_w^{SSD} variation is due to the difference of the scattered component of both water and SSD. As a result, RF_w^{SSD} depends on the determination of the primary dose ratios and scattered factors (SF_{SSD}, SF_w). However, it could not be easy to evaluate the primary and scattered doses separately in experiments, especially for high-energetic photons, because it needs massive buildup of material, which is necessary to achieve CPE to introduce significant attenuation and wide contribution [51]. Nevertheless, the response factor could be evaluated in a small field where CPE is still achieved. So in small-field dosimetry, the evaluated RF_w^{SSD} is close to the D_{SSD}^{pr}/D_w^{pr} since the main primary contribution component is dominant. Rewriting Eq. (9) for the last condition of small-field irradiation as reference condition to the following equation:

$$RF_w^{SSD} = \frac{D_{SSD}^{ref}(1+\gamma_{SSD})}{D_w^{ref}(1+\gamma_w)} \tag{10}$$

where D_{SSD}^{ref}/D_w^{ref} is the dose–response factor of SSD to the water in the reference condition (small field). γ_{SSD} andγ_w are introduced instead of SF_{SSD} *and* SF_w in Eq. (9), respectively, and could be written as follows:

$$\gamma_{SSD} = \frac{D_{SSD}}{D_{SSD}^{ref}} - 1 \tag{11}$$

$$\gamma_w = \frac{D_w}{D_w^{ref}} - 1 \tag{12}$$

where D_{SSD} and D_w correspond to the dose response of SSD and water in an arbitrary requirement. Both factors are used to describe primary component variation with respect to the scattering component in the reference condition. To calculate the response factor by interpolation or extrapolation, measure both the dose in water by ionization chamber and in SSD to establish a response factor table. So in experimental measurement setup as illustrated in **Figure 5**, choosing small-field area to be a reference condition that avoids scattering component for dose response of SSD. PMMA sheets could be arranged around the solid-state dosimeter to establish homogenous tissue equivalent material. Mentioning that, at least 10 cm thickness of PMMA should be placed below the detector to create a homogeneous volume for the backscattered radiation. However, the measurement of the dose at a reference point in water phantom is established by ionization chamber. In small-field dosimetry beyond the buildup region, the relative difference of dose response between SSD and ionization chamber in water should be minimum, as low as possible as the result of the stability of primary component of radiation. Therefore, it is easy to explore the scattering factors in a large field. On the other hand, the

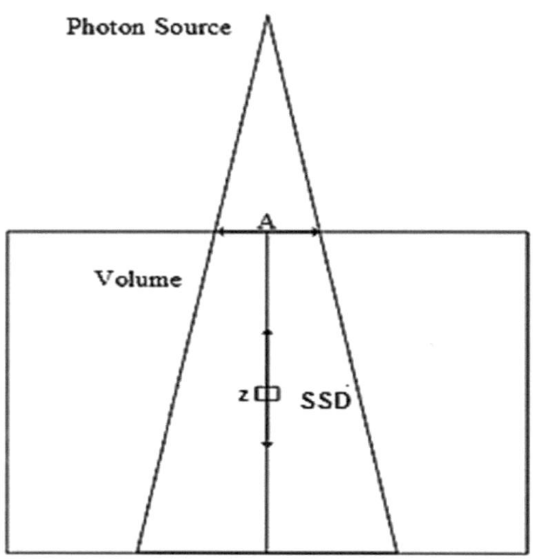

Figure 5.
Geometrical configuration.

spectral variation between SSD and ionization chamber is also affected by the depth of dosimeter. γ_{SSD} and γ_w could be evaluated from representing normalized maximum dose ratio or percentage depth dose for both dosimeters.

The relationship between γ_{SSD} and γ_w in small-field sizes may be linear due to the main contribution primary component. But the response factor linearity allows us to separate two sources that vary the local spectrum at the position of the detector: The size of the square field (A) and depth (z). Therefore, the response factor can be modeled by:

$$RF_{SSD} = 1 + k(z) \times \left(A - A_{ref}\right) \tag{13}$$

where the factor k(z) is a function of depth and A_{ref} corresponds to the size of the reference field (small-field size). Modeling of k(z) could be established from the slopes of plotted $RF_{SSD}(A)$ against the depth.

The previous characterization method of RF_{SSD} can be applied for a series of square field sizes with orthogonal collimators. However, in the case of irregular or circular fields, it must be expressed in terms of an equivalent square field for the interpolation. The method of equivalent square field is a simple empirical method for calculating the dose of irregular field size [52]. There are several ways to calculate the equivalent square field according to the literature: Equivalent tables for rectangular fields [53], sum of the small rectangles [54], and Clarkson integration of [55, 56]. Sterling's formula [57] can be used to calculate the equivalent square fields of the two rectangular fields:

$$ESQ = \frac{2WL}{(W + L)} \tag{14}$$

where ESQ is the side length of the equivalent square field, W is the width of the rectangle, and L is the length of the rectangle.

This method of empirical compensation consists primarily of establishing a response correction factors table by the experimental approach. It is based on the separation of primary and scattering contribution parts of photons and electrons in the beam. However, the primary contribution part to the SSD cannot be evaluated through the measurement in the air as the local spectral variation in the air with respect to that in the water causes a large SSD response difference. Therefore, an arbitrary square field should be selected as a reference field for a given energetic beam. In this reference field, the maximum tissue ratio of SSD is compared with that measured of water by ionization chamber. Although it is possible to apply this method of compensation in irregular fields, it is difficult to implement it in more complex fields such as IMRT or non-rectangular fields, because this method requires a lot of effort for measuring, adjustments, and approximations that could be uneasy in more complex fields.

3.3.2 Cavity theory approach

The cavity theory was originally developed to convert the absorbed dose in the ionization chamber to the absorbed dose in the medium of interest [58]. When the measurement is performed with a solid-state dosimeter, the material of the detector, in general, is different from that of the medium in which it is introduced. If we consider the detector as a cavity introduced into the uniform medium of interest, the absorbed dose in the detector D_{det} is different with respect to the absorbed dose in the medium at this position in the absence of the detector, D_{med}. The main objective of the cavity theory is to determine the response factor RF_Q, given by Eq. (15):

$$RF_Q = \left(\frac{D_{det}}{D_{med}}\right)_Q \tag{15}$$

where Q corresponds to a given beam quality. **Figure 6** illustrates the schematic application of cavity theory to convert detector absorbed dose for a given beam quality to the dose in the medium of interest by RF_Q [59].

There are two possible cavities where RF_Q could be derived, the large cavity and small cavity. The terms "small and large" refer to the size of the cavity relative to the bearing surfaces of secondary particles, i.e., the electrons and positrons.

3.3.3 Small cavity theory (SCT)

Small cavity theory is also referred to as Bragg-Gray cavity theory. First, William Bragg proposed it then Louis Harold Gray completed it [60]. Bragg-Gray proposed two conditions: (a) Cavity size should be small enough compared to the range of the charged particles inside the irradiated volume. So that, the fluence of charged particles and local fluence are not disturbed by the presence of the cavity in the middle (see **Figure 7**). (b) The absorbed dose in the cavity is completely deposited by charged particles which pass through the cavity.

The realization of the first condition ensures that the local influence is invariant, with or without the existence of this detector is to say $\Phi_{det}(E) = \Phi_{med}(E)$. The

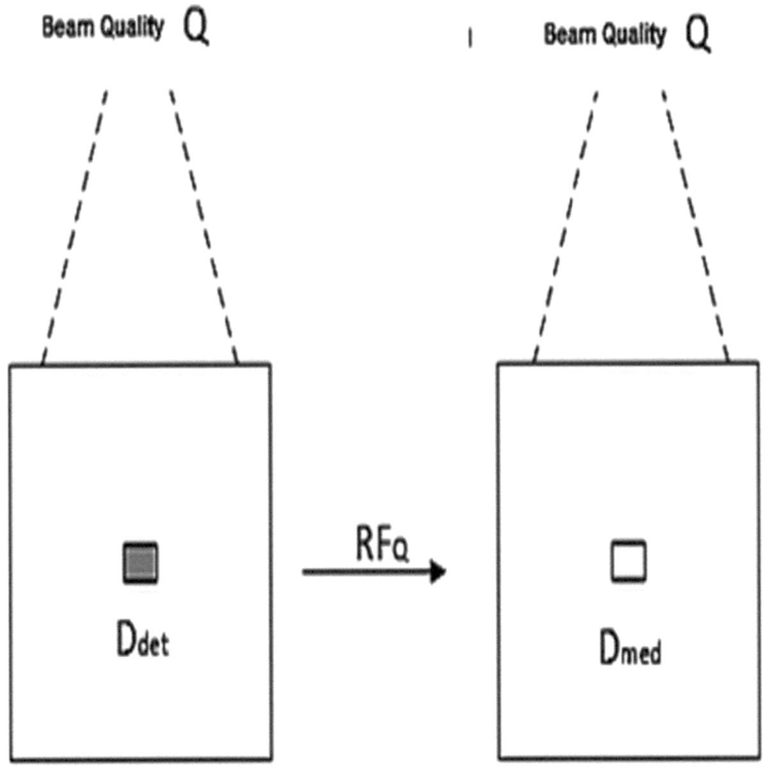

Figure 6.
Application of the cavity theory: The detector's absorbed dose for a given beam quality converted to the dose in the medium of interest by RF_Q [11].

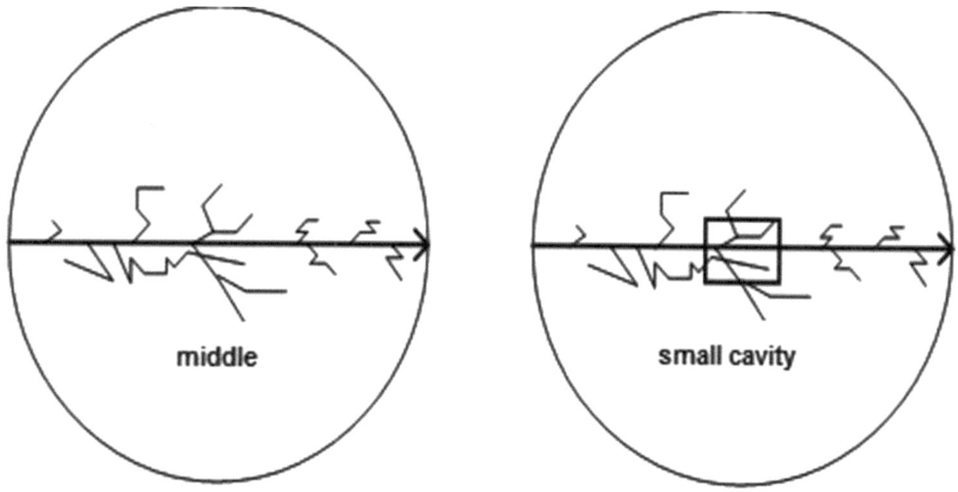

Figure 7.
A schematic illustration of small cavity behavior under high energetic photon irradiation.

second condition ensures that the dosimetric contribution from the photon is negligible. This is a valid condition for high-energy photon beams in most situations [61]. Under these conditions, D_{med} is related to D_{det} as:

$$\frac{D_{det}}{D_{med}} = \frac{\int_0^{E_{max}} \Phi_{med}(E)(S_{col}(E)/\rho)_{det} dE}{\int_0^{E_{max}} \Phi_{med}(E)(S_{col}(E)/\rho)_{med} dE} \tag{16}$$

where $(s_{col}(E)/\rho)_{det}$ and $(s_{col}(E)/\rho)_{med}$ are collision stopping power of the detector and the medium, respectively, and E_{max} is the maximum energy in the spectrum of ionization chamber fluence.

Secondary particles (delta rays) are considered prerequisite to assess the dose by the stopping power that reaches a balance in the cavity. Another way to express this requirement is that the electron is considered to lose energy in the continuous slowdown cavity. However, it could generate high-energy secondary electrons by hard collisions in the cavity. These secondary electrons will come out of the cavity, and thus the delta ray balance is no longer valid. To take into account the effects of delta rays in an approximate way, Spencer and Attix proposed an extension of the cavity of theory [62]. Spencer-Attix theory considered the separation of electron particles into two parts: The fast electrons with an energy greater than a threshold (Δ) and slow electrons with energy below the threshold. Slow electrons are considered to deposit the energy locally inside the cavity, while the fast electrons are considered completely capable of crossing the cavity. The dose contribution by fast electrons is estimated by the restricted stopping power, $L_\Delta/\rho(E)$. The restricted stopping power is defined as the stopping power limited to lose energy below the threshold energy (Δ). The total dose in the cavity can be written as:

$$D = \int_\Delta^{E_{max}} \Phi(E)\left(\frac{L_\Delta(E)}{\rho}\right) dE + (E.T.) \tag{17}$$

The first term on the right side of Eq. (17) corresponds to the dose deposited by fast electrons, and the second term takes into account the dose deposited by slow electrons, often termed as end track term (ET) suggested by Nahum [63] to estimate the contribution of slow electrons:

$$E.T. = \Phi(\Delta)\frac{S_{col}(\Delta)}{\rho}\Delta \tag{18}$$

where $\Phi(\Delta)$ is the electron differentiated fluence energy valued at Δ and $\frac{S_{col}(\Delta)}{\rho}$ is the nonrestricted stopping power evaluated at Δ. Instead of estimating the dose ratio in the detector and the medium by Bragg-Gray theory, it can be expressed as:

$$\frac{D_{det}}{D_{med}} = \frac{\int_0^{E_{max}} \Phi_{med}(E)(L_\Delta(E)/\rho)_{det}dE + \Phi(\Delta)(S_{col}(\Delta)/\rho)_{det}\Delta}{\int_0^{E_{max}} \Phi_{med}(E)(L_\Delta(E)/\rho)_{med}dE + \Phi(\Delta)(S_{col}(\Delta)/\rho)_{det}\Delta} \tag{19}$$

Δ is defined as the minimum energy needed for electron to pass through the cavity of interest. The value of Δ depends on the size and the material of the cavity. There are many studies based on determining Δ to apply the Spencer-Attix theory to some ionization chambers where Δ = 10 keV is used [64–66].

3.3.4 Large cavity theory (LCT)

On the other hand, large cavity is opposite to small cavity, whenever the size of the detector is much larger than the range of the electron that passes through the cavity. In this case, the range of delta ray is small in large cavity compared to the size of the cavity (see **Figure 8**). Hence, electronic equilibrium is established in most of the cavity size [59]. If the radiation source is a photon, it interacts with the material in the cavity and hence produces secondary electrons. As these created electrons are unable to pass through the cavity, the electronic control is established in the cavity of the detector. It should be noted that the electronic balance is not

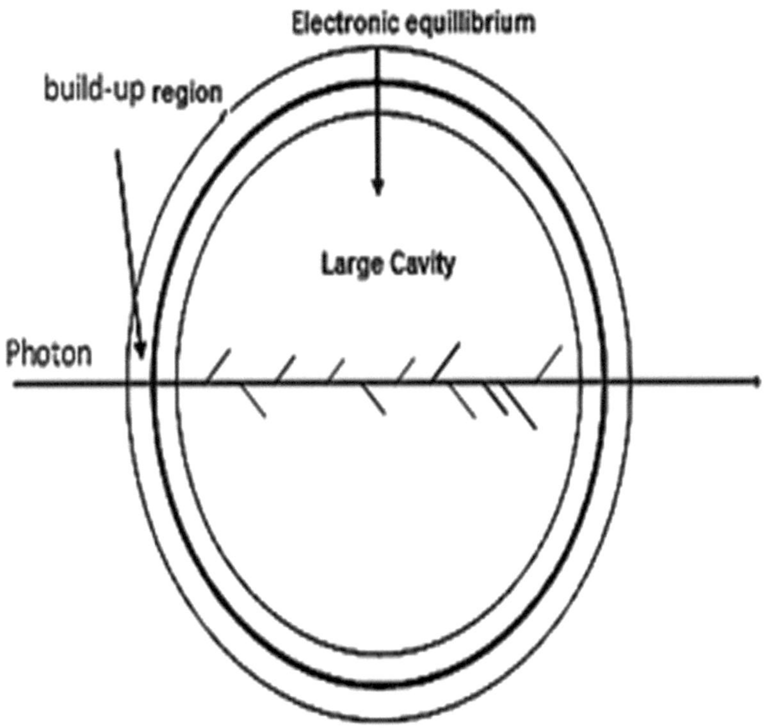

Figure 8.
Large cavity of high energetic photon beam deposition in a type of detector.

achieved in the border regions of the large cavity, due to the difference in the material around the border. However, the electronic balance is achieved in most of the cavity and the average absorbed dose in the detector can be determined using the following equation:

$$D = \int_0^{E_{max}} \left(\frac{\mu_{en}(E)}{\rho}\right)_{det} \cdot \Psi_{det}(E)dE \tag{20}$$

where $(\mu_{en}(E)/\rho)_{det}$ is the mass absorption coefficient of the detector and $\Psi_{det}(E)$ is energy fluence of photon energy E in the detector.

3.4 Dose model for the SSD crystal in the photon beam

3.4.1 Spectrum convolution calculation

To apply cavity theory, the first step is to obtain the spectrum at the position of interest. Fluence pencil kernels may be used to calculate the local spectrum in a homogeneous phantom. This model had been extensively used to calculate the dose in treatment planning system (TPS) [55, 67–69]. Its idea is to convolute the energy depositions for each pencil beam energy through wide beam spectrum. The most interesting approach to pencil beam fluence has been proposed by [47, 70] which calculated the local spectra via dividing it into high and low energies using small and large cavity theory approximations, respectively. However, it could be easy to calculate other physical quantities, such as the fluence spectrum in an irradiated water phantom as in **Figure 9**. Eklund and Ahnesjö [28, 70] use fluence pencil kernel database to evaluate the spectrum. In this database, the fluence pencil kernel has been defined as the spatial distribution of fluence, resulted from the irradiation of semi-infinite water slab with point of the monodirectional and monoenergetic beam in water phantom of infinite thickness. Monte Carlo simulation had a good feature of interaction for the evaluation of these spectra. As the energy deposited in the phantom is laterally symmetric, the parameters to describe the fluence pencil can be reduced to three parameters, as shown in schematic geometry for fluence pencil kernel acquisition of monoenergetic beam (see **Figure 10**).

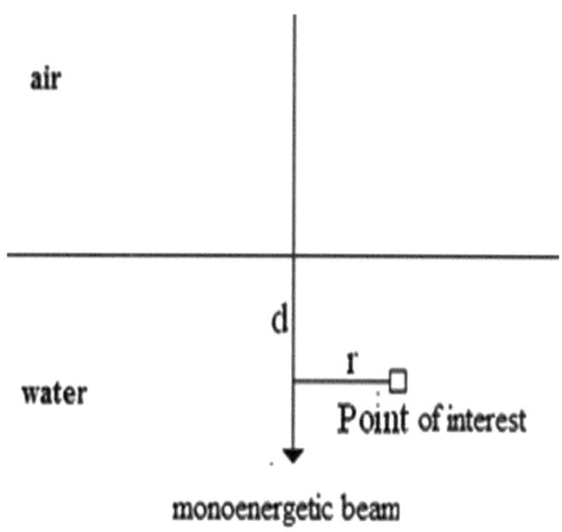

Figure 9.
A schematic geometry for fluence pencil kernel acquisition.

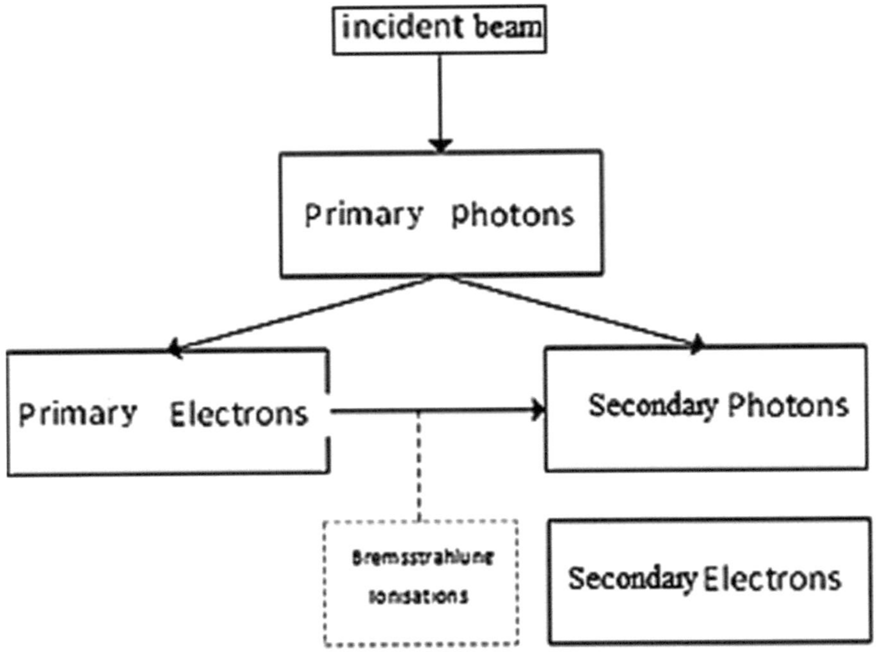

Figure 10.
Particles categories as defined in [70].

Here r is the lateral distance of the axis of irradiation from the position of interest; z is the depth of the point of interest; E is the energy of monoenergetic ionization chamber beam. Also, these database separated particles into four categories, depending on their histories of interaction, as shown in **Figure 5**:

- The incident photons, without any interaction are primary photons.
- The electrons created in interactions of primary photons are primary electrons.
- All other photons are scattered that are created by primary photon or secondary electrons such as Rayleigh and Compton effect, bremsstrahlung, and pair production.
- The electrons created by the scattered photons are scattered electrons.

The first two types of particles (primary photons and electrons) are the main component of the beam, while the last two are the scattered component. This separation of particles is only possible with the feature of tracking the particle's interaction history in Monte Carlo simulation. To obtain the spectrum of charged particle fluence $\Phi_E(x,y,z)$ at the point of interest (x, y, and z) at a given irradiation field size, a convolution integration on energy is applied, as follows:

$$\Phi_E(x,y,z) = \int_0^{E_{max}} \iint \Psi(x',y',E)\phi(x-x',y-y',z,E)dx'dy'dE \quad (21)$$

where $\Psi(x',y',E)$ is the lateral distribution photon energy fluence of the beam and $\phi(x-x',y-y',z,E)$ is the fluence pencil kernels to position (x, y, z). Note also that $\Psi(x',y',E)$ may vary depending on the dose deposition in the irradiation field, which is the case of IMRT.

3.5 Response model of SSD

In reality, the response behavior of any dosimeter deviates in two cavity theories, because the extreme conditions for both theories are never completely filled. To determine if the dosimeter cavity is large or small, the size of the cavity is compared with the range of the electrons. If the dosimeter is irradiated with a polyenergetic beam, the cavity of theories cannot be applied directly due to the varied response to particles of different energies. In 2004, Yin et al. [30] proposed a method to treat the primary and scattered components separately by different cavity theories, assuming that the primary particles satisfy conditions of SCT while the scattered particles satisfy the LCT. The total dose measured in the Si-diode dosimeter [30] considered the sum of primary and scattered contributions using Eq. (22):

$$D^{cav} = \int_{\Delta}^{E_{max}} \Phi^{p}_{cav}(E) \cdot \frac{L_{\Delta}^{cav}(E)}{\rho} dE + \Phi^{p}_{cav}(\Delta) \cdot \frac{L_{\Delta}^{cav}(\Delta)}{\rho} \cdot \Delta + \int_{0}^{E_{max}} \Psi^{s}_{cav}(E) \cdot \frac{\mu_{en}^{cav}(E)}{\rho} dE \tag{22}$$

where $\Phi^{p}_{cav}(E)$ is the primary electron fluence and $\Psi^{s}_{cav}(E)$ is the energy of the scattered photon fluence. $\frac{L_{\Delta}^{cav}(E)}{\rho}$ is the restricted stopping power, and $\frac{\mu_{en}^{cav}(E)}{\rho}$ is the mass absorption coefficient of material in the cavity. This model proved quite precisely the dose in water, verified by measurement [27]. Eklund and Ahnesjö [26] introduced some solution to calculate dose response through the two assumptions: (1) Ensuring all primary electrons satisfy the SCT condition if the detector size is rather small. Nevertheless, there are still low-energetic electrons in the spectrum that cannot pass through the cavity of the dosimeter. (2) The scattered photons are considered to satisfy the condition of LCT, indicating that CPE is assumed to be located in the cavity of the dosimeter. The validity of this assumption depends on the energy of the scattered photon. To solve this situation, Eklund and Ahnesjö [71] introduced two solutions for the condition of the hypothesis is closer to reality: Instead of calculating the primary low-energetic electron contribution by LCT, they calculate the contribution from primary photons in LCT that create low-energetic primary electrons. From this calculation of the fluence spectra, it is possible to find the low-energetic primary photons. Therefore, a partitioning of the primary electrons was performed, where the high-energetic primary electrons followed the SCT and the contribution of low-energy electron primary was calculated using their father or primary photons. Ideally, the scattered photons should be partitioned in the same way to treat low component of high energy differently. $K(E)$ correction had been introduced, which is defined as follows:

$$K(E) = \frac{D_{p}^{cav}(E)}{\Psi(E) \cdot \frac{\mu_{en}^{cav}(E)}{\rho}} \tag{23}$$

where $D_{p}^{cav}(E)$ is the dose deposited in the cavity of the detector, by the primary photons of energy E (or primary electrons) with a fluence of photons $\Psi(E)$ and its primary electrons. The denominator of this expression represents the collision kerma of the cavity, which is equivalent to the dose if CPE exists locally. Computing $D_{p}^{cav}(E)$ is only possible by a total particle transport calculation as by Monte Carlo simulation. With the introduction of partitioning primary electron and the approximation, factor CPE $K(E)$ in Eq. (21) gives:

$$D^{cav} = \int_{\Delta}^{E_{max}} \Phi_{cav}^{[E_A,E_{max}],p}(E) \cdot \left(\frac{L_{\Delta}^{cav}(E)}{\rho}\right) dE + \Phi_{cav}^{[E_A,E_{max}],p}(\Delta) \cdot \left(\frac{L_{\Delta}^{cav}(\Delta)}{\rho}\right) \cdot \Delta + \int_{0}^{E_{max}} K(E)\left(\Psi_{cav}^{[0,E_A],p}(E) + \Psi_{cav}^{s}(E)\right) \cdot \left(\frac{\mu_{en}^{cav}(E)}{\rho}\right) dE \quad (24)$$

where $\Phi_{cav}^{[E_A,E_{max}]p}(E)$ is the fluence of primary electrons produced by the photon with a higher energy E_A *and* $\Psi_{cav}^{[0,E_A],p}(E)$ is the fluence of primary photons with smaller energy E_A. Applying Eq. (24), one can calculate the water dose, SSD dose, and response factor of Eq. (19). In order to compare the calculated response factor with the measured one, it is necessary to normalize the response factor determined for a reference, which gives:

$$RF_{norm}^{calc}(A, r) = \frac{RF^{calc}(A, r)}{RF^{calc}(A_{ref}, r_{ref})} \quad (25)$$

The reference value of field size is square field of 10 cm × 10 cm, and the reference position from the axis is at a depth of 10 cm in the phantom.

Crop et al. [2] had conducted one of the most detailed studies on the response of air-filled detectors in small photon beams. Author's considered the effect of different perturbation effects: (a) perturbation caused by differences in the composition of detector with respect to water (p_{wall}), (b) perturbation caused by replacement of water by detector ($p_{a,w}$), (c) effect caused by the existence of central electrode of the air-filled detectors, and (d) volume averaging effect for two detectors with different volume. The results of the study are illustrated in **Figure 11**; it was a Monte Carlo-based study for 6 MV photon beam considering photon beams down to 0.8 cm × 0.8 cm. The maximum variation was reported for P_{vol} and $P_{a,w}$.

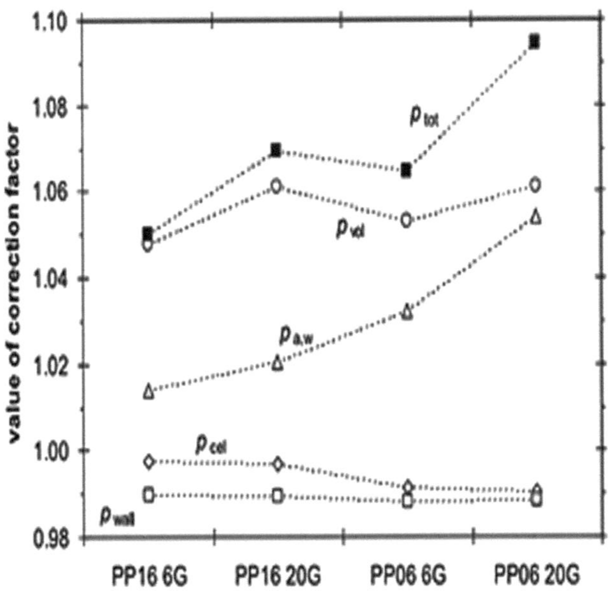

Figure 11.
Results reported by Crop et al. for different perturbation effects. Maximum deviation was reported for the volume averaging effect and perturbation caused by replacement of water by detector media.

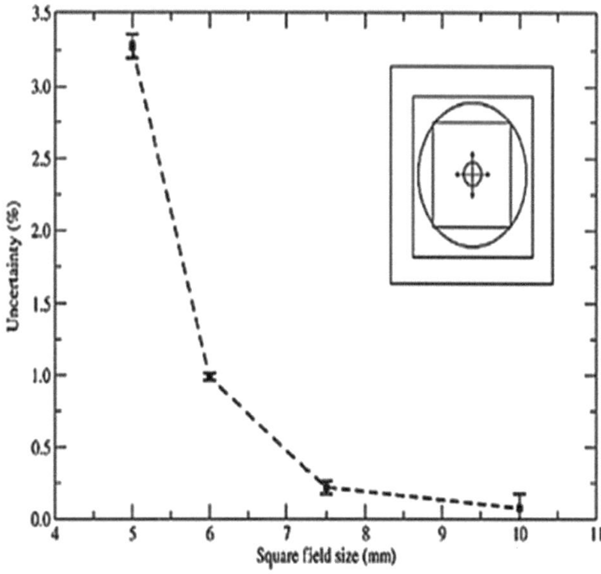

Figure 12.
Uncertainty observed in absorbed dose determination using PTW 60012 diode, due to uniformly distributed displacement error of 1 mm in all directions perpendicular to the beam axis.

In general case of large radiation beam, the value of total perturbation factor is approximately 0.99. However, for small photon beams, these perturbation factors become extremely large and no longer remain independent. Hence, Monte Carlo calculation of perturbation factors must be preferred over the use of SCT. Along with this, the size of the detector with respect to the source size and incorrect alignment can result in large values of correction factors. The perturbation caused by the displacement error in calculation of absorbed dose using Monte Carlo for PTW 60012 diode is illustrated in **Figure 12**. Similar results have been reported by various authors, for the Monte Carlo-based studies for computation of different perturbation factors [37, 72–77].

4. Energy spectrum and beam quality for small photon beams

4.1 Energy spectrum

The collimating devices utilized to project small photon beams result in blockage of photon source and scattered component of photon beam generated from the interaction of primary photon beam with other components of linear accelerator head, as a consequence of which the low energy photons are removed from the central axis of the beam. However, there may be probable increase in the amount of secondary component of beam for off-axis fields. The material composition of flattening filter is a deciding factor about whether the radiation beam will be softened or hardened. Along with this, there is a decrement in phantom scatter in small beams in comparison to the large field sizes. However, the decrement in phantom scatter is more noticeable than head scatter. Both effects are responsible for making the photon spectrum hard along the central axis of the beam. As a result the mass energy coefficient ratio and stopping power ratio of water and material of the detector are changed. Also in the small beams and the absence of LCPE, the low-energy electrons reaching the axis of the beam will be reduced. Hence, the mean electron energy is increased, as a result of which stopping power ratio is also affected.

However, various Monte Carlo-based studies have revealed that the charged particle spectrum generated inside water is not much affected by the change in photon fluence. Hence, the stopping power ratio of water to air does not vary more than 0.5% at 10 cm of depth for 6 MV photon beam for field sizes ranging from 10 cm × 10 cm to 0.3 cm × 0.3 cm or circular fields of 0.3 cm diameter [78, 79], for depth ranging up to 30 cm maximum variation of 1% has been reported [70]. However, the response of diode detectors is affected by this hardening of the photon beam due to the noticeable change in the mass-energy absorption coefficient ratio of water and silicon. For field sizes ranging from 10 cm × 10 cm to 0.5 cm × 0.5 cm, the variation of 3–4% has been reported in the response of the unshielded diodes as a result of reduction in phantom scatter [71, 80].

4.2 Beam quality

For reference dosimetry in photon beams of high energy and large field sizes of beam quality Q using the air-filled detectors calibrated with respect to beam quality Q_0, the radiation quality correction factor k_{Q,Q_0} is required. There are two methods defined to account for beam quality [1, 3, 7]. First is the tissue phantom ratio at the depth of 20 and 10 g/cm^2 using water as a medium for 10 cm × 10 cm beam size and source-to-detector distance (SDD) of 100 cm, $TPR_{20,10}(10,10)_x$ [1]. The second method is based on percentage depth dose at a depth of 10 cm to 10 cm × 10 cm beam size and source to surface distance of 100 cm, $\%dd(10,10)_x$. These beam quality indices are utilized to calculate .

For some calibration laboratories, it is possible to provide calibration of air-filled detectors using clinical linear accelerator photon beam from calibration laboratories. This methodology for calibration of measurement equipment is much more realistic as there are small variations on the absorbed dose to water calibration factor for radiation equipment of the same kind, as the quality of beam varies moderately between the modern equipment of the same type. Therefore, it is possible to use the same radiation beam quality correction factor for similar model of air-filled detectors and radiation emitting equipment of the same kind. Hence, the dosimetric measurements on such machines can be performed without correction for beam quality. This methodology has been applied at some level for Gamma Knife® (Elekta AB, Stockholm), Cyberknife®, and TomoTherapy® (Accuray Inc., Sunnyvale, CA) radiation generators. Also, the components of the clinical linear accelerators such as secondary jaws and multi-leaf collimators are employed for having better machine uniformity and accurate small-field size definition [25–27]. It is important to remember that by the above method of calibration of equipment, there is no requirement for beam quality correction factors, and even then beam quality indices are crucial from commissioning and quality check procedure perspectives. Since the nominal photon beam energies used for intensity-modulated radiation therapy (IMRT), volumetric modulated arc therapy (VMAT), and stereotactic methods are below 10 MV, and the variation of $k_{Q,Q0}$ to quality of the beam is small [1, 2]. A large number of add-ons are utilized in IMRT and stereotactic radiotherapy treatment methods, which makes it impossible to prepare tables for beam quality correction factors for each and every combination of radiation emitters, add-ons, and detector types. Hence, $k_{Q,Q0}$ is not available in all machine/detector combinations. As a result the beam quality index or beam quality correction factor is required to relate the beam quality used for the detector calibration and the beam quality of the user machine. Since, it is sometimes not possible to calibrate the detector in beam quality similar to that of user, and hence the values for all combination of machine/detector are not available. In that case the question arises, whether it is fine to use $TPR_{20,10}(10,10)_x$ or $\%dd(10,10)_x$ for dose measurements in fields smaller than 10 cm × 10 cm on the same radiation emitter. As discussed above the stopping power ratio variation with change in field size is small. Hence, the beam quality indices measured for large photon beams can be utilized for small beams. The variation of stopping power ratios with beam size and other perturbation factors can be merged together into an output correction factor.

In the conditions where the conventional beam size of 10 cm × 10 cm, a number of methods have been proposed to determine the beam quality:

a. A concept of machine-specific reference field (msr), f_{msr}, has been proposed by Alfonso et al. [81].

b. Machine-specific beam quality index has been proposed for TomoTherapy [82]. According to this methodology beam quality index is measured using similar methods as used for determination of the $\%dd(10, 10)_x$ in the conditions achievable in case of TomoTherapy. In this proposed methodology, authors calculated correction factors for beam quality with the help of Monte Carlo techniques and compared them with measurements as a function of conventional index to establish a relation between the machine-specific beam quality index and the conventional beam quality index [83].

c. In the third method, it is proposed to measure $TPR_{20,10}(S)$, the ratio of dose deposited at 20 and 10 g/cm^2 depths for an S cm × S cm square field size at source-to-detector distance of 100 cm. The measurement of $TPR_{20,10}(S)$ is performed on the machine where 10 cm × 10 cm field size is not achievable for series of square field sizes S, and comparison is made with the measurements performed using radiation emitter where 10 cm × 10 cm beam size is achievable; the measurement data is extrapolated [78, 79, 84]. Using this extrapolated data relationship for the beam quality index of 10 cm × 10 cm beam size, $TPR_{20,10}(10)$ and $TPR_{20,10}(S)$ are derived [85].

It was observed by Sauer et al. that the third methodology to measure beam quality index in nonstandard field sizes is effective for circular or rectangular fields using the concept of equivalent square field method [79, 85] and for flattening filter-free beams by surety of correction factor for deficiency in the lateral scatter because of conical beam profiles. It must be noted that the relation between the stopping power ratio and beam quality index in case of FFF radiation fields and WFF beams is not similar [86–89]. The relations to calculate $TPR_{20,10}(10)$ and *%dd* $(10,10)_x$ can be derived for small beams (S lying between 4 and 12 cm) [90]. **Figure 13** illustrated the variation of $TPR_{20,10}(S)$ for beam size of S cm × S cm for field sizes ranging from 4 cm × 4 cm to 12 cm × 12 cm with energy of photon beam ranging from 4 and 10 MV [79, 90] (squares representing the measurement data [79] and curved representing Monte Carlo results [90]).

4.3 Measurement of $TPR_{20,10}(10)$

The determination of $TPR_{20,10}(10)$ from the measurements obtained for $TPR_{20,10}(S)$, where S is the equivalent square f_{msr}, by using the measurement data in the analytic expression given by Palmans (Eq. (26)) [90]. **Figure 14** shows the experimental set-up to be used for measurement of $TPR_{20,10}(S)$, with source-to-detector distance of 100 cm and at a depth of 20 g/cm^2 and 10 g/cm^2.

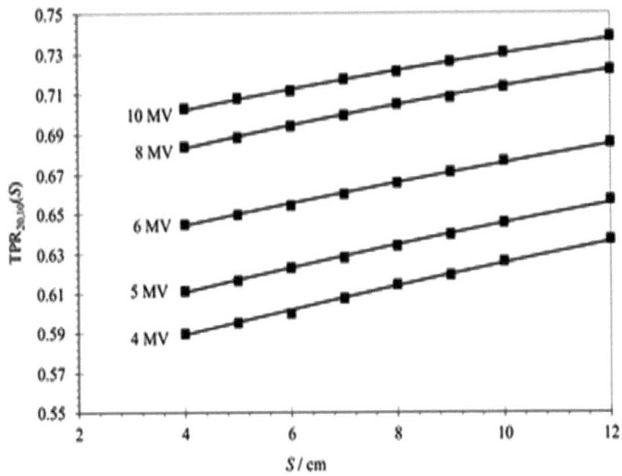

Figure 13.
Dependence of $TPR_{20,10}(S)$ on the field size S, for beam size ranging between 4 and 12 cm and photon energies between 4 and 10 MV.

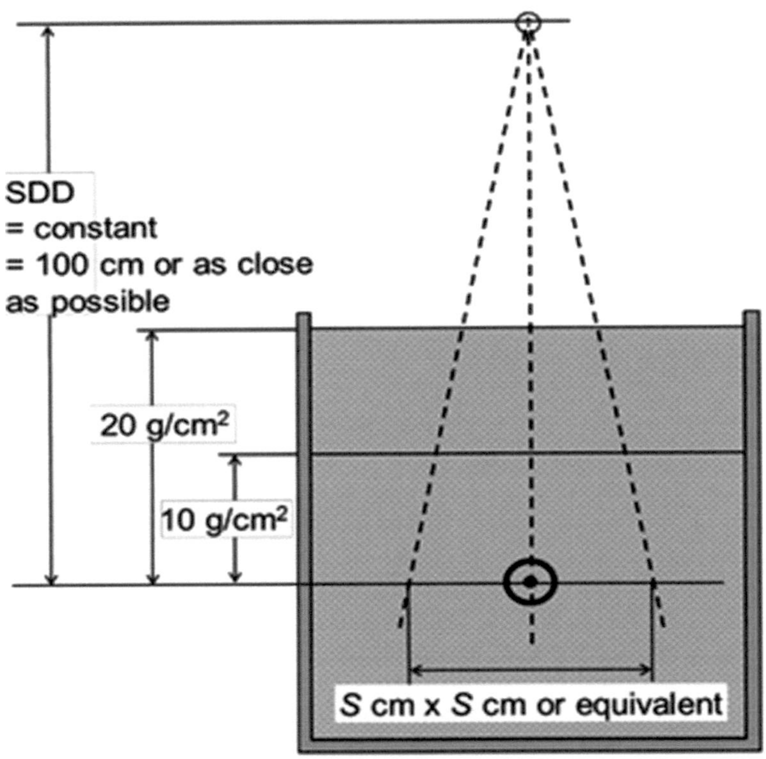

Figure 14.
The experimental set-up to be used for measurement of $TPR_{20,10}(S)$.

$TPR_{20,10}(10)$ for 10 cm × 10 cm can be derived using the following relationship:

$$TPR_{20,10}(10) = \frac{TPR_{20,10}(S) + c(10 - S)}{1 + c(10 - S)} \tag{26}$$

This relation is valid when 4 cm ≤ S ≤ 12 cm, where C = (16.15 ∓ 0.12) × 10^{-3}.

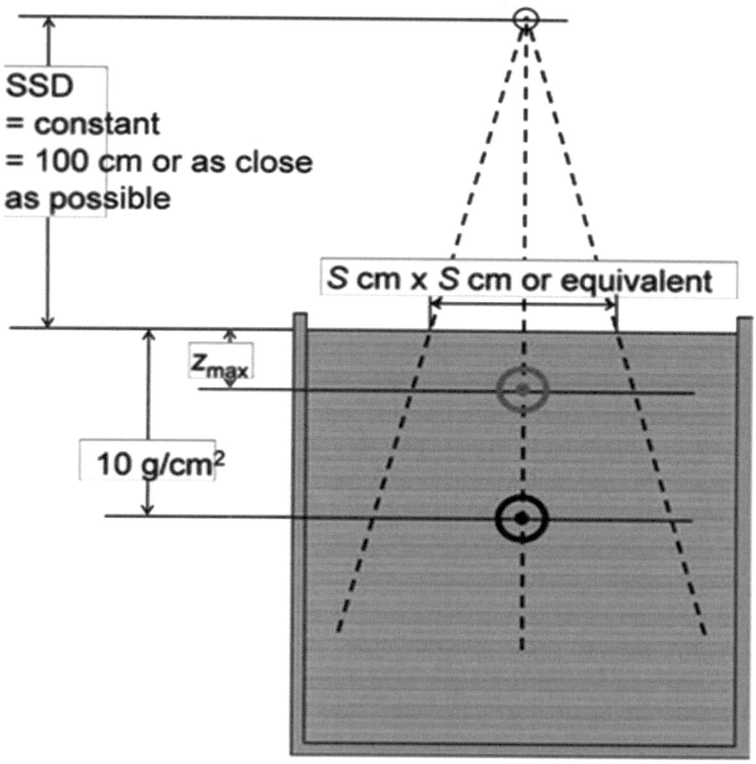

Figure 15.
Measurement setup for %dd(10,S).

4.4 Measurement of $\%dd(10,10)_x$

Similar to the determination of $TPR_{20,10}(10)$ from measurements of $TPR_{20,10}(S)$, the $\%dd(10,10)_x$ can be determined from the %dd(10) for S cm × S cm msr field size using the analytic relation provided by Palmans [90]. **Figure 15** illustrates the experimental setup for the measurement of %dd(10, S) for S cm × S cm beam size and measurement depths of maximum dose (z_{max}) and 10 g/cm^2 at a source-to-surface distance of 100 cm.

Lead foil is not required in the measurements of %dd(10,S) for WFF radiation beams (below 10 MV). However, the use of lead foil of 1 mm thickness is recommended for %dd(10,S) measurements in FFF radiation beams; in order to remove the electron contamination and analytic expression, Eq. (27) is used to calculate $\%dd(10,10)_{Pb}$. Then $\%dd(10,10)_x$ can be obtained from $\%dd(10,10)_{Pb}$ using the relation provided by AAPM Task Group report 21.

The $\%dd(10,10)_x$ can be calculated using the following expression:

$$\% \, dd(10, 10) = \frac{\% \, dd(10, S) + 80c(10 - S)}{1 + c(10 - S)} \tag{27}$$

where 4 cm ≤ S ≤ 12 cm and C = (53.4 ∓ 1.1) × 10^{-3}.

5. Determination of absorbed dose

In case of radiation-emitting equipment, where field beam of 10 cm × 10 cm (f_{ref}) can be established, the dose measurement is performed using the recommendation provided by task group series (TRS) 398 and other equivalent protocols [1–7]. However, in radiation equipment where f_{ref} setting is not feasible, f_{msr} is used. The full width at half maximum of f_{msr} must satisfy small-field condition.

$$FWHM \geq 2\, r_{LCPE} + d \tag{28}$$

5.1 Measurement of absorbed dose in f_{msr}

5.1.1 *Calibration coefficient for f_{msr} is available*

In situations where calibration coefficient in terms of absorbed dose to water ($N_{D,w,\,Q_{msr}}{}^{f_{msr}}$) is available for machine-specific reference field (f_{msr}) and beam quality similar to that of the user beam (Q_{msr}), the absorbed dose to water at depth of reference (z_{ref}) in the nonexistence of detector in water can be determined using the following relation:

$$D_{w,Q_{msr}}{}^{f_{msr}} = M_{Q_{msr}}{}^{f_{msr}} N_{D,w,\,Q_{msr}}{}^{f_{msr}} \tag{29}$$

where $M_{Q_{msr}}{}^{f_{msr}}$ is the detector reading f_{msr} beam corrected for influential quantities, such as temperature, pressure, perturbation factors, etc.

5.1.2 *Calibration factor available for f_{ref} (10 cm × 10 cm) and beam quality (Q_0) correction factor*

In conditions where calibration coefficient ($N_{D,w}{}^{f_{ref}}$) is provided by calibration laboratory in terms of f_{ref} and correction factor quality of beam Q_0. The absorbed dose to water can be calculated using the following relation:

$$D_{w,\,Q_{msr}}{}^{f_{msr}} = M_{Q_{msr}}{}^{f_{msr}} N_{D,w,Q_0}{}^{f_{ref}} k_{Q_{msr},Q_0}{}^{f_{msr},f_{ref}} \tag{30}$$

where $M_{Q_{msr}}{}^{f_{msr}}$ is the detector reading reworked for influential quantities and $k_{Q_{msr},Q_0}{}^{f_{msr},f_{ref}}$ is the correction factor for difference in beam quality and field size.

5.1.3 *Calibration factor available for f_{ref} (10 cm × 10 cm) without beam quality (Q_0) correction factor*

In the situation where the correction factor for the generic quality of beam, correcting for the difference in beam quality and effect of difference in field size, is not provided by the calibration laboratory, the dose deposited can be determined using the following relation:

$$D_{w,Q_{msr}}{}^{f_{msr}} = M_{Q_{msr}}{}^{f_{msr}} N_{D,w,Q_0}{}^{f_{ref}} k_{Q,Q_0}{}^{f_{ref}}\, k_{Q_{msr},Q}{}^{f_{msr},\,f_{ref}} \tag{31}$$

where $M_{Q_{msr}}^{f_{msr}}$ is the detector reading for f_{msr} reworked for influential quantities, $N_{D,w,Q_0}^{f_{ref}}$ is the detector calibration factor in terms of absorbed dose to water in f_{ref} beam and Q_0 quality of beam, $k_{Q,Q_0}^{f_{ref}}$ is the correction factor for difference in detector response of detector in beam quality Q_0 in field size f_{ref} and response of detector in beam quality Q in f_{ref} beam size, and $k_{Q_{msr},Q}^{f_{msr},f_{ref}}$ is the beam quality correction factor to account for the difference between the response of detector in beam quality Q, f_{ref} beam size and beam quality Q_{msr}, and beam size of f_{msr}.

In order to determine the dose deposited in water for FFF radiation beam, the following relation can be used:

$$D_{w,Q_{msr}^{FFF}}^{f_{msr}} = M_{Q_{msr}^{FFF}}^{f_{msr}} N_{D,w,Q_0}^{f_{ref}} k_{Q^{WFF},Q_0}^{f_{ref}} k_{Q^{FFF},Q^{WFF}}^{f_{ref}} k_{Q_{msr},Q}^{f_{msr},f_{ref}} \quad (32)$$

where $k_{Q^{WFF},Q_0}^{f_{ref}}$ is the correction for beam quality for difference in response of the detector in beam Q^{WFF}, beam size f_{ref} and response of detector in quality of beam Q_0, and beam size of f_{ref}. It can be taken from the international dosimetry protocols [1, 2, 7], and $k_{Q^{FFF},Q^{WFF}}^{f_{ref}}$ is the factor of correction for variation in response of the detector in the FFF and WFF radiation fields. It can be obtained from Monte Carlo studies. **Figure 16** summarizes the different conditions discussed above for the determination of dose deposited in water.

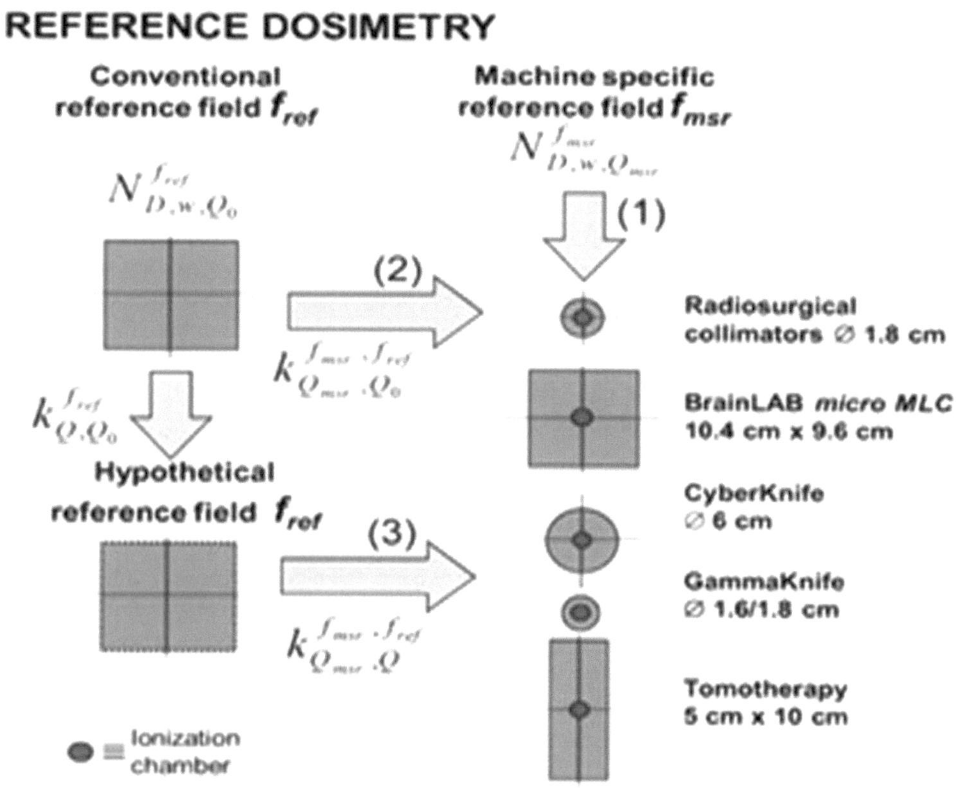

Figure 16.
Schematic summary of the determination of absorbed dose in case of small beams considering the case of machine specific reference field according to the formalism given by TRS 483. The arrows and formulas labeled (1), (2) and (3) refer to Section 6.1.1, 6.1.2 and 6.1.3, respectively.

5.2 Measurement of field output factors

To measure the dose deposited by clinical radiation beams with respect to the msr field in Ref. dosimetry, field output factors ($\Omega_{\Omega_{clin}\Omega_{msr}}^{f_{clin}f_{msr}}$) are determined. They are also known as relative dose factors [91] or total scatter factors [1, 56, 79]. It is defined as the ratio of dose deposited in water by clinical beam (f_{clin}) with the quality of beam (Q_{clin}) to the dose deposited in water in msr field (f_{msr}) with quality of beam Q_{msr}:

$$\Omega_{\Omega_{clin}\Omega_{msr}}^{f_{clin}f_{msr}} = \frac{D_{w,Q_{clin}}^{f_{clin}}}{D_{w,Q_{msr}}^{f_{msr}}} \tag{33}$$

The output factors are utilized to calculate the dose deposited to water in clinical beams (f_{clin}) from the dose deposited to water in machine-specific reference beams (f_{msr}). $\Omega_{\Omega_{clin}\Omega_{msr}}^{f_{clin}f_{msr}}$ can be determined using the detector readings by using the following relation:

$$\Omega_{\Omega_{clin}\Omega_{msr}}^{f_{clin}f_{msr}} = \frac{M_{Q_{clin}}^{f_{clin}}}{M_{Q_{msr}}^{f_{msr}}} k_{Q_{clin},Q_{msr}}^{f_{clin},f_{msr}} \tag{34}$$

where $k_{Q_{clin},Q_{msr}}^{f_{clin},f_{msr}}$ is the output correction factor; it can be determined either by direct measurements or using Monte Carlo techniques.

6. Monte Carlo simulation in small-field dosimetry

Monte Carlo techniques are widely used as an alternative in situations where measurements are either difficult or are not possible. Many authors have reported about the possibility of using MC techniques for small-field dosimetry [92–98]. Monte Carlo techniques can be used to calculate the correction factors as discussed in Section 6 of this chapter. It can also be used as a reference or standard with respect to different techniques of relative and absolute dose measurements with acceptable accuracy. With the use of Monte Carlo techniques, the dosimetry in low-density materials can be understood where it is difficult to perform measurements due to the presence of non-equilibrium conditions [99–105]. In radiation dosimetry two approaches are followed for the use of MC techniques. First approach is to calculate correction factors for the dosimeters to be used for dosimetric measurements. In the second approach, the dosimetric quantities are directly calculated, which is equivalent to performing measurements in ideal conditions. However, it is important to verify the MC model against the beam modeling parameters before using it for radiation dosimetry calculations.

6.1 General purpose of Monte Carlo codes for radiation dosimetry

It is possible to explicitly model the interaction of every particle using Monte Carlo techniques. The main characteristics of Monte Carlo techniques used for radiation dosimetry are:

1. The generation of particles is based on the distribution function used to describe the radiation source.

2. The random numbers are obtained in the range of (0, 1) using the pseudorandom number generators.

3. The probability distribution functions are sampled using interaction cross sections.

4. The step of a particle is defined as the distance between two consecutive events (collision/scatter).

5. "Scoring" for each and every outcome is performed to calculate quantities, such as dose deposited in a medium.

6. In order to reduce the statistical uncertainty in the calculation, it is recommended to perform simulations using a large number of particles ($\sim 1 \times 10^9$).

There are various Monte Carlo codes available which can be used in radiation dosimetry of stereotactic fields. The most commonly used MC codes are Electron Gamma Shower [106], GEANT4 [107], and the Monte Carlo N-Particle code [108]. Due to highly accurate radiation transport algorithm for electrons and photons and easy to use BEAM package, EGSnrc is one of the most frequently used Monte Carlo codes for small-field dosimetry.

6.2 Monte Carlo studies for small-field dosimetry

Heydarian et al. [109] performed a study using diamond detectors, diodes, films, and EGS4 Monte Carlo code, for field sizes ranging from 7 to 23 mm on Siemens Mevatron linac. Scielzo et al. [110] investigated the application of Monte Carlo-based calculation algorithm for treatment planning in stereotactic radiosurgery for Varian 2100C. Authors reported large difference between the treatment planning system (TPS) and MC calculation, especially near the inhomogeneous regions. Verhaegen et al. [92] performed a dosimetric study using the BEAM/EGS4 Monte Carlo code for 6 MV SRS unit for circular field sizes with diameter ranging from 1.25 to 5 cm at isocenter. The authors reported a good agreement between the measurement and computational results for most of the detectors in terms of cone factor. De Vlamynck et al. [111] performed clinical dosimetry using Markus parallel plate ion chamber and diamond detector in 6 MV photon beam of SL 25 (Elekta) linac and compared the results with Monte Carlo calculations. The depth dose distributions for measured and calculated data were found in good agreement with each other; however slight discrepancies were reported for lateral beam profiles. Cheung et al. [112] verified the accuracy of treatment planning system (Leksell GammaPlan) using Gafchromic films and Monte Carlo methods for field sizes ranging from 4 to 18 mm on a Gamma Knife unit. Variations up to 10% were observed for Gafchromic films which were attributed to the energy dependency of films. Westermark et al. [113] performed a comparative study using diamond detector, liquid ion chamber, plastic scintillator, silicon diode, and Monte Carlo techniques for small-field sizes ($\varphi > 4$ mm) of 6 and 18 MV photon beams in order to study the response of various dosimeters. Deng et al. [114] generated a multiple source model by following the procedure of beam commissioning for Cyberknife unit for Monte Carlo-based treatment planning. Authors reported largest variation of 9.5% for ionization chamber IC-10 and attributed this variation to the volume averaging effect of the chamber. Paskalev et al. [115] investigated the dose distribution for circular field (1.5 and 3 mm) for 10 MV photon beam using Varian Clinac-18 and reported maximum variation of 0.3 mm between the measured and calculated 50% isodose surface. Tsougos et al. [116] performed a Monte Carlo-based dosimetric study for in-house developed 6 MV SRT unit and compared it against conventional dosimetric techniques. Francescon et al. [117] investigated total scatter factor for Cyberknife unit for three different collimator opening diameters ranging from 5 to 10 mm. Comparison was made between the experimental and Monte Carlo results. Heydarian et al. [118] investigated the dosimetric parameters of a SRS linac using experimental measurements and Monte Carlo methods and reported good agreement between the Monte Carlo and experimental data. Scott et al. [29] investigated the effect of source occlusion on output of the linac for small-field sizes and large focal spot sizes and found that output factors are sensitive to the dimensions of the electron spot size hitting the target. Sargison et al. [119] proposed a methodology for measurement and reporting of relative output factors for small fields using both experimental and Monte Carlo methods. In 2014, Sargison et al. [120] presented two scientific quantitative definitions of very small-field size and reported that careful methodology is required for setting of field sizes and placement of detectors for field sizes less than 12 mm for 6 MV photon beams. In 2019, Francescon et al. [121] investigated the sensitivity of dosimetric correction factors to interunit variation and reported variation up to 9% between the measured data corrected using the recommendations of TRS-483 and Monte Carlo results. Casar et al. [122] provided detector-specific output correction factors for small-field sizes using the recommendations of TRS-483.

6.3 Monte Carlo codes optimized for radiation therapy and out-of-field doses for small fields

Considering the ability of Monte Carlo techniques to calculate absorbed dose in non-equilibrium conditions, it can be an ideal tool for clinical use. However, due to its lengthy computational sessions, it is difficult to use them in clinic. In the above section, we discussed about the general purpose of Monte Carlo tools which can model different types of particles (gamma, electron, positron, etc.) and different kinds of physics models to simulate the interactions of particles over the large range of energy of incident particles. The introduction of Monte Carlo-based treatment planning systems, which uses some approximations and simplification in comparison to full Monte Carlo codes, can help to overcome the limitations of contemporary TPS. In Monte Carlo-based TPS, a part of dose calculation is performed using Monte Carlo methods, and the remaining part is performed using approximation-based algorithms [123, 124]. Another option is to use Monte Carlo codes that are optimized specially for radiation therapy applications. TG105 report can provide more information about the use of Monte Carlo methods for clinical applications [125]. However, it is possible that the highly efficient Monte Carlo codes that can completely simulate the radiation transport within acceptable timeframe will be still required. Hence, the use of Monte Carlo methods in small-field dosimetry will increase the confidence in the accuracy of calculation of dose distributions.

Apart from the difficulty in calculating dose deposited within the field, TPS algorithms are also not able to calculate the doses out-of-field accurately, since the measurement data obtained to be used for commissioning of TPS extends only a few centimeters beyond the edges of the field. Penumbra region is defined as a region of steep dose fall, where radiation dose falls from 80 to 20% of maximum dose within the field. The dose protruding beyond the field is not considered in the calculation of the dose distribution or its contribution to the procedure of inverse optimization. Hence, the dose distribution obtained from TPS is expected to be inaccurate in regions beyond the edges of the primary field. The predictions in low-dose regions near the primary field by TPS have been shown to be inaccurate as well. Jang et al. [126] investigated the inaccuracies in dose calculation in low-dose regions for intensity-modulated radiotherapy (IMRT) and reason behind these inaccurate calculations by comparing their results against Monte Carlo methods. Authors reported error up to 25% in low-dose regions and found that the inadequate modeling of transmission through MLC leaves and leaf scatter in TPS to be the main cause of error. In the treatments performed using IMRT techniques, doses of 2 Gy per fraction is delivered over large fractions to deliver a total dose of 60–70 Gy to the tumor volume. However, stereotactic radiotherapy follows hypofractionated regime, in which doses of 10–20 Gy per fraction is delivered. Hence, the dose deposited out-of-field due to each fraction is of concern. Petti et al. [127] investigated the doses outside the treatment field and cause of it for treatment using Cyber Knife and compared them against the doses obtained using Gamma Knife and IMRT for similar treatment. The out-of-field doses were found higher by a factor of two to five for Gamma Knife and by a factor of four for IMRT treatments. According to the authors, the leakage radiation is the main cause of out-of-field doses. Chuang et al. [128] investigated for the reduction in out-of-field doses after installation of shielding upgrade and reported the reduction of 20–50% in out-of-field doses. Comparison of difference in peripheral doses absorbed using different equipment for stereotactic treatment was made by Di Betta et al. [129] and used the data for estimation of risk of stochastic effects. Authors reported that the risk of adverse side effects for treatment using 5 Gy per fraction due out-of-field doses is negligible. Lastly, there are relatively fewer studies available on out-of-field doses due to the small fields. More studies are required on it, which can be helpful to investigate the effects of out-of-field doses.

7. Conclusion

Considering the importance of accurate small-field dosimetry, this chapter discusses all important aspects related to it in details. It includes the physics of small radiation fields, cavity theory, and methodology of small-field dosimetry to understand the response of dosimeters and brief discussion on several dosimeters. It also discusses the recommendations of COP for dosimetry of small radiation fields. Moreover, it discusses the small and long cavity theories for computing the accurate dose response. In addition, pencil beam algorithms as a tool for the dose response evaluation is reported, and uses of Monte Carlo simulation in categorizing the primary and scattering components of the radiotherapeutic photon beam are handled. Also this chapter focuses on the application and importance of Monte Carlo techniques in small-field dosimetry and treatment methods that are based on small fields, such as stereotactic treatments and IMRT. Available general purpose Monte Carlo codes used for applications in radiotherapy is also mentioned. Such Monte Carlo codes have the ability to simulate transport of radiation within a medium in great details. EGSnrc, Geant4, PENELOPE, and MCNP are some of the most commonly used Monte Carlo codes for small-field dosimetry studies. Its accurate algorithm to model the transport of radiation and easy-to-use graphical user interface of BEAM code of EGSnrc makes it one of the most widely used MC code. A thorough recent literature review is performed on the small-field dosimetric studies performed using Monte Carlo codes. The studies on out-of-field doses, limitation of contemporary treatment planning systems, use of Monte Carlo codes optimized specially for their use in radiation therapy simulation, and need of use of full Monte Carlo for dose calculations are also reviewed. It was concluded that still more studies on these issues are required in order to investigate the effects related to inaccurate dosimetry in depth. Hence, it can be concluded from the above discussion that the user must select a suitable dosimeter and follow the recommendations provided by TRS-483 for accurate beam data collection and accurate dosimetric measurements.

Author details

Hossam Donya[1,2]*, Baljeet Seniwal[3], Reem Darwesh[1] and Telma C.F. Fonseca[3,4]

1 Department of Physics, Faculty of Science, King Abdulaziz University, Jeddah, Saudi Arabia

2 Physics Department, Faculty of Science, Menoufia University, Shebin El-Koom, Egypt

3 Programa de Pós-graduação em Ciências e Técnicas Nucleares - UFMG BH/MG, Brasil

4 Departamento de Engenharia Nuclear — DEN BH/MG, Brasil

*Address all correspondence to: hdunia@kau.edu.sa; donyavip@yahoo.com

References

[1] Godson HF, Ravikumar M, Ganesh KM, Sathiyan S, Ponmalar YR. Small field output factors: Comparison of measurements with various detectors and effects of detector orientation with primary jaw setting. Radiation Measurements. 2016;**85**:99-110

[2] Crop F, Reynaert N, Pittomvils G, Paelinck L, De Wagter C, Vakaet L, et al. The influence of small field sizes, penumbra, spot size and measurement depth on perturbation factors for microionization chambers. Physics in Medicine & Biology. 2009;**54**(9):2951

[3] Institute of Physics and Engineering in Medicine. Small Field MV Photon Dosimetry, IPEM Rep. 103. York: IPEM; 2010

[4] McEwen M et al. Addendum to the AAPM's TG-51 protocol for clinical reference dosimetry of high-energy photon beams. Medical Physics. 2014; **41**:041501

[5] Lillicrap SC, Owen B, Williams JR, Williams PC. Code of practice for high-energy photon therapy dosimetry based on the NPL absorbed dose calibration service. Physics in Medicine and Biology. 1990;**35**:1355-1360

[6] International Atomic Energy Agency. Absorbed Dose Determination in External Beam Radiotherapy: An International Code of Practice for Dosimetry Based on Standards of Absorbed Dose to Water, Technical Reports Series No. 398. Vienna: IAEA; 2000

[7] Netherlands Commission on Radiation Dosimetry. Code of Practice for the Absorbed Dose Determination in High Energy Photon and Electron Beams, Rep. NCS-18. Delft: NSC; 2008

[8] Andreo P. Monte Carlo simulations in radiotherapy dosimetry. Radiation Oncology. 2018;**13**(1):121

[9] IAEA. Dosimetry of Small Static Fields Used in External Beam Radiotherapy: An International Code of Practice for Reference and Relative Dose Determination. IAEA; 2017

[10] Das IJ, Ding GX, Ahnesjö A. Small fields: Nonequilibrium radiation dosimetry. Medical Physics. 2008;**35**: 206-215

[11] Papaconstadopoulos P. On the detector response and the reconstruction of the source intensity distribution in small photon fields [PhD thesis]. Montreal, Canada: McGill University; 2016

[12] Kalach NI, Rogers DW. Which accelerator photon beams are 'clinic-like' for reference dosimetry purposes? Medical Physics. 2003;**30**:1546-1555

[13] Wuerfel J. Dose measurements in small fields. Medical Physics International. 2013;**1**:81-90

[14] Ralston A, Liu P, Warrener K, McKenzie D, Suchowerska N. Small field diode correction factors derived using an air core fibre optic scintillation dosimeter and EBT2 film. Physics in Medicine and Biology. 2012;**57**: 2587-2602

[15] Sibata CH, Mota HC, Bedder AS, Higgins PD, Shin KH. Influence of detector size in photon beam profile measurements. Physics in Medicine and Biology. 1991;**36**:621-631

[16] Higgins PD, Sibata CH, Siskind L, Sohn JW. Deconvolution of detector size effect for small field measurement. Medical Physics. 1995;**22**:1663-1666

[17] Garcia-Vicente F, Delgado JM, Peraza C. Experimental determination of the convolution kernel for the study of the spatial response of a detector. Medical Physics. 1998;**25**:202-207

[18] Pantelis E et al. Dosimetric characterization of CyberKnife radiosurgical photon beams using polymer gels. Medical Physics. 2008;**35**: 2312-2320

[19] Azangwe G et al. Detector to detector corrections: A comprehensive experimental study of detector specific correction factors for beam output measurements for small radiotherapy beams. Medical Physics. 2014;**41**:072103

[20] McEwen MR. Measurement of ionization chamber absorbed dose kQ factors in megavoltage photon beams. Medical Physics. 2010;**37**: 2179-2193

[21] Georg D, Knöös T, McClean B. Current status and future perspective of flattening filter free photon beams. Medical Physics. 2011;**38**:1280-1293

[22] Pantelis E et al. On the implementation of a recently proposed dosimetric formalism to a robotic radiosurgery system. Medical Physics. 2010;**37**:2369-2379

[23] Kawachi T et al. Reference dosimetry condition and beam quality correction factor for CyberKnife beam. Medical Physics. 2008;**35**:4591-4598

[24] Le Roy M et al. Assessment of small volume ionization chambers as reference dosimeters in high-energy photon beams. Physics in Medicine and Biology. 2011;**56**:5637-5650

[25] Li XA, Soubra M, Szanto J, Gerig LH. Lateral electron equilibrium and electron contamination in measurements of head-scatter factors using miniphantoms and brass caps. Medical Physics. 1995;**22**:1167-1170

[26] Laub WU, Wong T. The volume effect of detectors in the dosimetry of small fields used in IMRT. Medical Physics. 2003;**30**:341-347

[27] Eklund K, Ahnesjö A. Modeling silicon diode energy response factors for use in therapeutic photon beams. Physics in Medicine and Biology. 2009; **54**:6135-6150

[28] Eklund K. Modeling silicon diode dose response in radiotherapy fields using fluence pencil kernels [PhD thesis]. Uppsala, Sweden: Uppsala University; 2010

[29] Scott AJ, Nahum AE, Fenwick JD. Monte Carlo modeling of small photon fields: Quantifying the impact of focal spot size on source occlusion and output factors, and exploring miniphantom design for small-field measurements. Medical Physics. 2009; **36**:3132-3144

[30] Yin Z, Hugtenburg R, Beddoe AH. Response corrections for solid-state detectors in megavoltage photon dosimetry. Physics in Medicine and Biology. 2004;**49**:3691-3702

[31] McKerracher C, Thwaites DI. Verification of the dose to the isocentre in stereotactic plans. Radiotherapy and Oncology. 2002;**64**:97-107

[32] Betzel GT, Lansley SP, Baluti F, Reinisch L, Meyer J. Clinical investigations of a CVD diamond detector for radiotherapy dosimetry. Physica Medica. 2012;**28**:144-152

[33] Ciancaglioni I et al. Dosimetric characterization of a synthetic single crystal diamond detector in clinical radiation therapy small photon beams. Medical Physics. 2012;**39**:4493-4501

[34] Marsolat F et al. A new single crystal diamond dosimeter for small beam: Comparison with different commercial active detectors. Physics in Medicine and Biology. 2013;**58**:7647-7660

[35] Ralston A, Tyler M, Liu P, McKenzie D, Suchowerska N.

Over-response of synthetic microDiamond detectors in small radiation fields. Physics in Medicine and Biology. 2014;**59**:5873-5881

[36] Lechner W, Palmans H, Sölkner L, Grochowska P, Georg D. Detector comparison for small field output factor measurements in flattening filter free photon beams. Radiotherapy and Oncology. 2013;**109**:356-360

[37] Scott AJ, Kumar S, Nahum AE, Fenwick JD. Characterizing the influence of detector density on dosimeter response in non-equilibrium small photon fields. Physics in Medicine and Biology. 2012;**57**:4461-4476

[38] Archambault L, Beddar AS, Gingras L, Roy R, Beaulieu L. Measurement accuracy and Cerenkov removal for high performance, high spatial resolution scintillation dosimetry. Medical Physics. 2006;**33**: 128-135

[39] Gagnon J-C et al. Dosimetric performance and array assessment of plastic scintillation detectors for stereotactic radiosurgery quality assurance. Medical Physics. 2012;**39**: 429-436

[40] Morin J et al. A comparative study of small field total scatter factors and dose profiles using plastic scintillation detectors and other stereotactic dosimeters: The case of the CyberKnife. Medical Physics. 2013;**40**:011719

[41] Liu PZY, Suchowerska N, Lambert J, Abolfathi P, McKenzie DR. Plastic scintillation dosimetry: Comparison of three solutions for the Cerenkov challenge. Physics in Medicine and Biology. 2011;**56**: 5805-5821

[42] Devic S. Radiochromic film dosimetry: Past, present, and future. Physica Medica. 2011;**27**:122-134

[43] Bekerat H et al. Improving the energy response of external beam therapy (EBT) GafChromic™ dosimetry films at low energies (≤100 keV). Medical Physics. 2014;**41**:022101

[44] Alnawaf H, Butson MJ, Cheung T, Yu PKN. Scanning orientation and polarization effects for XRQA radiochromic film. Physica Medica. 2010;**26**:216-219

[45] Araki F, Moribe N, Shimonobou T, Yamashita Y. Dosimetric properties of radiophotoluminescent glass rod detector in high-energy photon beams from a linear accelerator and cyber-knife. Medical Physics. 2004;**31**: 1980-1986

[46] Perks J, Gao M, Smith V, Skubic S, Goetsch S. Glass rod detectors for small field, stereotactic radiosurgery dosimetric audit. Medical Physics. 2005; **32**:726-732

[47] Donya H. Pencil-beam fluence evaluation based on Monte Carlo simulations algorithm of high energetic treatment photons. Journal of Medical Signals and Sensors. 2018;**8**:81

[48] Seniwal B, Fonseca TC, Singh R. Monte-Carlo modelling for evaluation of two different calculation algorithms. Brazilian Journal of Radiation Sciences. 2019;7(1):1-14

[49] Cunningham JR. Scatter-air ratios. Physics in Medicine and Biology. 1972; **17**(1):42-51

[50] Gupta SK, Cunningham JR. Measurement of tissue-air ratios and scatter functions for large field sizes, for cobalt 60 gamma radiation. The British Journal of Radiology. 1966;**39**(457):7-11

[51] Drouard J, Rosenfeld J-C, Simonian M. Generation of primary and scatter tables for dose computation in high energy photon beams. In:

Proceedings of the 5th ESTRO Meeting on Radiotherapy and Oncology; 1986

[52] ICRU. ICRU Report 23: Measurement of Absorbed Doses in a Phantom Irradiated by a Single Beam of X or Gamma Rays. Bethesda, MD: ICRU; 1973

[53] Kim S, Zhu TC, Palta JR. An equivalent square field formula for determining head scatter factors of rectangular fields. Medical Physics. 1997;**24**(11)

[54] Day MJ. A note on the calculation of dose in X-ray fields. The British Journal of Radiology. 1950;**23**(270): 368-369

[55] Clarkson JR. A note on depth doses in fields of irregular shape. The British Journal of Radiology. 1941;**14**(164): 265-268

[56] Khan FM. The Physics of Radiation Therapy. Baltimore: Williams and Wilkins; 1984

[57] Sterling TD, Perry H, Katz L. Automation of radiation treatment planning—IV. Derivation of a mathematical expression for the per cent depth dose surface of cobalt 60 beams and visualisation of multiple field dose distributions. The British Journal of Radiology. 1964;**37**(439):544-550

[58] Greening JR. Fundamentals of Radiation Dosimetry. Bristol: Adam Hilger; 1981

[59] Mayles P, Nahum A, Rosenwald J-C. Handbook of Radiotherapy Physics: Theory and Practice. New York: Franionization Chambers & Taylor; 2007. p. 1432

[60] Gray LH. The experimental determination by ionization methods of the rate of emission of beta- and gamma-ray energy by radioactive substances. The British Journal of Radiology. 1949;**22**(264):677-697

[61] Ma C, Nahum AE. Bragg-Gray theory and ion chamber dosimetry for photon beams. Physics in Medicine and Biology. 1991;**36**(4):413-428

[62] Spencer LV, Attix FH. A theory of cavity ionization. Radiation Research. 1955;**3**(3):23-54

[63] Nahum AE. Water/air mass stopping power ratios for megavoltage photon and electron beams. Physics in Medicine and Biology. 1978;**23**(1): 24-38

[64] Siebers JV, Keall PJ, Nahum AE, Mohan R. Converting absorbed dose to medium to absorbed dose to water for Monte Carlo based photon beam dose calculations. Physics in Medicine and Biology. 2000;**45**(4):983

[65] Janssens A. Modified energy-deposition model, for the computation of the stopping-power ratio for small cavity sizes. Physical Review A. 1981; **23**(3):1164-1176

[66] Andreo P. Depth-dose and stopping-power data for mono-energetic electron beams. Nuclear Instruments & Methods in Physics Research Section B Beam Interactions with Materials and Atoms. 1990;**51**(2): 107-121

[67] Ahnesjö A, Andreo P, Brahme A. Calculation and application of point spread functions for treatment planning with high energy photon beams. Acta Oncologica. 1987;**26**(1):49-56

[68] Mohan R. Differential pencil beam dose computation model for photons. Medical Physics. 1986;**13**(1):64

[69] Mackie TR. A convolution method of calculating dose for 15-MV X rays. Medical Physics. 1985;**12**(2):188

[70] Eklund K, Ahnesjö A. Fast modelling of spectra and stopping-power ratios using differentiated fluence pencil kernels. Physics in Medicine and Biology. 2008;**53**(16): 4231-4247

[71] Eklund K, Ahnesjö A. Modeling silicon diode dose response factors for small photon fields. Physics in Medicine and Biology. 2010;**55**(24): 7411-7423

[72] Fenwick JD, Kumar S, Scott AJ, Nahum AE. Using cavity theory to describe the dependence on detector density of dosimeter response in non-equilibrium small fields. Physics in Medicine and Biology. 2013;**58**: 2901-2923

[73] Czarnecki D, Zink K. Monte Carlo calculated correction factors for diodes and ion chambers in small photon fields. Physics in Medicine and Biology. 2013; **58**:2431-2444

[74] Czarnecki D, Zink K. Corrigendum: Monte Carlo calculated correction factors for diodes and ion chambers in small photon fields. Physics in Medicine and Biology. 2014;**59**:791-794

[75] Francescon P, Cora S, Satariano N. Calculation of for several small detectors and for two linear accelerators using Monte Carlo simulations. Medical Physics. 2011;**38**:6513-6527

[76] Francescon P, Kilby W, Satariano N, Cora S. Monte Carlo simulated correction factors for machine specific reference field dose calibration and output factor measurement using fixed and iris collimators on the CyberKnife system. Physics in Medicine and Biology. 2012;**57**:3741-3758

[77] Sanchez-Doblado F et al. Ionization chamber dosimetry of small photon fields: A Monte Carlo study on stopping-power ratios for radiosurgery and IMRT beams. Physics in Medicine and Biology. 2003;**48**:2081-2099

[78] Sharma SC, Ott JT, Williams JB, Dickow D. Commissioning and acceptance testing of a CyberKnife linear accelerator. Journal of Applied Clinical Medical Physics. 2007;**8**:119-125

[79] British Institute of Radiology. Central Axis Depth Dose Data for Use in Radiotherapy Departments: 1996, BJR Supplement 25. London: BIR; 1996

[80] Sauer OA, Wilbert J. Measurement of output factors for small photon beams. Medical Physics. 2007;**34**: 1983-1988

[81] Alfonso R et al. A new formalism for reference dosimetry of small and nonstandard fields. Medical Physics. 2008;**35**:5179-5186

[82] Thomas SD, MacKenzie M, Rogers DWO, Fallone BG. A Monte Carlo derived TG-51 equivalent calibration for helical tomotherapy. Medical Physics. 2005;**32**:1346-1353

[83] Langen KM et al. QA for helical tomotherapy: Report of the AAPM task group 148. Medical Physics. 2010;**37**: 4817-4853

[84] Zeverino M, Agostinelli S, Pupillo F, Taccini G. Determination of the correction factors for different ionization chambers used for the calibration of the helical tomotherapy static beam. Radiotherapy and Oncology. 2011;**100**:424-428

[85] Sauer OA. Determination of the quality index (Q) for photon beams at arbitrary field sizes. Medical Physics. 2009;**36**:4168-4172

[86] Andreo P. On the beam quality specification of high-energy photons for radiotherapy dosimetry. Medical Physics. 2000;**27**:434-440

[87] Xiong G, Rogers DWO. Relationship between %dd(10)x and stopping-power ratios for flattening filter free accelerators: A Monte Carlo study. Medical Physics. 2008;**35**:2104-2109

[88] Palmans H, National Physical Laboratory. Personal Communication; 2015

[89] Dalaryd M, Knöös T, Ceberg C. Combining tissue-phantom ratios to provide a beam-quality specifier for flattening filter free photon beams. Medical Physics. 2014;**41**:111716

[90] Palmans H. Determination of the beam quality index of high-energy photon beams under nonstandard reference conditions. Medical Physics. 2012;**39**:5513-5519

[91] Podgorsak EB. External photon beams: Physical aspects. In: Radiation Oncology Physics: A Handbook.

[92] Verhaegen F, Das IJ, Palmans H. Monte Carlo dosimetry study of a 6 MV stereotactic radiosurgery unit. Physics in Medicine & Biology. 1998;**43**(10): 2755

[93] Ding GX, Duggan DM, Coffey CW. Comment on "Testing of the analytical anisotropic algorithm for photon dose calculation" [Med. Phys. 33, 4130-4148 (2006)]. Medical Physics. 2007;**34**(8): 3414

[94] Kijewski PK, Bjärngard BE, Petti PL. Monte Carlo calculations of scatter dose for small field sizes in a 60Co beam. Medical Physics. 1986;**13**(1):74-77

[95] Ding GX, Duggan DM, Coffey CW. Commissioning stereotactic radiosurgery beams using both experimental and theoretical methods. Physics in Medicine & Biology. 2006; **51**(10):2549

[96] Ding GX. Dose discrepancies between Monte Carlo calculations and measurements in the buildup region for a high-energy photon beam. Medical Physics. 2002;**29**(11): 2459-2463

[97] Ding GX. Using Monte Carlo simulations to commission photon beam output factors—A feasibility study. Physics in Medicine & Biology. 2003; **48**(23):3865

[98] Ahnesjö A. Collimator scatter in photon therapy beams. Medical Physics. 1995;**22**(3):267-278

[99] Jones AO, Das IJ, Jones FL Jr. A Monte Carlo study of IMRT beamlets in inhomogeneous media. Medical Physics. 2003;**30**(3):296-300

[100] Jones AO, Das IJ. Comparison of inhomogeneity correction algorithms in small photon fields. Medical Physics. 2005;**32**(3):766-776

[101] Saitoh H, Fujisaki T, Sakai R, Kunieda E. Dose distribution of narrow beam irradiation for small lung tumor. International Journal of Radiation Oncology Biology Physics. 2002;**53**(5): 1380-1387

[102] Al-Hallaq HA, Reft CS, Roeske JC. The dosimetric effects of tissue heterogeneities in intensity-modulated radiation therapy (IMRT) of the head and neck. Physics in Medicine & Biology. 2006;**51**(5):1145

[103] Paelinck L, Reynaert N, Thierens H, De Neve W, De Wagter C. Experimental verification of lung dose with radiochromic film: Comparison with Monte Carlo simulations and commercially available treatment planning systems. Physics in Medicine & Biology. 2005;**50**(9):2055

[104] Krieger T, Sauer OA. Monte Carlo- versus pencil-beam-/collapsed-cone-dose calculation in a heterogeneous multi-layer phantom. Physics in Medicine & Biology. 2005;**50**(5):859

[105] Chetty IJ, Charland PM, Tyagi N, McShan DL, Fraass BA, Bielajew AF. Photon beam relative dose validation of the DPM Monte Carlo code in lung-equivalent media. Medical Physics. 2003;**30**(4):563-573

[106] Rogers DWO, Kawrakow I, Seuntjens JP, Walters BRB, Mainegra-Hing E. NRC user codes for EGSnrc. NRCC Report PIRS-702 (Rev. B). 2003

[107] GEANT Collaboration, Agostinelli S. GEANT4—A simulation toolkit. Nuclear Instruments and Methods A. 2003;**506**(25)

[108] MCNP—A General Monte Carlo. N-Particle Transport Code. Vol. I: Overview and Theory. Los Alamos, NM: Los Alamos National Laboratory; 2003. LA-UR-03-1987

[109] Heydarian M, Hoban PW, Beddoe AH. A comparison of dosimetry techniques in stereotactic radiosurgery. Physics in Medicine & Biology. 1996; **41**(1):93

[110] Scielzo G, Grillo FR, Schwarz M, Rivolta A, Brunelli B, Surridge M, et al. The Monte Carlo method and parallel estimation in the drawing up of radiosurgery treatment plans. La Radiologia Medica. 1998;**95**(6): 647-655

[111] De Vlamynck K, Palmans H, Verhaegen F, De Wagter C, De Neve W, Thierens H. Dose measurements compared with Monte Carlo simulations of narrow 6 MV multileaf collimator shaped photon beams. Medical Physics. 1999;**26**(9):1874-1882

[112] Cheung YC, Yu KN, Ho RTK, Yu CP. Stereotactic dose planning system used in Leksell gamma knife model-B: EGS4 Monte Carlo versus GafChromic films MD-55. Applied Radiation and Isotopes. 2000;**53**(3): 427-430

[113] Westermark M, Arndt J, Nilsson B, Brahme A. Comparative dosimetry in narrow high-energy photon beams. Physics in Medicine & Biology. 2000; **45**(3):685

[114] Deng J, Ma CM, Hai J, Nath R. Commissioning 6 MV photon beams of a stereotactic radiosurgery system for Monte Carlo treatment planning. Medical Physics. 2003;**30**(12):3124-3134

[115] Paskalev KA, Seuntjens JP, Patrocinio HJ, Podgorsak EB. Physical aspects of dynamic stereotactic radiosurgery with very small photon beams (1.5 and 3 mm in diameter). Medical Physics. 2003;**30**(2):111-118

[116] Tsougos I, Theodorou K, Bazioglou M, Stathakis S. Kappas C. a comparison of Monte Carlo simulation with experimental dosimetric techniques for a 6 MV stereotactic radiotherapy unit. Journal of BUON. 2004;**9**:451-564

[117] Francescon P, Cora S, Cavedon C. Total scatter factors of small beams: A multidetector and Monte Carlo study. Medical Physics. 2008;**35**(2): 504-513

[118] Heydarian M, Asnaashari K, Allahverdi M, Jaffray DA. Dosimetric evaluation of a dedicated stereotactic linear accelerator using measurement and Monte Carlo simulation. Medical Physics. 2008;**35**(9):3943-3954

[119] Cranmer-Sargison G, Charles PH, Trapp JV, Thwaites DI. A methodological approach to reporting corrected small field relative outputs. Radiotherapy and Oncology. 2013; **109**(3):350-355

[120] Charles PH, Cranmer-Sargison G, Thwaites DI, Crowe SB, Kairn T, Knight RT, et al. A practical and theoretical definition of very small field size for radiotherapy output factor measurements. Medical Physics. 2014; **41**(4):041707

[121] Francescon P, Kilby W, Satariano N, Orlandi C, Elshamndy SK. The impact of inter-unit variations on small field dosimetry correction factors, with application to the CyberKnife system. Physics in Medicine and Biology. 2018

[122] Casar B, Gershkevitsh E, Mendez I, Jurković S, Huq MS. A novel method for the determination of field output factors and output correction factors for small static fields for six diodes and a microdiamond detector in megavoltage photon beams. Medical Physics. 2019; **46**(2):944-963

[123] Freud N, Letang JM, Mary C, Boudou C, Ferrero C, Elleaume H, et al. A hybrid approach for fast simulation of dose deposition in stereotactic synchrotron radiotherapy. IEEE Transactions on Nuclear Science. 2008; **55**(3):1008-1017

[124] Freud N, Letang JM, Mary C, Boudou C, Ferrero C, Elleaume H, et al. Fast dose calculation for stereotactic synchrotron radiotherapy. In: 2007 29th Annual International Conference of the IEEE Engineering in Medicine and Biology Society. IEEE; 2007. pp. 3914-3917

[125] Chetty IJ, Curran B, Cygler JE, DeMarco JJ, Ezzell G, Faddegon BA, et al. Report of the AAPM Task Group No. 105: Issues associated with clinical implementation of Monte Carlo-based photon and electron external beam treatment planning. Medical Physics. 2007;**34**(12):4818-4853

[126] Jang SY, Liu HH, Mohan R. Underestimation of low-dose radiation in treatment planning of intensity-modulated radiotherapy. International Journal of Radiation Oncology Biology Physics. 2008;**71**(5):1537-1546

[127] Petti PL, Chuang CF, Smith V, Larson DA. Peripheral doses in CyberKnife radiosurgery. Medical Physics. 2006;**33**(6 Part 1):1770-1779

[128] Chuang CF, Larson DA, Zytkovicz A, Smith V, Petti PL. Peripheral dose measurement for CyberKnife radiosurgery with upgraded linac shielding. Medical Physics. 2008; **35**(4):1494-1496

[129] Di Betta E, Fariselli L, Bergantin A, Locatelli F, Del Vecchio A, Broggi S, et al. Evaluation of the peripheral dose in stereotactic radiotherapy and radiosurgery treatments. Medical Physics. 2010;**37**(7 Part 1):3587-3594

Chapter 4

Monte Carlo's Core and Tests for Application Developers: Geant4 and XRMC Comparison and Validation

Gabriela Hoff, Bruno Golosio, Elaine E. Streck and Viviana Fanti

Abstract

In this chapter, the Monte Carlo (MC) core is presented, particularly its cross-sectional libraries and random generators. The main idea is to introduce validation and reliability of MC applications and to explore its limitations. As an example, a comparison between two MC toolkits, namely XRMC (version 6.5.0–2) and Geant4 (version 10.02.p02), and a validation between each of them and experimental data applied to mammography (external dosimetry) are presented. The simulated quantities compared are exposure, kerma, half-value layer, and backscattering. Limitations, advantages, and disadvantages of using a general and specific MC toolkit are commented too.

Keywords: Monte Carlo, mammography, medical physics, XRMC, Geant4

1. Introduction

The Monte Carlo (MC) method history began two centuries before its computational implementation that happened in the period of World War II (1939–1945). The MC method conception starts in 1733 with the *Probléme de l'aiguille* (Needle's problem) by Georges-Louis Leclerc, known as the Comte de Buffon [1], which is enunciated as:

> *Sur un plancher qui n est formé que de planches égales & parallèles, on jette une Baguette d'une certaine longueur, & qu'on suppose sans largeur. Quand tombera-t-elle franchement ſur une seule planche? Leclerc [1], p. 44*

or, translated to English:

> *On the floor formed only of equal boards placed in parallel, one throws a needle of a certain length which and supposed without width. When will this needle fall on one specific board?*

The first solution proposed by Leclerc [2], in 1777, is considered one of the oldest geometrical probability solutions. The method basically consists in generating successive random samples N that will be tested in a statistical model representing the statistical probability. To use this method, one needs to satisfy the main condition: the random variable evaluated must be independent, which means that previous events of interest may not have (may have the minimum) an influence on the successive tryings. In the needle case, Leclerc ([2], pp. 100–104), presented a solution considering the distance D of the limits of each wood board and the length l of the needle ($l < D$) taking the probabilities of crossing zero lines and one line as [3].

$$p_0 = 1 - 2r\theta \text{ and } p_1 = 2r\theta, \text{ where } r = \frac{l}{D} \text{ and } \theta = \frac{1}{\pi}.$$

It seems to be a simple problem, but its solution ensued a sequence of different mathematical methodologies [3]. For example, in 1812, Laplace, using his theory of probability and theoretical calculations based on this methodology to determine an approximation to the π value [3, 4], presented a generalized solution in 3D space [3–5].

Following the main condition of independence for random variable enunciated by Leclerc [2], the MC method was proposed as an alternative solution to analytical mathematics to evaluate the behavior of random samples to predict a statistic sample distribution or a statistic behavior. This behavior can be assessed by empirical processes of drawing sequences of independent random samples and observing its behavior [6]. The strategy is simple in concept, but it is time-consuming, being the first computerized MC simulation developed and implemented by the working team of John and Klara von Neumann and Nick Metropolis with the advent of the computers in 1947–1948 [7].

There are different algorithms [8–10] implemented to apply different MC solutions by using different computational tools. Since the objective of this chapter is to present MC validation and/or reliability for application developers (AD), on a specific study case, we will not detail the different MC algorithms.

There are several characteristics that can be used to classify MC computational tools (MCCT); however, based on the objective of this chapter, the available ones will be classified according to its applicability as general and specific MCCTs. So, in section 2, the general concepts and MCCT code core (cross-sectional libraries and pseudorandom generators), including the specific and general MCCTs characteristics and some codes available nowadays, are going to be presented. In section 3, the validation and reliability of MCCT code concepts and main methods, including its limitations on the implementations of cross-sectional libraries and random generators, are going to be discussed. To illustrate this, a case study of validation for dosimetry in mammography using two MCCT methods for radiation transport (Geant4 and XRMC) is going to be presented. In the last section, the final considerations on choosing a MCCT and important issues on validation or reliability tests will be presented.

2. Monte Carlo general concepts and core

The MC method may be used to solve different kinds of problems. It may be used to solve problems that could also be solved by deterministic calculations, but it is usually more time-consuming than those and can increase the complexity of the solution. MC must to be applied, generally, when the change in the model follows a "time dependence" and is suitable for a stochastic calculation, which depends on a sequence of random numbers generated during the simulation. It means that a new execution of the solution with a new (different) sequence of random numbers for the same simulation will not give identical results. However, it will return values that agree with the results obtained from the previous sequence within some "statistical error" or in a statistical fluctuation range [11].

In a general manner, the problems that are in essence managed by random phenomena can be solved by applying MC [11, 12]. The main idea of MC method is to estimate a quantity, based on systems that use random numbers to simulate random walks [11], with an estimator computed from observed/experimental data [12]. Considering this idea, the core system of a MCCT is based on a randomized algorithm (random number generator) to manage probabilities (libraries of sampling distribution) [12]. A MCCT has other tools implemented, but for an AD, the knowledge of the MC core limitations is essential to estimate the accuracy and precision of the results.

Taking into account the proposition of MCCT for transport radiation, one may define core as the computational random number generator (randomized algorithm) and the cross sections for each possible process of interaction (probabilities, in the case of photons that can be the total attenuation cross sections for each possible process, or the differential cross sections—if applicable—or the energy transfer cross sections or the energy absorption cross sections). Let's think about a traditional MC simulation as is represented in the following scheme (**Figure 1**). It is important to keep in mind that this is a simplified scheme of transport radiation designed to aid the understanding of the basics of MC processing. Before one starts to run[1] an event[2] in a MCCT, one may define the simulation universe (or world), including the geometry, material composition of the simulated objects, and, if necessary, the additional information needed for the interaction.

The run starts always with the generation of a primary particle (emitted by the radiation source), and it finishes when all histories were run. As one may observe in **Figure 1**, the system starts the run, after the geometry built and physics definition, by initializing the counter of the number of histories (*VARnh*). This variable is compared to the expected total number of histories (*nh*), so if the *VARnh* is equal to *nh*, then the termination of run is performed, or if *VARnh* is smaller than *nh*, then a new history is started by generating a new primary particle. In the generation of primary particle, if the source is defined by an energy distribution and/or position distribution (linear, planar, or volumetric source) and/or momentum direction distribution, the random number generator will be evoked (one to each distribution needed). After the primary particle of the source is generated, the information about this particle is recorded at the beginning of step (pre-step information). Following the step execution, the end of the step information will be generated (post-step information) and tested. The traditional MCCT tests are:

a. Is this particle inside the world? In MC simulation, the geometrical limits to follow the transport of radiation are the limits described on the geometry by the larger volume (the world) that will contain the other volumes. Some MCCTs have no world volume defined; usually if they are specific MC using variance reduction techniques that force the radiation to interact with the

---

[1] RUN: word used to define the execution of the MC code.

[2] EVENT: every interaction that happened to one primary particle or its secondaries until they die or leave the universe of simulation. It is defined as the collections of steps performed by one particle.

defined volumes, then the logic is different than the presented in the scheme in **Figure 1**.

b. Is this particle alive? In MCCT for transport radiation, there is a minimum energy to proceed the transportation, so if the particle kinetic energy is smaller than this minimum energy, then this particle will die, which means in MCCT all residual energy will be locally deposited and the particle will stop.

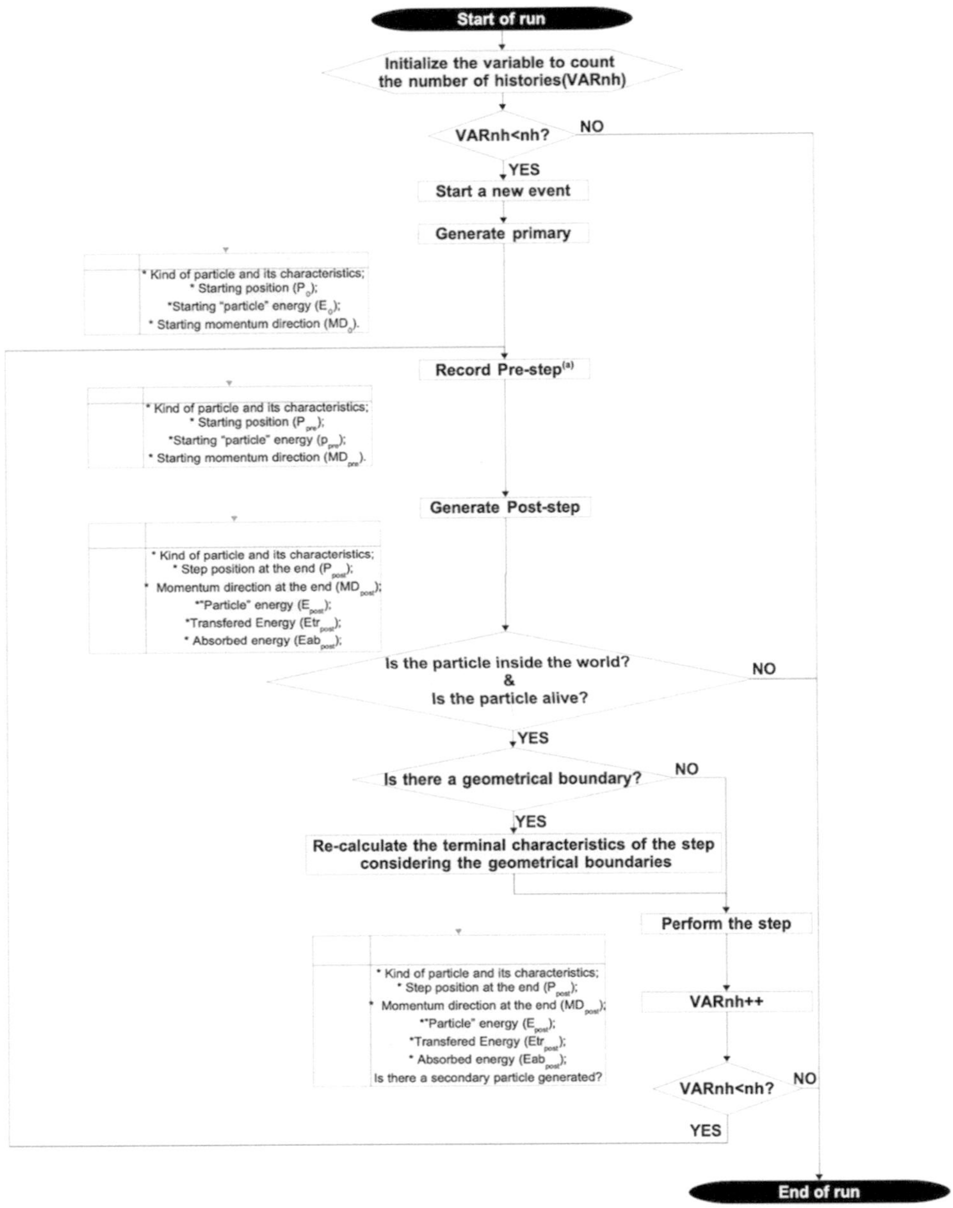

[a] RECORD PRE-STEP: on this stage the information to start a new step will be recorded. If it is a new event then the information of the primary particle will be recorded, if it is a continuation of the particle walk (which means a intermediate step) then the infomration of the end of particle (post-step information) are going to be recorded.

Figure 1.
Simplified scheme of a traditional Monte Carlo simulation.

If the particle is alive and inside the world, then it is important to know if this particle will find a geometrical boundary and/or a different material in its path during the step. If the answer is *no* to both pre-defined questions, then the code will proceed with the step. If the answer is *yes*, the code will calculate the length until this boundary and check if the other volume has or does not have a new material, and the step will proceed until the boundary; after that the residual kinetic energy of the particle will be recalculated for the next volume material. At the end of the step, the post-step information is recorded. Then, the *VARnh* is increased of a unit and is compared to *nh*. If *VARnh* is equal to *nh*, the termination of run is performed. If *VARnh* is smaller than *nh*, a new step procedure is started by recording the post-step information of the previous step as initial information of the new one, proceeding with the verifications and implementations for this new step. It is important to note that all secondary particles generated, as product of an interaction, will be transported following the same procedure starting in *Record Pré-Step* with the exception that *VARnh* will not be incremented and these particles will be followed until they die or leave the world.

To illustrate the selection of random number, let's create a hypothesis of a 40 keV photon interacting with a liquid water medium. In this case, the total attenuation cross section is 0.2683 cm^2/g, being composed by coherent scattering (0.02874 cm^2/g), incoherent scattering (0.1827 cm^2/g), and photoelectric effect (0.05680 cm^2/g).[3] **Figure 2** shows the simplified scheme that defines the process of interaction.

Considering the information in **Figure 2**, one may see that among the three possible processes of interaction a probability of approximately 10.71% for coherent scattering, 68.11% for incoherent scattering, and 21.18% for photoelectric effect. Then, the normalization of the probabilities for each process between 0 and 1 is performed, considering the total attenuation cross section as the normalizing factor,

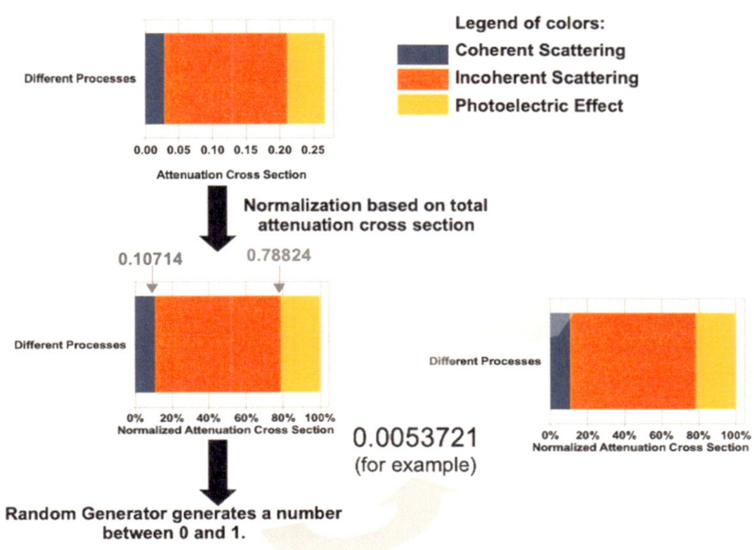

Figure 2.
Scheme of the random generator logic to define a probability of interaction of a 40 keV photon into liquid water medium.

---

[3] All attenuation cross sections used were from XCOM NIST (https://physics. nist.gov/cgi-bin/Xcom/xcom3_2).

and these normalized probabilities are organized in a sequence of real values. The possible number of values between 0 and 1 depends on the variable type defined in the MCCT implementation for the random generator number. On the presented example, the random numbers in the intervals [0; 0.10714) identify coherent scattering [0.10714; 0.78824), incoherent scattering, and [0.78824; 1) photoelectric effect. It is important to note that the probability of occurrence is proportional to the quantity of random numbers in the sequence of values. In the case exemplified in **Figure 2**, the number 0.0053721 is in the range [0; 0.10714) and defines the photon transport by coherent effect. If the random number were 0.78824, the photoelectric effect would be simulated since this value is in the range [0.78824; 1).

During the simulation several processes may need to have a random number generated such as process of interaction (used in the above example), momentum direction of the particle, secondary particle momentum and kinetic energy, atomic effect (if considered in the simulation), probability of Auger effect, and momentum direction of the Auger electron or auto-absorption of the Auger electron, among others. After the random definition of some of the abovementioned characteristics, deterministic equations are applied to keep the Principle of Energy and Momentum Conservation. Regarding the core of MCCT, it is important to know, as an AD, the main validity and limitations of the random number generator and the cross-sectional libraries.

The random number generator may be classified as pseudorandom number generator (PRNG) or true random number generator (TRNG) [13]. The so-called PRNG uses a deterministic process to generate a series of outputs from an initial seed state which means that for the same input "seed" one may have the same output number [13–15]. As an example one may cite the <cstdlib> head of C++ rand() function. In this case, usually the random number generated is an integer, and to know the range of possible numbers, it helps the AD to understand the limitations of the number of histories that can be run without compromising the randomicity of the simulation [13, 14], the so-called period of random number generator [16]. **Table 1** presents the different range of values generated among the possible integer variables according to [14].

Based on the value range presented in **Table 1**, one may see that different possible variable definitions of the random generator can affect the resolution of the simulation, which means that there is a limit of histories with a proper random behavior for a PRNG. The PRNG is used in several applications [15], and one advantage of using it on MCCT is the capability of reproducing the same sequence of pseudorandom numbers [14] that can be used to validate an application and/or to validate and test different installations of a MCCT under different environments (evaluating the accuracy and precision of the simulation in different conditions) [16].

The TRNG uses a non-deterministic source to produce randomness [13], and its advantage is that TRNG is unpredictable, unbiased, and independent [16]. The

Type	Storage size	Values range
Short	2 bytes	−32,768 to 32,767
Int	2 bytes or 4 bytes	−32,768 to 32,767 or −2,147,483,648 to 2,147,483,647
Long	4 bytes	−2,147,483,648 to 2,147,483,647
Unsigned short	2 bytes	0 to 65,535
Unsigned integer	2 bytes or 4 bytes	0 to 65,535 or 0 to 4,294,967,295
Unsigned long	4 bytes	0 to 4,294,967,295

Table 1.
Type of integers, storage size, and range of possible values in C++ programming language.

disadvantage on developing TRNG is that it is implemented in hardware, which limits the flexibility of this random number generator and since additional verification of randomness is required with every change of environment [16]. Because of the hardware implementation of TRNG, computers without a hardware random number generator will require a peripheral that will generate a TRNG seed to be used as incoming data for PRNG [16].

Sometimes, an association of random number generators (PRNG-PRNG and PRNG-TRNG) is implemented to increase the period of a random generator, but the randomness of the number generated must be tested and verified. Special care must to be taken attention on running MCCT in computational grids or clusters to ensure that every processor will have an independent random seed to start the process. If this requirement is not kept, inconsistencies in the results may happen turning them unrealistic and carrying with them statistical tendencies that do not represent the expected probabilities. Therefore, to guarantee the reliability of results of a MCCT, the AD must understand the random number generator and its period and limitations.

Considering the reliability of the MCCT in the example described above, when it is applied to low-energy radiation transport, the probabilities (e.g., cross-sectional libraries—total and differential—for photons), the distribution functions, and the transport models for particles, such as electrons, are indispensable. As a general rule, it is important to know the processes simulated and if there are one or more models to be evoked. To validate these characteristics, the MCCT requires a microscopic validation[4] that in turn requires experimental data of the cross sections or distribution functions for different material and energy range. The microscopic validation is hard work to be performed by an AD; however, one may find the validation of the data libraries in the literature and/or online libraries [17–27] and on independent validations published for specific MC codes [21, 28–30].

2.1 General *versus* specific Monte Carlo toolkit for radiation transport

The MCCT may be classified according to its applicability as general purpose (GP) [31–33] or specific purpose (SP) [33–35]. It is important to understand that this classification refers to the possibility of using MCCT in different applications and not the kind of solution generated by the MCCT. All MCCTs present a general solution to the study case, when applied to the same particle types, degrees of freedom, and simulated quantities, taking into account the limitations of the implemented code and libraries.

Some MCCTs are developed considering the simulation of a wide range of particles and/or quantities. Usually these MCCTs simulate detailedly the radiation transport of primary and secondary particles using minimal approximations as possible. These MCCTs are called general purpose Monte Carlo toolkit (GPMCT), and they may be applied to solve a wide range of radiation transport problems: large energy range, different particle types, different geometries, and a large range of simulated processes. As examples, one may cite Geant4, MCNP, or FLUKA.

The geometry and tracking (Geant4) [36–38] is a MCCT that has a complete range of functionalities including tracking, geometry, physics models, and hits [36]. It was developed based on object-oriented technology and implemented in C++ programming language. The physics processes available cover a comprehensive range, including electromagnetic, hadronic, and optical ones with a large set of

[4] Microscopic validation: refers to the detailed validation of microscopic quantities (usually the libraries) used by the MC code to generate the quantitative results. See more information on Section 3. Verification, validation, comparison, and reliability of Monte Carlo toolkit.

materials, chemical elements, and long-lived particles, over a wide energy range starting from 250 or 990 eV and extending to a few TeV. The extended package Geant4-DNA adds processes for the modeling of induced biological damage by ionizing radiation at DNA scale, which transports all particles using a discrete model [39–42] extending the possibility of transport particles down to a few eV (the range is different to each particle and process). On Geant4, the AD may access a large cross-sectional library database, making possible to choose different radiation processes and, to each process, to select different transport models. On Geant4, the AD may implement different variance reduction methods and set different parameters to transport primary and secondary particles [43] among the more than 35 particles[5] allowed [43]. AD may use Geant4 classes to create collections of interactions, named hits (G4VHit or G4THitsCollection), and/or evoke sensitive detector counters (G4MultiFunctionalDetector or G4VPrimitiveScorer) and/or implement his/her own personal class (a new sensitive detector or hit file) [44].

The Monte Carlo N-particle (MCNP6) [45–49] MCCT includes a powerful general source, a criticality source, and a surface source. In addition to that, this MCCT includes both geometry and output counter (named tally) plotters. MCNP is implemented on GNU Fortran and C/C++ compilers [49] being a continuous-energy, generalized-geometry, time-dependent, MC radiation-transport code designed to track many particle types over broad ranges of energies. This MCCT may simulate neutron, photon, electron, or coupled neutron/photon/electron transport and heavy ions [49]. It simulates different energy ranges for different particles: neutron energy range from 10^{-11} to 20 MeV for most of isotopes and up to 150 MeV for some others, photon energy range from 1 keV up to 100 GeV, and electron energy range from 1 keV to 1 GeV [50]. It has a rich collection of variance reduction techniques with an extensive collection of cross-sectional data. In addition, MCNP contains numerous tallies: surface current and flux, volume flux (track length), point or ring detectors, particle heating, fission heating, pulse height tally for energy or charge deposition, mesh tallies, and radiography tallies [46, 49]. This MCCT makes it possible to change transport parameters by command lines [46, 50].

The Fluktuierende Kaskade (FLUKA) [51–53] MCCT was implemented and presents a number of ADs interface routines in Fortran 77. It simulates accurately the interaction and propagation of radiation in matter of about 60 different particles,[6] including photons and electrons from 100 eV or 1 keV to thousands of TeV, neutrinos, muons of any energy, hadrons of energies up to 20 TeV and all the corresponding antiparticles, neutrons down to thermal energies, and heavy ions. Efficiency on radiation transport has been achieved using a frequent access table look-up sampling, and accuracy is maximized by systematic use of double precision variables. It is provided with a large number of available options for an AD and has been completely restructured introducing dynamical dimensioning. It has the double capability to be used in a biased mode as well as a fully analogue code which means that while it can be used to predict fluctuations, signal coincidences, and other correlated events, a wide choice of statistical techniques is also available to investigate punch through or other rare events in connection with attenuations by many orders of magnitude [52]. FLUKA can generate several output cards: a main (standard) output file, two scratch files, a file with the last random number seeds, an error messages file (if any), and any number (including zero) of estimator

[5] The Geant4 list of particles and its identifications number may be found at https://www.star.bnl.gov/public/comp/simu/newsite/gstar/Manual/particle_id.html).

[6] The FLUKA list of particles and its identifications number may be found at http://www.fluka.org/content/manuals/online/5.1.html.

output files. Generally, the AD may choose between formatted and unformatted output and may generate a personalized routine for additional outputs [53].

However, some MCCTs are developed to solve problems considering specific particles or specific geometrical conditions or specific simulated quantities. These MCCTs are called specific purpose Monte Carlo toolkit (SPMCT) and are usually optimized to use several approximations and variance reduction techniques. They are developed considering restrictions on applications, and very specific quantities are simulated. In general, the SPMCTs are faster than the GPMCTs to solve the same problem. As examples, one may cite XRMC, ITS TIGER series, PENELOPE, EGS, and ETRAN.

The X-Ray Monte Carlo (XRMC) [54] simulates accurately X-ray imaging and spectroscopy experiments of heterogeneous samples. This MCCT is implemented in C++ and is capable of simulating, in detail, complex experiments on generic samples using different variance reduction techniques by default. It was developed initially to simulate X-ray fluorescence and photon imaging. XRMC simulates the transport of photons only and makes it possible to simulate the following quantities: total fluence and fluence with energy binding and total energy fluence and energy fluence with energy binning. As output, it may generate a raw file with the transmission image [55], and if energy binning is evoked, the AD may define the bin size. On transport possibilities, the AD may define maximum scattering order number, maximum scattering order as transmission, first-order scattering or fluorescence emission, and second-order scattering or fluorescence emission or higher order. It also has the flexibility of activating or inactivating fluorescence [54, 55] process. The cross-sectional library evoked by XRMC is the *xraylib* [56], a library for X-ray matter interactions generally used for XRF applications.

The integrated tiger series (ITS) [57–59], version 6, allows solutions of linear time-independent coupled electron/photon radiation transport problems. This MCCT employs accurate cross sections, sampling distributions, and physical models to describe the production and transport of the electron/photon cascade from 1.0 keV to 1.0 GeV [58, 59]. The ITS, version 6, was converted to Fortran 90 [59] with C++ links to CAD software. The availability of the source code allows the AD to tailor this MCCT to specific applications and to extend its capabilities to more complex applications. Overlaps in CAD geometry may be evaluated and reported in an output file [58]. The AD may set different parameters by command line like to define the cross section for different data sets, to deactivate the coherent photon scattering, to include (or not) binding effects in incoherent photon scattering, and/or to apply (or not) energy-loss straggling to electrons [59]. The AD may set different output information such as the energy and charge deposited in every subzone, the detailed energy and charge deposited in every subzone, and the geometry-dependent input settings [58]. ITS' cross-sectional [58] suite of codes includes a multigroup version along with the multigroup cross-sectional generator CEPXS and a continuous-energy (XGEN) cross sections [58, 59]. In ITS, photons below 1 keV are locally absorbed, an alternative algorithm to electron transport was implemented named Generalized Boltzmann Fokker-Planck (GBFP), and the full transport capability for photons and electrons using the Livermore database is under development [58].

The penetration and energy loss of positrons and electron (PENELOPE) [60], version 2014, MCCT simulates the coupled electron-photon transport as well as photons, electrons, and positrons. The PENELOPE simulation algorithm is based on a scattering model combining numerical databases with analytical cross-sectional models for the different interaction mechanisms being applicable to energies from few hundred eV up to approximately 1 GeV. Photon transport is simulated by means of the standard, detailed simulation method. Electron and positron transports are simulated based on a mixed procedure, which combines a detailed simulation with a condensed one [60–63]. The implementation of the cross-sectional libraries considers EPDL[7] total cross sections for photoelectric absorption and Rayleigh scattering, XCOM[8] cross sections for pair production, and SUMGA[9] function for total atomic cross sections and Compton scattering. PENELOPE can simulate the emission of characteristic X-rays and Auger electrons resulting from vacancies produced in K, L, M, and N shells by photoelectric absorption, Compton scattering, triplet production, and electron/positron impact. In PENELOPE 2014, the elastic collisions of electrons and positrons are simulated, using numerical partial-wave cross sections for free neutral atoms by elastic scattering of electrons and positrons by atoms (ELSEPA) program that is a database distributed by ICRU Report 77 (2007) [60]. The output may be defined using Fortran subroutines, where the AD may get different quantities such as number of materials that were loaded, mass density of specific materials, characteristics of the slowing down for charged particles, energy of the particle at the beginning of the track segment, effective stopping power of soft energy-loss interactions, and energy lost along the step, among others [61].

The electron gamma shower (EGS) MCCT may be found on different main versions, EGS5 and EGSnrc. Both versions of EGS are implemented in Mortran3 language, which is a preprocessor for Fortran [64, 65]. The origins of EGS MCCT are documented in NRC-PIRS-0436 report [66]. The EGS5 simulates the coupled transport of electrons and photons in an arbitrary geometry for particles with energies from a few keV up to a several hundred GeV [64] depending on the atomic numbers of the target materials. The EGSnrc[10] (Electron Gamma Shower from National Research Council) is an extended and improved version of the EGS MCCT, having specific modeling implementations to electron and photon transport through matter. It includes the BEAMnrc software component that models beams traveling through consecutive material components, ranging from a simple slab to the full treatment head of a radiotherapy linear particle accelerator (linac). EGSnrc is particularly well-suited for medical physics applications (research and devices development) being used for medical radiation detection, medical image based on x-radiation, and dosimetry for a specific volume. However, due to the flexibility of this MCCT, the AD may use it for different applications such as in industrial linac beams, X-ray emitters, radiation shielding, and more. The EGSnrc simulates the radiation transport in homogeneous materials for photons, electrons, and positrons with energies between 1 keV and 10 GeV. It incorporates significant refinements in charged particle transport and better low energy cross sections and makes it possible to define elaborated geometries and particle sources [65].

The electron transport (ETRAN) MCCT transports electrons and photons through extended media being developed by the National Bureau of Standards. This MCCT has various versions representing mainly refinements, embellishments, and different geometrical treatments that share the same basic simulation algorithm based on random sampling the path of electrons and photons as they travel through matter. The algorithms and computational tools written at other laboratories, such

---

[7] EPDL: Photon and Electron Interaction Data is available at https://www-nds.iaea.org/epdl97.

[8] XCOM: Photon Cross-sectional Database is available at https://www.nist.gov/pml/xcom-photon-cross-sections-database.

[9] Additional information about SUGMA function access SectionB.2 in Appendix B of the PENELOPE-2014: A Code System for Monte Carlo Simulation of Electron and Photon Transport at https://www.oecd-nea.org/science/docs/2015/nsc-doc2015-3.pdf

[10] The EGSnrc has its official page associate to National Research Council Canada at https://nrc.canada.ca/en/research-development/products-services/software-applications/egsnrc-software-tool-model-radiation-transport.

as Sandia's older SANDYL code and their more current series of the TIGER, CYLTRAN, and ACCEPT codes, together have been called ETRAN model too.

When an AD chooses a MCCT, it is important to consider:

a. The characteristics of the application: type of primary and secondary particles and their energy range, quantities to be simulated, geometry and material composition of the simulated universe;

b. The capabilities of the MC code: if the code can handle properly the transport of primary and (if necessary) secondary particles in the energy range of interest, if it is possible to simulate the necessary quantities, and if it can handle the transport simulation in all material compositions expected and how it simulates the geometry of interest;

c. The limitations of the MC code: transport processes and models simulated in the energy range of interest (search for microscopic validation of the cross-sectional libraries published) and how accurate the MCCT is on simulating the dosimetric quantities and the particle fluxes (search for macroscopic validation published), being recommended that the AD proceeds his/her own macroscopic validation;

d. The computational performance: verifying the running time to get an acceptable statistical fluctuation in the results for the cases of interest and, in some cases, checking the RAM memory used to build the virtual universe and the memory used to save the output files;

Considering those minimal guidelines on choosing a MCCT, there is a good chance for the AD to not have unresolvable problems during the development of an application. Now, if you, as an AD, still have questions about the proper MCCT to choose, keep in mind the best one is the MCCT able to solve your "problem" (accuracy of the results) with an adequate statistical fluctuation (precision of the results). In addition to that, an AD at least should be able to install and to use the MCCT interface, being aware of the common limitation of it. All these characteristics may be found, usually, in the manual (user manual and physics process manual).

3. Verification, validation, comparison, and reliability of Monte Carlo toolkits

To guarantee that one application is realistic, it is important to test it (computational code) in different ways. There are several known ways to test a computational code and its parts; however, in this section, the focus is to present the concepts applied on developed applications for MCCTs such as verification, validation, comparison, and reliability.

When one is working in an application for MCCT, it is important to understand the concepts that may guarantee its internal consistency and accuracy. The IEEE 1012–2016 gives a general description of software verification and validation, and the IEEE 24765–2017 gives a detailed description of these concepts defining these terms. *Verification* is defined as a "confirmation by examination and provisions of objective evidence that specified requirements have been fulfilled" (IEEE 1012–2016), and lately this concept was detailed as "the process of evaluating a system or component to determine whether the products of a given development phase satisfy the conditions imposed at the start of that phase" (IEEE 24765–2017). *Validation* is defined as a "confirmation by examination and provisions of objective evidence that the particular requirements for a specific intended use are fulfilled" (IEEE 1012–2016), and lately this concept was detailed as "the process of evaluating a system or component during or at the end of the development process to determine whether it satisfies specified requirements" (IEEE 24765–2017). So, one may say that a validation was performed when this one answers affirmatively the question: "Are we building the right product?" In the other hand, one may affirm that one is doing a verification by answering the question: "Are we building the product right?" [67].

According to [68], "*Validation* involves the system and acceptance testing during the test phase, whereas *verification* involves reviews and audits, software unit testing, and other techniques to evaluate intermediate work products such as the *software requirements specification, software design description*, and individual modules during earlier project phases." In MC, the AD does the *verification* of the application developed to guarantee that this application is reproducing the system (or geometry) and general conditions as close as possible to the reality, and the AD does the *validation* to guarantee that the MC application (considering the geometry material, particles if interaction and energy range of the particles) gives realistic results when compared statistically to experimental data, when a consistent amount of quantitative experimental data is available. In this context, it is fundamental to understand the setup and the experimental limitations of the instruments and measurements used in the experiments to take it into account on the data analyses to explain observed differences and similarities on the results.

When experimental data is not available, it is possible to use other MCCT or deterministic models to compare to the MC application results. In this way, one is performing a *comparison* between models and not a *validation*. This *comparison* must be based on quantitative statistical tests. In this case, to know and understand the main conceptions involved in the models and databases used, including its limitations and previous validations, it is fundamental to explain the observed differences and similarities on the results.

A *reliability* evaluation is recommendable when there are neither experimental data on specific trustable models nor amount of data to perform a *validation* or a *comparison*. The IEEE 982.1–2005 provides information used as indicators of *reliability* defining software *reliability* as "the probability that software does not cause the failure of a system for a specified time under specified conditions." In this context, the software *reliability* represents an effective measurement of the more general concept of software quality, using derived quantities and experimental models that are partially consistent to the application of interest. It is important to know the systematic errors and map all differences on the contour limitations of the application and the theory involved in this comparison.

It is possible to combine *validation* results, *comparison* between models, and software *reliability* to evaluate an application. Additional information about statistical tests and specific recommendations for software *verification*, *validation*, *reliability,* and *comparison* may be found in international documents. Thus, it is important to study the international standard regulations/recommendations when one wants to validate any software, including the MCCTs themselves and applications developed using them. The standard lists of active documents from IEEE, International Electrotechnical Commission (IEC), and International Organization for Standardization (ISO) may be searched online.[11] Additional detailed information about this subject may be studied at:

---

[11] Search for the active standards was performed at https://standards.ieee.org; https://www.en-standard.eu and https://www.iso.org/about-us.html.

- IEEE 730–2014—IEEE Standard for Software Quality Assurance Processes
- IEEE 982.1–2005—IEEE Standard Dictionary of Measures of the Software Aspects of Dependability
- IEEE 1012–2016—IEEE Standard for System, Software, and Hardware Verification and Validation (corrigendum 1012–2016/Cor 1–2017)
- IEEE 1016–2009—IEEE Standard for Information Technology-Systems Design —Software Design Descriptions
- IEEE 12207–2017—ISO/IEC/IEEE International Standard—Systems and software engineering—Software life cycle processes
- IEEE 14764–2006—ISO/IEC/IEEE International Standard for Software Engineering—Software Life Cycle Processes—Maintenance
- IEEE 15026–1—Revision-2019—ISO/IEC/IEEE Approved Draft International Standard—Systems and Software Engineering—Systems and Software Assurance—Part 1: Concepts and Vocabulary
- IEEE 15026–2-2011—IEEE Standard—Adoption of ISO/IEC 15026–2:2011 Systems and Software Engineering—Systems and Software Assurance—Part 2: Assurance Case
- IEEE 15026–3-2013—IEEE Standard Adoption of ISO/IEC 15026–3—Systems and Software Engineering—Systems and Software Assurance—Part 3: System Integrity Levels
- IEEE 15026–4-2013—IEEE Standard Adoption of ISO/IEC 15026–4—Systems and Software Engineering—Systems and Software Assurance—Part 4: Assurance in the Life Cycle
- IEEE 24765–2017—ISO/IEC/IEEE International Standard—Systems and software engineering—Vocabulary
- IEEE 29119–1-2013—ISO/IEC/IEEE International Standard—Software and systems engineering—Software testing—Part 1: Concepts and definitions
- IEEE 29119–2-2013—ISO/IEC/IEEE International Standard—Software and systems engineering—Software testing—Part 2: Test processes
- IEEE 29119–3-2013—ISO/IEC/IEEE International Standard—Software and systems engineering—Software testing—Part 3: Test documentation
- IEEE 29119–4-2015—ISO/IEC/IEEE International Standard—Software and systems engineering—Software testing—Part 4: Test techniques
- IEEE 29119–5-2016—ISO/IEC/IEEE International Standard—Software and systems engineering—Software testing—Part 5: Keyword-Driven Testing
- IEC 61508–0 (2005–2101)—Functional safety of electrical/electronic/ programmable electronic safety-related systems—Part 0: Functional safety

- IEC 61508–1 (2010–2104)—Functional safety of electrical/electronic/ programmable electronic safety-related systems—Part 1: General requirements
- IEC 61508–2 (2010–2104)—Functional safety of electrical/electronic/ programmable electronic safety-related systems—Part 2: Requirements for electrical/electronic/programmable electronic safety-related systems
- IEC 61508–3 (2010–2104)—Functional safety of electrical/electronic/ programmable electronic safety-related systems—Part 3: Software requirements
- IEC 61508–4 (2010–2104)—Functional safety of electrical/electronic/ programmable electronic safety-related systems—Part 4: Definitions and abbreviations
- IEC 61508–5 (2010–2104)—Functional safety of electrical/electronic/ programmable electronic safety-related systems—Part 5: Examples of methods for the determination of safety integrity levels
- IEC 61508–6 (2010–2104)—Functional safety of electrical/electronic/ programmable electronic safety-related systems—Part 6: Guidelines on the application of IEC 61508–2 and IEC 61508–3
- IEC 61508–7 (2010–2104)—Functional safety of electrical/electronic/ programmable electronic safety-related systems—Part 7: Overview of techniques and measures
- IEC 61511–1 (2003–2101)—Functional safety—Safety instrumented systems for the process industry sector—Part 1: Framework, definitions, system, hardware and software requirements
- IEC 61511–2 (2003–2007)—Functional safety—Safety instrumented systems for the process industry sector—Part 2: Guidelines for the application of IEC 61511–1
- IEC 61511–3 (2003–2003)—Functional safety—Safety instrumented systems for the process industry sector—Part 3: Guidance for the determination of the required safety integrity levels
- ISO/IEC 25010:2011—Systems and software engineering—Systems and software Quality Requirements and Evaluation (SQuaRE)—System and software quality models

There are two ISO documents under development at the moment: the ISO/DTR 11462–3 Guidelines for implementation of statistical process control (SPC)—Part 3: Reference data sets for SPC software validation and ISO/NP TR 11462–4 Guidelines for implementation of statistical process control (SPC)—Part 4: Reference data sets for measurement process analysis software validation.

3.1 Example of application for macroscopic validation, comparison, and reliability for XRMC and Geant4

On this section a comparison between XRMC version 6.5.0-2 (henceforth called XRMC) [54, 55] and Geant4 version 10.02.p02 (henceforth called Geant4) [36–38] is presented, as well as the validation of both MCCTs using experimental data collected on three different mammographs. For validation the following measurements were performed: exposure (X), kerma, half-value layer (HVL), inverse square law (ISL), and backscattering (BS). Limitations, advantages, and disadvantages of using a general and specific MCCT will be commented too. Absolute and normalized quantities were selected because it is important to know the correction factor for total number of photons generated per mAs per total irradiated area for each equipment (this number is characteristic of each X-ray tube and will change with the time), and the combination of these quantities helps to define the best approximation for this correction factor in the simulation to get results closer to the clinical reality.

It is important to inform that each setup had the data collected with calibrated equipment (electrometers and ionizing chambers) available at their institutions and performed by the same person that developed the application with both MCCTs. The simulated geometries are the same used on the data collection. In the following, a brief description of the measurement equipment and simulated setup is presented:

- Mammomat Inspiration [69, 70] (henceforth called Inspiration)—measurements were performed with electrometer and ionizing chamber TNT 12000 kit (Fluke) and Al 99% purity filters. SIMULATION: dry air-sensitive volume of 15 cm^3; focal spot as point-source irradiating homogeneously on circular surface of 2.08 cm of radius; spectra for acceleration voltages 25, 30, and 35 kVp; track-additional filtration combination Mo-Mo (30 μm) and Mo-Rh (25 μm); spectra of ripple 0%; target tilt angle of 20°; and a window of 0.8 mm of beryllium (Be). The HVL calculations are based on a source-to-detector distance of 41.0 cm for different Al thickness filtration; and X data were collected and simulated to source-to-detector distances 26, 40, 50, and 60 cm.

- Mammomat 3000 [71] (henceforth called M3000)—measurements were performed with electrometer Victoreen model 660–1 (1315REV) and ionizing chamber Victoreen model 660-4A (512REV). SIMULATION: dry air-sensitive volume of 4 cm^3; focal spot as point-source irradiating homogeneously on a circular surface of 10.0 cm^2; spectra of ripple 0%; target tilt angle of 22°; a Be window 0.8 mm thick; track-additional filtration combinations of Mo-Mo (30 μm), Mo-Rh (25 μm), and W-Rh (50 μm); and spectrum acceleration voltages of 24 up to 32 kVp, in steps of 2 kVp. The BS was calculated considering simulators of BR12 epoxy and polymethilmetacrilate, considering a source-to-detector distance of 60.0 cm and simulator thicknesses of 4, 5, 6, and 8 cm.

- Lorad MIII [72] (henceforth called Lorad)—measurements were performed with electrometer Modified Keitlhy (model 602) and ionizing chamber for mammography MPT SN 442. SIMUALTION: dry air-sensitive volume of 6.0 cm^3; focal spot as point-source irradiating homogeneously on a rectangular surface of (18.0×24.0) cm^2; spectra for acceleration voltages from 26 to 34 kVp, in steps of 2 kVp; track-additional filtration combination of Mo-Mo (30 μm) and Mo-Rh (25 μm); spectra of ripple 0%; target tilt angulation of 16°; and a Be window 0.8 mm thick. The X measurements were performed with compression paddle and by minimizing the BS effects by increasing the distance between the bucky and the ionizing chamber.

It is important to evaluate all the available possibilities on the MCCT to get a realistic perspective of the configurations. Because of that, two modes to describe the transport model were evaluated on XRMC (transmission (T) and with scattering for dosimetry (D)). In Geant4, the different radiation transport physics models recommended for low energy photons and electrons (standard-option3 (*std*), penelope (*pen*), and Livermore (*liv*)) were also evaluated. Since measurements of the experimental spectra were not possible, different descriptions of the incident spectra modeled by two different references [73, 74] were explored. When nonexperimental spectra are used to simulate dosimetric quantities, it is necessary to take into account the validation of normalized quantities and, if possible, to use semiempirical correction factors to get accurate values for the average number of photons per mAs per total irradiated area. There are different ways on doing it, but the usual are:

i. to use the ratio of the simulated and experimental KERMA to get a correction factor, generally using primary beam with different kVp and mAs, in the range of energy of interest, collecting the KERMA with the minimization of scattering effects or

ii. to use a normalized quantity, for example, normalized HVL, to evaluate the proximity of the behavior of the simulated and experimental curves and then use a good of fit (GoF) test on the non-normalized HVL to estimate the best correction factor to fit the amplitude of the simulated to the experimental data.

In both cases, the error estimation of the experimental data as well as the quantification of the statistical fluctuations of the MC method must be taken into account.

The XRMC does not return the absorbed energy or dose as an output information, so to make the comparison of quantities calculated in same conditions possible, the calculations are based on the incoming spectra on the surface of the sensitive volume. The Geant4 application was planned to collect the spectra on the surface of the sensitive volume, and the same calculations applied to XRMC results were used. On the other hand, for Geant4 validation, the absorbed energy in the sensitive volume was used. The statistical fluctuations were based in a sequence of 10 runs with different seeds for each evaluated case, for both MCCTs, and the average and standard deviation of the data were calculated and used on data analyses.

It is important to compare quantitatively experimental to simulated data for validation. Several statistical tests usually may be applied generally: Chi-square (χ^2), Anderson-Darling, Kolmogorov-Smirnov, and Walt-Wolfowitz, among others. However, when one has data with error or statistical fluctuation associated, the χ^2 must be applied since it considers this in the nonparametric evaluation between the statistical populations of interest. Another simple way to start an evaluation of the results is to generate comparative plots. **Figure 3** presents the graphical comparison of MCCT validations, and **Tables 2** and **3** present the χ^2 p value for the validation and the comparison for all simulated conditions and normalized data.

The graphics in **Figure 3** present a visual interesting result for the evaluation of the relative difference between experimental and simulated data taking experimental data as reference. It shows that different systems may be better represented by different modeled spectra. The Inspiration setup (**Figure 3a**) shows similar results for both modeled spectra since all relative differences for median, first and third quartiles, are between −10 and −2%. A small number of outlier data are observed in this case. The M3000 (**Figure 3b**) evaluation clearly presents better accuracy and precision using spectra from Barnes et al. [74], since it presents all median data closer to 0% and the lowest data dispersion among the three

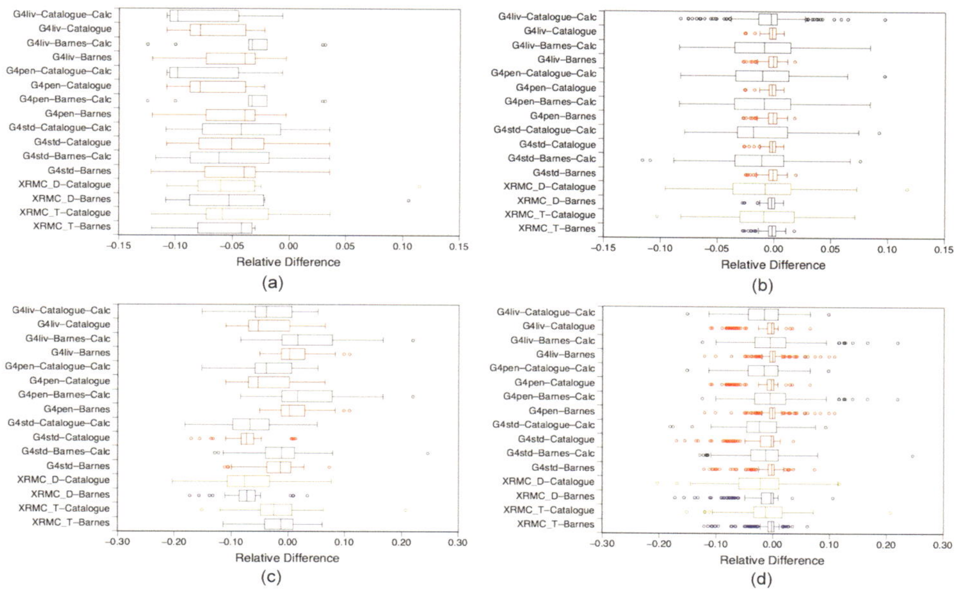

Figure 3.
Relative difference between simulated and experimental data considering normalized data, with outliers, for different modeled spectra and all studied mammographs: Inspiration (a), M3000 (b), Lorad (c), and all equipment (d).

mammographs represented by smallest first and third quartiles (in the range of −3 and 2%). For Lorad (**Figure 3c**) a better accuracy of the results is visible when spectrum from Barnes et al. [74] is used specially with Geant4, because all data for these spectra presented median closer to 0% and the data for catalogued spectra [73] presented medians between −6 and −3%. However, for this mammograph, there is no difference on precision when both modeled spectra are used, being observed that the data between first and third quartiles for Barnes et al. [74] are in the range of −4 and 8% and for catalogued spectra [73] between −10 and 1%. These differences between spectra are more evident in Geant4 simulations. All mammographs presented outliers for the evaluation of the relative differences. In an evaluation of all mammographs studied, one may observe (**Figure 3d**) that the spectrum from [74] was generally more accurate and precise than the spectra from [73]. In the case of Geant4, the simulated absorbed energy seems to present smaller dispersion than the calculated data based on spectra at the detector entrance surface (observe the first and third quartiles in **Figure 3d**). Even observing this general tendency on data dispersion, it is not possible to conclude that one calculation methodology for the dosimetric quantities is better than the other, since this tendency was only observed for one of the three studied mammographs (**Figure 3b**).

It is important to note that these are qualitative observations valid for the database (equipment and setups) of this study or similar conditions of energy range and irradiation geometry. To have a quantitative evaluation, one needs to evaluate the statistical significance of the results. **Table 2** presents the χ^2 p value summary to all evaluated cases considering a significance level of 0.05.

The null hypothesis[12] is rejected if p value is smaller than the significance level (values highlighted in gray in **Table 2**). When the null hypothesis is rejected, in this

[12] χ^2 test null hypothesis: relationship between experimental and simulated data does not exist, which means these samples are presenting the same distribution.

Transport models and spectrum identification	Inspiration (HVL)	M3000 (BS)	Lorad (HVL)	All	M3000 (Mo30Mo)	M3000 (Mo25Rh)	M3000 (W-25Rh)	Lorad (Mo30Mo)	Lorad (Mo25Rh)
XRMC_T–Barnes	0.3025	NA	1.0000	0.9988	NA	NA	NA	1.0000	0.7265
XRMC_T–Catalogue	0.0687	NA	0.5859	0.3125	NA	NA	NA	0.9258	0.1466
XRMC_D–Barnes	NA	1.0000	NA	1.0000	1.0000	1.0000	1.0000	NA	NA
XRMC_D–Catalogue	NA	1.0000	NA	1.0000	1.0000	1.0000	1.0000	NA	NA
G4*std*–Barnes	0.2463	1.0000	0.0817	1.0000	1.0000	1.0000	1.0000	0.9998	<0.001
G4*std*–Barnes–Calc	0.1966	1.0000	0.0785	1.0000	1.0000	1.0000	1.0000	0.1049	0.2069
G4*std*–Catalogue	0.1481	1.0000	<0.001	0.3636	1.0000	1.0000	1.0000	<0.001	<0.001
G4*std*–Catalogue–Calc	0.0710	1.0000	<0.001	0.9993	1.0000	1.0000	1.0000	0.1811	<0.001
G4*pen*–Barnes	0.2397	1.0000	0.1113	1.0000	1.0000	1.0000	1.0000	0.9999	<0.001
G4*pen*–Barnes–Calc	0.1564	1.0000	0.7587	1.0000	1.0000	1.0000	1.0000	0.9997	0.0597
G4*pen*–Catalogue	0.3511	1.0000	<0.001	0.3811	1.0000	1.0000	1.0000	<0.001	<0.001
G4*pen*–Catalogue–Calc	0.2383	1.0000	0.0102	1.0000	1.0000	1.0000	1.0000	0.3842	0.0018
G4*liv*–Barnes	0.2494	1.0000	0.9703	1.0000	1.0000	1.0000	1.0000	1.0000	0.2405
G4*liv*–Barnes–Calc	0.3756	1.0000	0.0600	1.0000	1.0000	1.0000	1.0000	0.0328	0.3994
G4*liv*–Catalogue	0.1910	1.0000	0.0290	1.0000	1.0000	1.0000	1.0000	<0.001	0.9905
G4*liv*–Catalogue-Calc	0.0331	1.0000	0.6826	1.0000	1.0000	1.0000	1.0000	0.1454	0.9993

Table 2.
χ^2 p values for the validation for both MCCTs considering normalized quantities for all studied cases.

test, one may assume that the compared samples are not from the same population (or are not equal). In **Table 2**, one may see that, in a general evaluation of HVL, the data collected in Inspiration rejects the null hypothesis for Geant4, evoking *liv* physics list and spectra from Catalogue [73] for data calculated based on the spectrum that reaches the detector surface. The M3000 is not presenting any null hypothesis rejection. Lorad presents three cases of null hypothesis rejection for HVL values all calculated with Geant4 and the spectra from Catalogue [73]: *std* physics list considering both calculation methods used (based on spectra and simulated absorbed energy) and *pen* physics list for simulated absorbed energy. The data for Inspiration and Lorad were collected for different target track-additional filtration combination, so it makes it possible to evaluate the results considering this specific setup characteristic. For Lorad it was possible to observe the null hypothesis rejection for different setups simulated taking into account both target track-additional filtration combination. Comparing the MCCTs, the XRMC presented better agreement to the experimental dataset. In Geant4, the *liv* physics list presented the lowest, and the *std* physics list presented the largest number of null hypotheses rejection among the three evaluated Geant4 physics lists. The contingency table with χ^2 statistical test was used to evaluate the independence among the possible transport models evoked by each MCCT and the best modeled spectra. A χ^2 p value of 0.49136 for the comparison among the different transport models (XRMC, Geant4-*std*, Geant4-*pen*, Geant4-*liv*) and a χ^2 p value of 0.10068 for both modeled spectra were calculated. Both comparisons presented p values above the significance level, showing that not the transport models nor both modeled spectra simulated are not statistically different when normalized data is used (which means comparing the data independently of the total number of photons emitted per mAs for the irradiation area).

Table 3 presents the χ^2 p value summary comparing the results of XRMC to Geant4 for all evaluated cases considering a significance level of 0.05. Most of the cases evaluated (**Table 3**) present χ^2 p values larger than the significance level not rejecting the null hypothesis. It shows that the simulated data for both MCCTs are not statistically different. The exception was Lorad HVL for Geant4 *liv* Catalogue for absorbed energy calculation due to the track target-additional filtration combination Mo25Rh. This difference did not affect the evaluation considering all cases for each transport model. In a complete evaluation of the simulated data produced by XRMC, the results are statistically compatible (in agreement) to the ones simulated by Geant4 when normalized data are taken into account.

The evaluation same as before was performed with the absolute measurements, first applying the theoretical correction factor, and then the semiempirical correction factor was applied to estimate the number of photons emitted per mAs per total irradiated area. **Figure 4** presents the qualitative evaluation for all studied cases and absolute values considering the theoretical correction factor.

As expected, the relative differences increase when absolute values are compared. This was expected since under this condition the results are dependent of the number of photons emitted per mAs per total irradiated area, considering each setup configuration (peak tension, track target-add filtration combination, and stability of the electrical network associate to the wave rectification of the tube generator). All mammographs presented outlier data, and, in a general observation, one may see that Inspiration setup (**Figure 4a**) presented again a systematic behavior with median values between 0 and 30% and first and third quartiles between −10 and 80%. In this case, the simulated data overestimated the experimental data. Compared to the results presented in **Figure 3a**, it suggests that the simulated normalization factor is larger than the experimental one, causing this systematic behavior for normalized HVL to present simulated values that are always

Transport models and spectrum identification	Inspiration (HVL)	M3000 (BS)	Lorad (HVL)	All	M3000 (Mo30Mo)	M3000 (Mo25Rh)	M3000 (W-25Rh)	Lorad (Mo30Mo)	Lorad (Mo25Rh)
G4*std*–Barnes	0.9777	1.0000	1.0000	1.0000	1.0000	1.0000	1.0000	1.0000	0.9999
G4*std*–Barnes–Calc	0.9149	1.0000	0.9671	1.0000	1.0000	1.0000	1.0000	0.6334	0.9972
G4*std*–Catalogue	0.2139	1.0000	1.0000	1.0000	1.0000	1.0000	1.0000	0.9808	1.0000
G4*std*–Catalogue–Calc	0.1595	1.0000	0.9975	1.0000	1.0000	1.0000	1.0000	0.9200	0.9974
G4*pen*–Barnes	0.8606	1.0000	1.0000	1.0000	1.0000	1.0000	1.0000	1.0000	0.9999
G4*pen*–Barnes–Calc	0.7994	1.0000	1.0000	1.0000	1.0000	1.0000	1.0000	1.0000	0.9637
G4*pen*–Catalogue	0.1660	1.0000	1.0000	1.0000	1.0000	1.0000	1.0000	1.0000	1.0000
G4*pen*–Catalogue–Calc	0.1572	1.0000	1.0000	1.0000	1.0000	1.0000	1.0000	1.0000	0.9997
G4*liv*–Barnes	0.9767	1.0000	1.0000	0.9998	1.0000	1.0000	1.0000	1.0000	1.0000
G4*liv*–Barnes–Calc	0.6809	1.0000	1.0000	0.9998	1.0000	1.0000	1.0000	0.4828	1.0000
G4*liv*–Catalogue	0.7014	1.0000	<0.001	0.9965	1.0000	1.0000	1.0000	1.0000	<0.001
G4*liv*–Catalogue–Calc	0.6993	1.0000	0.1663	1.0000	1.0000	1.0000	1.0000	1.0000	1.000

Table 3.
χ^2 p values for the comparison between XRMC and Geant4 (references) considering normalized quantities for all studied cases.

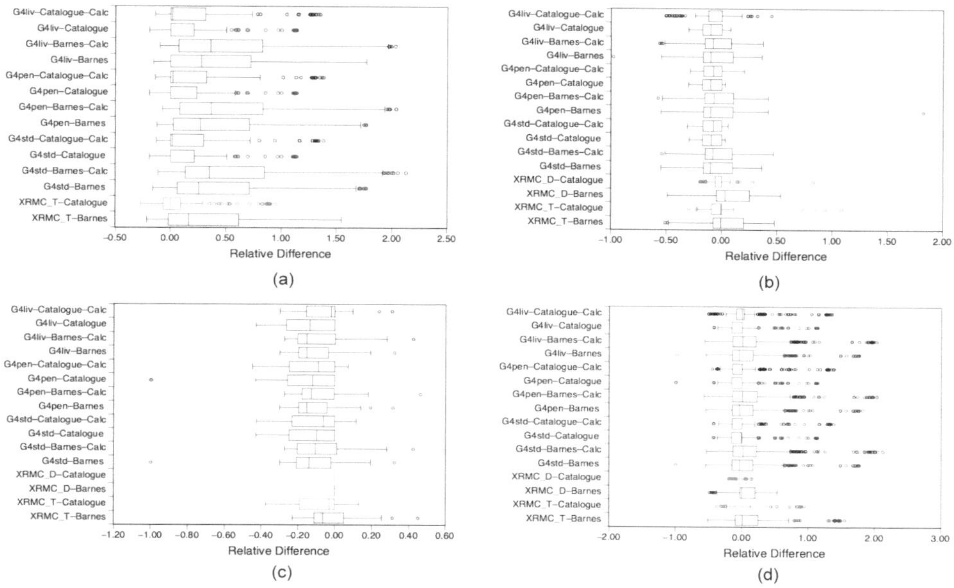

Figure 4.
Relative difference between simulated and experimental data considering absolute data, with theoretical correction and showing outliers, for the different modeled spectra and all studied mammographs: Inspiration (a), M3000 (b), Lorad (c), and all equipment (d).

smaller than experimental ones. M3000 (**Figure 4b**) presents few cases with outliers (Geant4 *pen* transport model and Barnes et al. spectra [74] and XRMC on T mode with Catalogue [73]). As was observed on normalized data (**Figure 3b**), it presents the best results with median closer to 0% and the first and third quartiles −10 and 35% for all mammographs and different setups evaluated. Lorad (**Figure 4c**) presents absolute values generally smaller than the experimental data with the median between −14 and 0% and first and third quartiles between −21 and 5% for all evaluated cases. In a general observation of absolute values (**Figure 4d**), both spectra presented median differences closer to 0%, probably a compensation for the positive systematic tendency presented by Inspiration and the negative systematic tendency presented by Lorad. It shows the importance of evaluating the whole and parts of the database, grouped by characteristics that may influence the simulation, to have better understanding of the curve behaviors and systematic tendencies of the simulated results.

To better evaluate the significance of the findings in **Figure 4**, it is important to apply a statistical evaluation. **Tables 4** and **5** are presenting χ^2 p values for the validation and the comparison of both MCCTs considering absolute quantities and all mammographs evaluated, applying the theoretical corrections.

Table 4 is presenting the validation for the mammographs that had at least one p value larger than 0.001. For this reason, the Inspiration (HVL), Inspiration (HVL W50Rh), Inspiration (ISL), Inspiration, (ISL Mo30Mo), Inspiration (ISL Mo25Rh), Inspiration (ISL W50Rh), M3000, M3000 (Mo30Mo), Lorad (Mo-XMo), Lorad (Mo-XRh), and Lorad are not presented.

Table 5 is presenting the χ^2 p values for the comparison of both MCCTs considering absolute quantities and all options evaluated, applying theoretical correction factor. It only presented the mammographs that had p values larger than 0.001. For this reason, Inspiration (HVL), Inspiration (HVL Mo25Rh), Inspiration (HVL W50Rh, Inspiration (ISL), Inspiration (ISL W50Rh), Inspiration, M3000 (Mo25Rh), M3000 (W50Rh), M3000, and Lorad are not presented.

Transport models and spectrum identification	Inspiration (HVL Mo30Mo)	Inspiration (HVL Mo25Rh)	M3000 (Mo25Rh)	M3000 (W-50Rh)
XRMC_T–Barnes	<0.001	0.1035	<0.001	<0.001
XRMC_T–Catalogue	<0.001	<0.001	<0.001	0,0453
XRMC_S–Barnes	NA	NA	<0.001	<0.001
XRMC_S–Catalogue	NA	NA	0.0028	0.8740
G4*std*–Barnes	0.1174	<0.001	<0.001	<0.001
G4*std*–Barnes–Calc	0.1250	<0.001	<0.001	<0.001
G4*std*–Catalogue	<0.001	0.9867	<0.001	<0.001
G4*std*–Catalogue–Calc	<0.001	<0.001	<0.001	<0.001
G4*pen*–Barnes	0.5026	<0.001	<0.001	<0.001
G4*pen*–Barnes–Calc	0.7886	<0.001	<0.001	<0.001
G4*pen*–Catalogue	<0.001	0.9854	<0.001	<0.001
G4*pen*–Catalogue–Calc	<0.001	<0.001	<0.001	<0.001
G4*liv*–Barnes	0.1907	<0.001	<0.001	<0.001
G4*liv*–Barnes–Calc	0.0224	<0.001	<0.001	<0.001
G4liv–Catalogue	<0.001	0.9869	<0.001	<0.001
G4liv–Catalogue–Calc	<0.001	<0.001	<0.001	<0.001

Table 4.
χ^2 p values for the validation for both MCCTs considering absolute quantities for all studied cases, applying the theoretical correction factors to define the number of photons emitted per mAs per total irradiated area.

Transport models and spectrum identification	Inspiration (HVL Mo30Mo)	Inspiration (ISL Mo30Mo)	Inspiration (ISL Mo25Rh)	M3000 (Mo30Mo)	Lorad (Mo-XMo)	Lorad (Mo-XRh)
G4*std*–Barnes	0.9841	0.84732	0.9999	1.000	0.8953	0.05693
G4*std*–Barnes–Calc	0.0894	0.06821	0.3586	0.5481	0.0249	0.0586
G4*std*–Catalogue	0.0676	0.0269	0.9685	0.0957	0.6954	0.0568
G4*std*–Catalogue–Calc	0.05832	0.0384	0.8437	0.7865	0.7864	0.6785
G4*pen*–Barnes	0.8284	0.0145	0.0725	0.8679	0.0978	0.6604
G4*pen*–Barnes–Calc	0.6983	0.9421	0.8796	0.5647	0.0413	0.0211
G4*pen*–Catalogue	0.6753	0.0261	0.2246	0.3540	0.7953	0.7894
G4*pen*–Catalogue–Calc	0.9485	0.8475	0.1000	0.0039	0.8796	0.6854
G4*liv*–Barnes	1.0000	0.6735	0.0516	0.7865	0.9999	1.0000
G4*liv*–Barnes–Calc	0.0768	0.1276	0.6875	0.5694	0.9574	1.0000
G4*liv*–Catalogue	0.0107	0.0554	0.1534	0.7865	0.7865	0.3451
G4*liv*–Catalogue–Calc	0.0544	0.0895	0.5674	0.6352	0.4731	0.8966

Table 5.
χ^2 p values for the comparison between XRMC and Geant4 (references) considering absolute quantities for all studied cases, applying the theoretical correction factors to define the number of photons emitted per mAs per total irradiated area.

The χ^2 test evaluation presented in **Table 5** for absolute values shows a similar result to the ones presented in **Table 3** but with a larger number of cases rejecting the null hypothesis and presenting lower p values for each of the studied cases which was expected due to the dependency of the number of photons per mAs for the total area estimated. Only Inspiration ISL Mo25Rh did not present null hypothesis rejection among all evaluated cases. The increase on null hypothesis rejection, comparing XRMC to Geant4, is related to the small statistical fluctuation presented by the MCCTs (between 0.2 and 1.5%) when compared to experimental data.

Based on the p values presented in **Table 4**, one could conclude that both MCCTs are not valid for this kind of simulation. However, the p values presented for normalized data (**Tables 2** and **3**) show that the tendencies of the normalized quantities for the simulated data using both MCCTs can be considered statistically non-different to the experimental data. Besides that, the absolute data comparison between both MCCTs (**Table 4**) presented no null hypothesis rejection. In this case, it is important to verify if the total number of photons defined by the theoretical correction factor applied to the spectra produced a systematic tendency on the expected curves. It is important as well to note that the evaluation is consistent when the normalized data shows no significant difference in the validation process. The curves used in this study to estimate the semiempirical correction factor were:

- HVL—the curve of KERMA as function of the additional Al filtration thickness for the same acceleration voltage
- ISL—the tendency of the KERMA as function of the distance between focal spot and detector surface for the same acceleration voltage
- BS—the tendency of the KERMA as function of the thickness of the scatterer considering the scatterer (or considering the backscattered radiation) and the tendency of the KERMA as function of the thickness of the scatterer without considering the scatterer (or not considering the backscattered radiation)

All cases used to generate the semiempirical correction factor considered the best GoF test results for the amplitude when applied to the simulated data for one acceleration voltage and track target-additional filtration combination for a specific mammograph. The best value for the amplitude in each case was used as semiempirical correction factor to be applied as a multiplication factor on the theoretical correction factor for the total number of photons per mAs per total irradiated area.

Tables 6 and 7 are presenting the χ^2 p values for the validation of both MCCTs considering absolute quantities and all cases evaluated, applying the semiempirical correction factors to define the number of photons emitted per mAs per total irradiated area.

The application of semiempirical correction factors shows a better approximation for absolute values. When one compares the results corrected by the theoretical factors (**Table 4**) to the results corrected by theoretical factors associated to semiempirical factors (**Table 6**), the increase of cases that did not reject the null hypothesis is visible. With the exception of Geant4 *std* (Barnes et al. [74]), all the other cases that rejected the null hypothesis are all from Catalogue [73] which shows that for absolute values and the semiempirical methodology used to generate the correction factor; spectrum of Barnes et al. [74] was the one that presented better agreement to experimental data. In the overall evaluation for each studied case comparing each MCCT and transport model, three cases simulated using Catalogue [73] spectra presented χ^2 p values below the significance level: Genat4 *std* and *liv* for Calculated absorbed energy and Geant4 *pen*. All the other χ^2 p values are above the

Transport models and spectrum identification	Inspiration (HVL)	Inspiration (ISL)	M3000 (BS)	Lorad (HVL)	All	M3000 (Mo30Mo)	M3000 (Mo25Rh)	M3000 (W-25Rh)	Lorad (Mo30Mo)	Lorad (Mo25Rh)
XRMC_T–Barnes	0.2502	0.0754	NA	1.0000	0.9889	NA	NA	NA	1.0000	0.7265
XRMC_T–Catalogue	0.0603	0.0564	NA	0.5859	0.2123	NA	NA	NA	0.82734	0.1466
XRMC_S–Barnes	NA	NA	1.0000	NA	1.0000	1.0000	0.8009	1.0000	NA	NA
XRMC_S–Catalogue	NA	NA	1.0000	NA	1.0000	0.9990	0.9990	1.0000	NA	NA
G4*std*–Barnes	0.2635	0.2384	0.9987	0.0817	0.7669	0.9871	0.9987	1.0000	0.8996	<0.001
G4*std*–Barnes–Calc	0.1006	0.0845	1.0000	0.0785	0.8876	0.8997	0.9946	1.0000	0.1073	0.2069
G4*std*–Catalogue	0.1182	<0.001	1.0000	<0.001	0.3636	0.9999	0.8954	1.0000	<0.001	<0.001
G4*std*–Catalogue–Calc	0.0653	<0.001	1.0000	<0.001	0.0457	1.0000	0.9997	1.0000	0.0819	0.0211
G4*pen*–Barnes	0.1398	0.1294	0.9998	0.1101	1.0000	1.0000	1.0000	1.0000	0.9989	0.0521
G4*pen*–Barnes–Calc	0.1263	0.5643	1.0000	0.7587	1.0000	1.0000	0.9982	1.0000	0.9897	0.0597
G4*pen*–Catalogue	0.2151	<0.001	0.9988	<0.001	0.0381	0.9675	0.9999	1.0000	0.0467	<0.001
G4*pen*–Catalogue–Calc	0.2299	<0.001	0.8999	0.0302	0.0569	0.9999	1.0000	1.0000	0.3747	0.0138
G4*liv*–Barnes	0.1946	0.1112	0.9979	0.9703	1.0000	1.0000	1.0000	1.0000	1.0000	0.1435
G4*liv*–Barnes–Calc	0.2384	0.1349	0.9977	0.0690	1.0000	1.0000	0.9734	1.0000	0.0528	0.2694
G4*liv*–Catalogue	0.7910	<0.001	0.0357	0.0490	0.0428	0.9863	1.0000	1.0000	0.0521	0.7092
G4*liv*–Catalogue–Calc	0.0301	<0.001	0.8073	0.5762	0.0665	1.0000	0.9763	1.0000	0.1454	0.8968

Table 6.
χ^2 p values for the validation for both MCCTs considering absolute quantities for all studied cases, applying the semiempirical correction factors to define the number of photons emitted per mAs per total irradiated area.

Transport models and spectrum identification	Inspiration (HVL)	Inspiration (ISL)	M3000 (BS)	Lorad (HVL)	All	M3000 (Mo30Mo)	M3000 (Mo25Rh)	M3000 (W-25Rh)	Lorad (Mo30Mo)	Lorad (Mo25Rh)
G4*std*–Barnes	0.9777	0.2463	1.0000	1.0000	1.0000	1.0000	1.0000	1.0000	1.0000	0.9999
G4*std*–Barnes–Calc	0.9149	0.1966	1.0000	0.9671	1.0000	1.0000	1.0000	1.0000	0.6334	0.9972
G4*std*–Catalogue	0.2139	0.1481	1.0000	1.0000	1.0000	1.0000	1.0000	1.0000	0.9808	1.0000
G4*std*–Catalogue–Calc	0.1595	0.0710	1.0000	0.9975	1.0000	1.0000	1.0000	1.0000	0.9200	0.9974
G4*pen*–Barnes	0.8606	0.2494	1.0000	1.0000	1.0000	1.0000	1.0000	1.0000	1.0000	0.9999
G4*pen*–Barnes–Calc	0.7994	0.3756	1.0000	1.0000	1.0000	1.0000	1.0000	1.0000	1.0000	0.9637
G4*pen*–Catalogue	0.1660	0.1910	1.0000	1.0000	1.0000	1.0000	1.0000	1.0000	1.0000	1.0000
G4*pen*–Catalogue–Calc	0.1572	0.0331	1.0000	0.0002	0.4832	1.0000	1.0000	1.0000	1.0000	0.0401
G4*liv*–Barnes	0.9767	0.1595	1.0000	1.0000	1.0000	1.0000	1.0000	1.0000	1.0000	0.9997
G4*liv*–Barnes–Calc	0.6809	0.8606	1.0000	0.8765	1.0000	1.0000	1.0000	1.0000	0.4828	1.0000
G4*liv*–Catalogue	0.7014	0.7994	1.0000	0.9212	0.9994	1.0000	1.0000	1.0000	1.0000	1.0000
G4*liv*–Catalogue–Calc	0.6993	0.1660	1.0000	0.1663	1.0000	1.0000	1.0000	1.0000	1.0000	1.0000

Table 7.
χ^2 p values for the comparison between XRMC and Geant4 (references) considering absolute quantities for all studied cases, applying the semiempirical correction factors to define the number of photons emitted per mAs per total irradiated area.

significance level. To conclude, the validation of absolute values for all studied cases (column "All" on **Table 6**), when semiempirical correction factors are applied for both MCCTs, Geant4 MCCT seems to present more sensitivity to the changes in the spectra showing significant differences (not agree) from experimental data for three simulated cases using spectra from Catalogue [73]. This can be due to the more detailed transport of primary and secondary particles. Considering Barnes et al.'s [74] spectra, there is no significant difference between experimental and simulated data considering the results for both MCCTs.

The comparison between both MCCTs after applying the semiempirical correction factor is presented in **Table 7**. As was expected there was an increase of the *p* values for the absolute value comparison of both MCCTs (**Table 7**) when compared to the validation of both MCCTs (**Table 6**). This is expected since the relative differences presented between simulated results (XRMC compared to Geant4) are smaller than the presented between each MCCT and experimental data. It is also important to note that for the comparison between both MCCTs only differences among the transport models evoked are significant. However, on a validation there may be differences associated to minimal discrepancies between experimental and simulated geometry, discrepancies among the transport models evoked (limitations of each model) and the repeatability of the X-radiation production and technical parameters of the mammograph. In the example presented in this section, the introduction of the modeled primary beam increases one variable to be considered in this context, increasing the error associated to the estimation of total number of proton emitted per mAs per total irradiated area. However, when one uses a code or model available on the X-ray equipment to estimate the dose in a radiological procedure, this person is using a modeled spectra or an estimated average spectra for the equipment and needs to pay attention to the limitations of this methodological choice.

To compare the results generated by both MCCTs directly, the χ^2 Pearson, Anderson-Darling, and Kolmogorov-Smirnov tests were applied on the simulated spectra at the entrance surface of the sensitive volume. These spectra were compared, and all of the studied cases presented *p* values above the significance level. For χ^2 Pearson test, all *p* values were 1.0000. The cases that presented larger differences on the validation, such as absolute values for M3000 XRMC and Geant4 based on Catalogue [73] (**Tables 8** and **9**), presented the lower *p* values in all statistical tests performed for the comparison of the MCCT.

Another important characteristic of MCCT to take into account is the running time. In this example, the XRMC Transmission mode reduced the running time around 2.5 times compared to Geant4 *std* physics list, 4 times compared to Geant4 *pen* physics list and 4.5 compared to Geant4 *liv* physics list. However, the limitations on simulating the absorbed energy and statistic fluctuations for this XRMC

Transport models and spectrum identification	Inspiration	M3000	Lorad	All
G4*std*–Barnes	0.9149	0.6566	0.9671	1.0000
G4*std*–Catalogue	0.1595	0.0521	0.9975	1.0000
G4*pen*–Barnes	0.7994	0.1182	1.0000	1.0000
G4*pen*–Catalogue	0.1572	0.0653	0.9975	0.4832
G4*liv*–Barnes	0.6809	0.1398	0.8765	1.0000
G4*liv*–Catalogue	0.6993	0.1263	0.1663	1.0000

Table 8.
Anderson-Darling p values for the comparison between XRMC and Geant4 (references) considering the spectrum at detector entrance surface for all physics lists and studied cases.

Transport models and spectrum identification	Inspiration	M3000	Lorad	All
G4*std*–Barnes	1.0000	0.8671	1.0000	0.9768
G4*std*–Catalogue	0.9999	0.9975	1.0000	0.9999
G4*pen*–Barnes	1.0000	1.0000	1.0000	1.000
G4*pen*–Catalogue	1.0000	1.0000	0.9999	1.0000
G4*liv*–Barnes	0.9998	0.8765	1.0000	0.9154
G4*liv*–Catalogue	1.0000	0.1663	1.0000	0.3687

Table 9.
Kolmogorov-Smirnov p values for the comparison between XRMC and Geant4 (references) considering the spectrum at detector entrance surface for all physics lists and studied cases.

version make the data treatment slower than that used on Geant4 and dependent of several external tools to perform data analyses that are not needed in Geant4.

When the experimental spectra of the X-ray equipment (in this example for mammographs) are available, it is better to use the experimental ones and the correction factors associated to it. However, it is important to keep in mind that it should be the spectra generated by the X-ray tube that is being used, since each tube (even the ones with the same characteristics produced by the same manufacturer) may have a difference on efficiency conversion due to minimal differences in its manufacturing. Besides that, a periodical verification of the amplitude correction factor for the number of photons generated per mAs per total irradiated area (or solid angle) must be applied since the tube wear can affect the conversion efficiency due to the deposition of atoms of the track-target on the window surface (by sputtering effect) or by the releasing of atoms from the track-target into the volume of the tube low pressure air.

4. Final considerations

The objective of this chapter was to present the main concepts of validation and reliability applied to MC application development to dosimetry and imaging, presenting a minimal validation that can be performed by MCCT ADs. It is important to note, as an AD in MC, that it is always valid to have your own experimental data to validate the application in the contour limitations of your problem. If experimental data for validation or modeled data for comparison are not available; at least a reliability test should be performed to ensure the quality of the results generated by the MCCT.

On choosing a MCCT, one needs to pay attention to the characteristics of the application, the capabilities and limitations of the MCCT code, and its computational performance. Besides that, the best MCCT is the one that the AD knows how to use (installing, developing applications, and extracting useful data). To do that the AD needs to have knowledge of a programing language or, at least, to understand the logic of input data in MCCT, to understand the experiment or clinical reality to be described in the simulation, and to have the notions of the processes and models of transport significant to the study case.

Regarding the results for the example used in this chapter the evaluation presented as follows:

- Validation—the statistical evaluation presented no null hypothesis rejection for XRMC results and presented the rejection of null hypothesis for few Geant4 cases evaluated considering normalized data. The XRMC presented the best agreement to the experimental data. Considering Geant4 the Livermore was the best physic list option. For absolute quantities calculated by applying semiempirical correction factors, all mammographs presented χ^2 p value under the significance level: one value for Inspiration (HVL) and one M3000 (BS) and few for Lorad (Mo25Rh and Mo30Mo) and Inspiration (ISL). Despite these particular cases of null hypothesis rejection, the overall evaluation for each transport model considering all studied cases presented few null hypothesis rejections for Geant4 MCCT using Catalogue spectra. So, it is recommendable to use spectra from Barnes et al. that were validated using both MCCTs (XRMC and Geant4). The use of only the theoretical correction factor for absolute quantities is not encouraged to perform validation, unless the AD knows pretty well the total number of photons emitted by the tube for the irradiation condition. Normalized data may be used associated to theoretical spectra to understand behaviors and tendencies of dosimetric quantities and to explore the influence of changes in the data acquisition but not to define absolute quantities.

- Comparison—the spectra generated at the entrance surface of the detector by both MCCTs always presented p values above the significance level of 0.05 for normalized data, showing that for this case the spectra generated by the same setup were from the same population (equal) within statistical significance. For absolute quantities calculated by applying semiempirical correction factors, one p value was under the significance level for Lorad (Mo25Rh) and one for Inspiration (ISL). Despite of these particular cases of null hypothesis rejection, the overall evaluation for each transport model considering all the evaluated cases presented no significant difference between XRMC and Geant4 which is compatible with the internal consistency of the transport models evoked.

- Reliability—the qualitative reliability evaluation based on graphics makes possible to observe that the more consistent data occurs for the simulation of the M3000. The graphics allowed to observe the tendencies when comparing simulated data to experimental data considering overall data and specific subgroups. This visual observation shows a consistency with the statistical tables, presenting sensitivity to help on data classification for a detailed analysis.

The methods to test a MCCT application are indispensable in the good practice of computational dosimetry and imaging because they guarantee the quality of the results, helping on the evaluation of the methodology limitations and making it possible to improve the trustability of the application and its results transposing with safety the "*computational world*" to the "*real world*."

Author details

Gabriela Hoff[1]*, Bruno Golosio[1,2], Elaine E. Streck[3] and Viviana Fanti[1,2]

1 Università degli studi di Cagliari, Cagliari, Italy

2 INFN Sezione, Cagliari, Italy

3 Independent Researcher, Brazil

*Address all correspondence to: ghoff.gesic@gmail.com

References

[1] Leclerc GL. Des Sciences: Géométrie. In: De L' Imprimerie Royale (France). Histoire de l'Académie Royale des Sciences. 1735. pp. 43–45. Available from: https://play.google.com/books/reader?id=GOAEAAAAQAAJ

[2] Leclerc GL. Essai D'Arithmétique Morale. In: De L' Imprimerie Royale (France). Histoire naturelle, générale et particulière, servant de suite à la Théorie de la Terre et d'introduction à l'Histoire des Minéraux. Supplément Tome premier [septième]. 1777. pp. 46–148. Available from: https://play.google.com/books/reader?id=AjhYD1vsVAIC&hl=pt&pg=GBS.PP9

[3] Siniksaran E. Throwing Buffon's needle with Mathematica. The Mathematic Journal. 2008;**11**(1):71-90. Available from: https://www.mathematica-journal.com/issue/v11i1/contents/BuffonsNeedle/BuffonsNeedle.pdf

[4] Birch CPD. Diagonal and orthogonal neighbors in grid-based simulations: Buffon's stick after 200 years. Ecological Modelling. 2006;**192**(3–4):637-644. DOI: 10.1016/j.ecolmodel.2005.07.017

[5] Zachary ED, Scott VF. The Buffon–Laplace needle problem in three dimensions. JSM: The.&Exp. IOP Publishing; 2009; P0900-P09010. DOI: 10.1088/1742-5468/2009/09/p09010

[6] Mooney CZ. Monte Carlo Simulation. Sage Publications; 1997. 103 p. ISBN: 0–8039–5943–5

[7] Haigh T, Priestley M, Rope C. Los Alamos Bets on ENIAC: Nuclear Monte Carlo Simulations, 1947-1948. IEEE Annals of the History of Computing. 2014;**36**(3):42-63. DOI: 10.1109/MAHC.2014.40

[8] Nicholas M, Ulam S. The Monte Carlo method. Journal of the American Statistical Association. 1949;**44**(247): 335-341. DOI: 10.1080/01621459.1949.10483310

[9] Geman S, Geman D. Stochastic relaxation, Gibbs distributions, and the Bayesian rof images. IEEE TPA&MI. 1984;(6):721-741. DOI: 10.1109/TPAMI.1984.4767596

[10] Jooyoung L. New Monte Carlo algorithm: Entropic sampling. Physical Review Letters. 1993;**71**(2):211-214; Erratum Physical Review Letters. 1993; **71**:2353. DOI: 10.1103/PhysRevLett.71.211

[11] Landau DP, Binder K. A Guide to Monte Carlo Simulations in Statistical Physics. 3rd ed. Cambridge University Press; 2014; 432 p. ISBN-13 978–0–511-65176-2

[12] Mooney CZ. Monte Carlo Simulation. Vol. 116. Sage Publications; 1997. 103 p. ISBN: 0–8039–5943–5

[13] Jun B, Kocher P. The Intel random number generator. White Paper. Vol. 27. Cryptography Research Inc. 1999. pp. 1–8. Available from: https://www.rambus.com/wp-content/uploads/2015/08/IntelRNG.pdf

[14] Hubbard JR. Programação em C++. 2nd ed. Coleção Schaum. Bookman. 2003. 392 p. ISBN: 85–363–0251-8

[15] Tang H, Qin T, Hui Z, Cheng P, Bai W. Design and implementation of a configurable and aperiodic pseudo random number generator in FPGA. In: 2018 IEEE 2nd ICCSS. Guangzhou, China. 2018. DOI: 10.1109/CIRSYSSIM.2018.8525964

[16] Lee K, Lee SY, Seo C, Yim K. TRNG (True Random Number Generator) method using visible spectrum for secure communication on 5G network. IEEE Access 6—Special Section on

Recent Advances on Radio Access and Security Methods in 5G Networks. 2018; **1**:12838-12847. DOI: 10.1109/ACCESS.2018.2799682

[17] Hubbell JH, Viegele WJ, Briggs EA, Brown RT, Cromer DT, Howerton RJ. Atomic form factors, incoherent scattering functions, and photon scattering cross section. Journal of Physical and Chemical Reference Data. 1975;**4**:471-538. DOI: 10.1063/1.555523

[18] Cullen D et al. EPDL97—The Evaluated Photon Data Library, Lawrence Livermore National Laboratory UCRL-50400. 1997;**6**(5). Available from: https://www.osti.gov/servlets/purl/295438

[19] Chadwick MC et al. ENDF/B-VII.1 Nuclear data for science and technology: Cross sections, covariances, fission product yields and decay data. Nuclear Data Sheets. 2011;**112**(12):2887-3152. Available from: https://www.sciencedirect.com/science/article/pii/S009037521100113X

[20] Cullen DE. Program SCATMAN: A code designed to calculate photon coherent scattering anomalous scattering factors and cross sections. In: Lawrence Livermore National Laboratory UCRL-ID-103422. 1989. Available from: https://www.osti.gov/biblio/5832494

[21] Han MC, Han SK, Pia MG, Basaglia T, Batic M, Hoff G, et al. Validation of cross sections for Monte Carlo simulation of the photoelectric effect. IEEE TNS. 2016;**63**(2):1117-1146. DOI: 10.1109/TNS.2016.2521876

[22] Pratt RH. Atomic photoelectric effect at high energies. Physical Review. 1960;**117**(4):1017-1028. DOI: 10.1103/PhysRev.117.1017

[23] Pratt RH. K-shell photoelectric cross sections from 200 keV to 2 MeV. Physical Review. 1964;**134**(4A):A898-A915. DOI: 10.1103/PhysRev.134.A898

[24] Rakavy G, Ron A. Atomic photoeffect in the range Eγ = 1–2000 keV. Physical Review. 1960; **159**(1):50-56. DOI: 10.1103/PhysRev.159.50

[25] Scofield JH. Theoretical Photoionization Cross Sections From 1 to 1500 keV. Lawrence Livermore Laboratory UCRL-51326; 1973. DOI: 10.2172/4545040

[26] Chantler CT. Theoretical form factor, attenuation and scattering tabulation for Z = 1–92 from E = 1–10 eV to E = 0.4–1.0 MeV. Journal of Physical and Chemical Reference Data. 1995;**24**(1):71-643. DOI: 10.1063/1.555974

[27] Hubbell JH. Photon Cross Sections, Attenuation Coefficients, and Energy Absorption Coefficients from 10 keV to 100 GeV. NSRDS-NBS 29. Washington, DC, USA: National Bureau of Standards; 1969 85p. Available from: https://nvlpubs.nist.gov/nistpubs/Legacy/NSRDS/nbsnsrds29.pdf

[28] Batic M, Hoff G, Pia MG, Saracco P. Photon elastic scattering simulation: Validation and improvements to Geant4. IEEE TNS. 2012;**59**(4):1636-1664. DOI: 10.1109/TNS.2012.2203609

[29] Tschalär C, Maccabee HD. Energy-straggling measurements of heavy charged particles in thick absorbers. Physical Review B: Condensed Matter and Materials Physics. 1970;**1**(7):2863-2869. DOI: 10.1103/PhysRevB.1.2863

[30] Wang H, Vassiliev NO. Radial dose distributions from protons of therapeutic energies calculated with Geant4-DNA. Physics in Medicine & Biology. 2014;**59**(14):3657. DOI: 10.1088/0031-9155/59/14/3657

[31] Iwase H, Niita K, Nakamura T. Development of general-purpose particle and heavy ion transport Monte Carlo code. Journal of Nuclear Science and Technology. 2002;**39**(11):1142-1151. DOI: 10.1080/18811248.2002.9715305

[32] Kling A, Barao FJC, Nakagawa M, Tavora L, Vaz P, editors. Advanced Monte Carlo for radiation physics, particle transport simulation and applications. In: Proceedings of the Monte Carlo Conference, Lisbon, 23–26 October 2000. Springer. 2014. 1192 p

[33] Martz HE, Logan CM, Schneberk DJ, Shull PJ. X-Ray Imaging: Fundamentals. Industrial Techniques and Applications: CRC Press; 2016. 574 p. ISBN: 9780849397721

[34] Gardner RP, Mickael MW, Verghese K. Specific purpose Monte Carlo code development for nuclear well logging applications. Progress in Nuclear Energy. 1991;**25**(2–3):245-264. DOI: 10.1016/0149-1970(91)90012-E

[35] Ao Q, Lee SH, Gardner RP. Development of the specific purpose Monte Carlo code CEARXRF for the design and use of in vivo X-ray fluorescence analysis systems for lead in bone. Applied Radiation and Isotopes. 1997;**48**(10–12):1403-1412. DOI: 10.1016/S0969-8043(97)00136-X

[36] Agostinelli S, Allisonas J, Amako K, Apostolakis J, Araujo H, Arce P, et al. Geant4—A simulation toolkit. Nuclear Instruments and Methods in Physics Research A. 2003;**506**(3):250-303. DOI: 10.1016/S0168-9002(03)01368-8

[37] Allison J, Amako K, Apostolakis J, Araujo H, Arce P, Asai M, et al. Geant4 developments and applications. IEEE TNS. 2006;**53**(1):270-278. DOI: 10.1109/TNS.2006.869826

[38] Allison J, Amako K, Apostolakis J, Arce P, Asai M, Asog T, et al. Recent developments in Geant4. Nuclear Instruments and Methods in Physics Research A. 2016;**835**(1):186-225. DOI: 10.1016/j.nima.2016.06.125

[39] Incerti S, Kyriakou I, Bernal MA, Bordage MC, Francis Z, Guatelli S, et al. Geant4-DNA example applications for track structure simulations in liquid water: A report from the Geant4-DNA Project. Medical Physics. 2018;**45**(8):e722-e739. DOI: 10.1002/mp.13048

[40] Bernal MA, Bordage MC, Brown JMC, Davídková M, Delage E, El Bitar Z, et al. Track structure modeling in liquid water: A review of the Geant4-DNA very low energy extension of the Geant4 Monte Carlo simulation toolkit. Physica Medica. 2015;**31**: 861-874. DOI: 10.1016/j.ejmp.2015.10.087

[41] Incerti S, Ivanchenko A, Karamitros M, Mantero A, Moretto P, Tran HN, et al. Comparison of Geant4 very low energy cross section models with experimental data in water. Medical Physics. 2010;**37**:4692-4708. DOI: 10.1118/1.3476457

[42] Incerti S, Baldacchino G, Bernal M, Capra R, Champion C, Francis Z, et al. The Geant4-DNA project. International Journal of Modelling, Simulation, and Scientific Computing. 2010;**1**:157-178. DOI: 10.1142/S1793962310000122

[43] Geant4 Collaboration. Physics Reference Manual—Release 10.5. Rev3.1: March 5th, 2019. 442 p. Available from: http://geant4-userdoc.web.cern.ch/geant4-userdoc/UsersGuides/PhysicsReferenceManual/fo/PhysicsReferenceManual.pdf

[44] Geant4 Collaboration. Geant4 Book For Application Developers—Release 10.5. Rev3.1: March 5th, 2019. 433 p. Available from http://geant4-userdoc.web.cern.ch/geant4-userdoc/UsersGuides/ForApplicationDeveloper/fo/BookForApplicationDevelopers.pdf

[45] Werner CJ et al. MCNP6.2 Release Notes. Los Alamos National Laboratory, LA-UR-18-20808. 2018. DOI: 10.2172/1419730

[46] Werner CJ, editor. MCNP Users Manual—Code Version 6.2, Los Alamos National Laboratory, LA-UR-17-29981. 2017. Available from: https://laws.lanl.gov/vhosts/mcnp.lanl.gov/pdf_files/la-ur-17-29981.pdf

[47] Goorley T, James M, Booth T, Brown F, Bull J, Cox LJ, et al. Initial MCNP6 Release Overview. Nuclear Technology. 2012;**180**(3):298-315. DOI: 10.13182/NT11-135

[48] Goorley T. MCNP6.1.1-Beta Release Notes, LA-UR-14-24680. 2014. Available from: https://laws.lanl.gov/vhosts/mcnp.lanl.gov/pdf_files/la-ur-14-24680.pdf

[49] Bull JS. How to Build MCNP 6.2—MCNP6 Development Team, LA-UR-17-30373. 2017. Available from: https://mcnp.lanl.gov/pdf_files/la-ur-17-30373.pdf

[50] X-5 Monte Carlo Team. MCNP—Version 5, Vol. I: Overview and Theory, LA-UR-03-1987. 2003. Available from https://mcnp.lanl.gov/pdf_files/la-ur-03-1987.pdf

[51] Böhlen TT, Cerutti F, Chin MPW, Fassò A, Ferrari A, Ortega PG, et al. The FLUKA code: Developments and challenges for high energy and medical applications. Nuclear Data Sheets. 2014;**120**(C):211-214. DOI: 10.1016/j.nds.2014.07.049

[52] Ferrari A, Sala PR, Fasso A, Ranft J. FLUKA: A multi-particle transport code. CERN-2005–10, INFN/TC_05/11, SLAC-R-773. 2005. Available from: https://www.slac.stanford.edu/pubs/slacreports/reports16/slac-r-773.pdf

[53] FLUKA Team 2000–2019. FLUKA Manual On-Line. FLUKA Team 2000–2019. Available from: http://www.fluka.org/content/manuals/online/INDEX-fluka2011.html. Last updated: 17th of November, 2018. [Accessed: April 10th 2019]

[54] Golosio B, Schoonjans T, Brunetti A, Oliva P, Masala GL. Monte Carlo simulation of X-ray imaging and spectroscopy experiments using quadric geometry and variance reduction techniques. Computer Physics Communications. 2014;**185**(3):1044-1052. DOI: 10.1016/j.cpc.2013.10.034

[55] Golosio B, Schoonjans T, Brunetti A, Masala GL, Oliva P. XRMC—The definitive manual (v6.4.5). 2014. Available from: http://lvserver.ugent.be/xrmc/files/xrmc_6.4.5_man.pdf.

[56] Schoonjans T, Brunetti A, Golosio B, Sanchez del Rio M, Solé VA, Ferrero C, et al. The x-raylib library for X-ray–matter interactions. Recent Developments in Spectrochimica Acta B. 2011;**66**(11–12):776-784. DOI: 10.1016/j.sab.2011.09.011

[57] Halbleib AJ, Kensek RP, Valdez GD, Seltzer SM, Berger MJ. ITS: The integrated TIGER series of electron/photon transport codes—Version 3.0. IEEE TNS. 1992;**39**(4):1025-1030. DOI: 10.1109/23.159753

[58] Laub TW, Kensek RP, Franke BC, Crawford MJ, Valdez GD. ITS version 6.4: The integrated TIGER series of Monte Carlo electron/photon radiation transport codes. In: ANS RPSD 2014—18th Topical Meeting of the Radiation Protection & Shielding Division of ANS Knoxville, TN, American Nuclear Society. 2014;**1**:1–4. Available from: https://www.osti.gov/servlets/purl/1141777

[59] Franke BC, Kensek RP, Thomas WL. ITS Version 6: The Integrated TIGER Series of Coupled Electron/Photon Monte Carlo Transport

Code—SAND2008–3331. Albuquerque: Sandia National Laboratories; 2008. 341 p. DOI: 10.2172/1028913

[60] Salvat F. PENELOPE-2014—A Code System for Monte Carlo Simulation of Electron and Photon Transport. In: Workshop Barcelona, Spain (2015) (NEA/NSC/DOC(2015)3) —Tutorial for PENELOPE (version 2014). Available from: https://www.oecd-nea.org/science/docs/2015/nsc-doc2015-3.pdf

[61] Salvat F, Fernandez-Varea JM, Acosta E, Sempau J. PENELOPE, a code system for Monte Carlo simulation of electron and photon transport. In: Proceedings of a Workshop/Training Course, OECD/NEA 5–7 November 2001 NEA/NSC/DOC. 2001. p. 19. ISBN: 92–64–18475-9

[62] Sempau J, Acosta E, Baro J, Fernandez-Varea JM, Salvat J. An algorithm for Monte Carlo simulation of the coupled electron-photon transport. Nuclear Instruments and Methods B. 1997;**132**(3):377-390. DOI: 10.1016/S0168-583X(97)00414-X

[63] Sempau J, Fernandez-Varea JM, Acosta E, Salvat F. Experimental benchmarks of the Monte Carlo code PENELOPE. Nuclear Instruments and Methods B. 2003;**207**(2):107-123. DOI: 10.1016/S0168-583X(03)00453-1

[64] Hirayama H, Namito Y, Bielajew AF, Wilderman SJ, Nelson WR. The EGS5 Code System. LAC number: SLAC-R-730 KEK (2005–8). Available from http://rcwww.kek.jp/research/egs/egs5_manual/slac730-150228.pdf [Revised version of February 27, 2015]

[65] Kawrakow I, Mainegra-Hing E, Rogers DWO, Tessier F, Walters BRB. The EGSnrc Code System: Monte Carlo Simulation of Electron and Photon Transport. NRCC PIRS-701. Canada: National Research Council; 2019; 3231 p. Available from: https://nrc-cnrc.github.io/EGSnrc/doc/pirs701-egsnrc.pdf

[66] Bielajew AF, Hirayama H, Nelsony WR, Rogers DWO. History, overview and recent improvements of EGS. Research Council of Canada —NRC-PIRS-0463. National Laboratory for High Energy Physics—KEK Internal 94-4. National Laboratory for High Linear Accelerator Center—SLAC-PUC 6499. 1994. 25 p. Available from http://rcwww.kek.jp/research/egs/docs/pdf/nrcpirs0436.pdf

[67] Dasso A, Funes A. Verification, Validation and Testing in Software Engineering. Idea Group Publishing; 2006; 428 p. ISBN: 1-59140-853-9

[68] Schmidt MEC. Implementing the IEEE Software Engineering Standards. Sams Publishing; 2000. 242 p. ISBN: 0672318571

[69] Lima NW, Hoff G. Impacto da pureza dos filtros de alumínio no valor de Camada Semi-Redutora em radiologia convencional e mamografia. Brazilian Journal of Radiation Sciences. 2016;**03**(2A):1-13. DOI: 10.15392/bjrs.v3i2A.92

[70] Hoff G, Lima NW. Aplicabilidade da Lei do Inverso do Quadrado da distância em radiologia convencional e mamografia. Brazilian Journal of Radiation Sciences. 2015;**03**(1A):01-16. DOI: 10.15392/bjrs.v3i1A.91

[71] Hoff G, de Assis JT, Brunetti A, Fanti V, Golosio B. Comparison of XRMC and Geant4 on dosimetry applied to mammography. In: 2017 IEEE Nuclear Science Symposium and Medical Imaging Conference (NSS/MIC). 2017. DOI: 10.1109/NSSMIC.2017.8532758

[72] Hoff G, de Almeida CE, Barnes GT. Behavior of subject contrast versus glandular dose in mammography: Determination of a semi-empirical

formalism for different target-filter combinations. Radiologia Brasileira. 2006;**39**(3):1-10. DOI: 10.1590/ S0100-39842006000300008

[73] Cranley K, Gilmore BJ, Fogarty GWA, Desponds L. Catalogue of diagnostic X-ray spectra & other data. In: (Report style) IPEM Report 78. New York: IPEM; 1997

[74] Barnes GT. Private communication. Medical Physics. 2000;**18**(2):211-218. Mar/Apr Medical Physics. 1991;**18**(3): 402–407; Radiology. May/Jun 1991;**179**: 143–148, April 1991

Section 2

Material

Chapter 5

How to Use the Monte Carlo Simulation Technique? Application: A Study of the Gas Phase during Thin Film Deposition

Fethi Khelfaoui and Oumelkheir Babahani

Abstract

Many physical phenomena can be modeled using Monte Carlo simulation (MCS) because it is a powerful tool to study thermodynamic properties. MCS can be used to simulate interactions between several particles or bodies in the presence of local or external fields. The main idea is to create a high number of different random configurations; statistics can be taken according to appropriate algorithms (Metropolis algorithm). In this chapter, we present basic techniques of MCS as the choice of potential, reaction rates, simulation cell, random configurations, and algorithms. We present some principal ideas of MCS used to study particle-particle collisions in the gas and in plasmas. Other MCS techniques are presented briefly. A numerical application is presented for collisions in gas phase during thin film deposition by plasma-enhanced chemical vapor deposition (PECVD) processes. Parameters and results of the simulation are studied according to a chosen reactor and mixture.

Keywords: MCS, potential, reaction rates, collisions, thin film deposition

1. Introduction

In statistical physics only a few problems can be solved exactly. For complex problems, numerical methods can give exact results for problems that could only be solved in an approximate way. Numerical simulation can be a way to test the theory. The numerical results can be compared to the experimental results. The numerical simulation is placed between the fundamental and the experimental treatment; it has a quasi-experimental character (numerical experience). For problems of statistical physics, the most widely used simulation methods are the Monte Carlo method and the molecular dynamics method.

The first Monte Carlo simulation (MCS) was proposed by Metropolis et al. in 1953 [1]. The second Monte Carlo simulation was proposed by Wood and Parker in 1957 [2]. The obtained results were in good agreement with the experimental results of Bridgman [3] and those of Michels et al. [4]. In this method we attribute a series of initial positions chosen randomly to a system of N particles interacting through a defined potential. A sequence of particle configurations is generated by giving successive displacements to particles; we only retain configurations to ensure that the probability density is that of the chosen.

Molecular dynamics simulation (MDS) has been first introduced to simulate the behavior of fluids and solids at the molecular or atomic level. MDS was used for the first time by Alder and Wainwright in the late 1950s [5, 6] to study the interactions of hard spheres. The principle is the resolution of equations of motion for a hard sphere system in a simulation cell. The basic algorithm is Verlet's algorithm [7].

In this chapter, we will present techniques of numerical simulations using the Monte Carlo method. We will present an application on the gas phase during plasma-enhanced chemical vapor deposition (PECVD) of thin films. The application concerns collisions between particles. Particles are in Brownian motion. Collisions, elastic or inelastic, are considered to be binary. Non-elastic collisions result in effective chemical reactions.

In Section 2, we cite some MCS and MDS works on PECVD processes. Section 3 presents general rules on numerical simulation methods. Section 4 presents how to simulate a physical problem using MCS? We present the Metropolis algorithm as a scheme to trait random configurations and different modules related to elaborate an MCS code. In Section 5, we apply the MCS on SiH_4/H_2 gas mixture during a PECVD process. Finally the conclusion summarizes the contents of the chapter.

2. Simulation works on the PECVD using MCS and MDS

The PECVD is the most widely used technique to produce hydrogenated amorphous silicon thin films (a-Si:H) for solar cells and for film transistors and electronic devices [8, 9]. Reactions during plasma deposition are complex and are not understood completely.

Gorbachev et al. [10–12] have developed a model that is based on chemical reactions and different processes in a PECVD reactor. The model takes into account the formation of Si_nH_m oligomers ($n \leq 5$). It presents a simulation of the growth of the films. Gorbachev et al. found that Si_2H_5 and Si_3H_7 strongly influence the growth of the film [11].

Valipa et al. [13] calculated the β reactivity of the SiH_3 radical on a surface of a silicon lattice plane during the growth of a-Si:H using MDS. The mechanisms of physical and chemical interactions of low temperature plasmas with surfaces can be explored using MDS [14].

For a CH_4/H_2 mixture, Farouk et al. used the Monte Carlo method (PIC/MC); they calculated the ionization rate of the plasma and the deposition rate of the thin layer [15]. Rodgers et al. [16] have developed three-dimensional Monte Carlo simulations of diamond (100) surface CVD. Other works on MCS are in [17–19].

In our previous works [20–24], we were interested in the study of the gas phase and the interaction of plasmas with the surface, for SiH_4/H_2 and CH_4/H_2 gas mixtures during PECVD processes. The used numerical simulation techniques were MCS and MDS. To complete the studies, we used the fluid model [25].

3. General rules for numerical simulation methods

The starting point of numerical simulation is a physical phenomenon; its purpose is to obtain useful physical results. Between these two points, several steps can be identified. These steps are general and they are applicable for MCS. The steps can be summarized as follows:

3.1 Definition of the physical phenomenon and main hypothesis

The physical phenomenon must be defined by the description of the dominant domain of physics. The main assumptions and simplifying approximations are necessary to understand the physical phenomenon and the design of the first model.

DOI: http://dx.doi.org/10.5772/intechopen.88559

3.2 Definition of the mathematical model

Mathematical model requires a mathematical formulation of the problem. It may be a problem of elements or discrete object or a problem of a continuous medium; it may be a spatiotemporal problem or frequency problem and may be a deterministic or probabilistic problem.

It would be interesting to know the mathematical equations that govern the phenomenon:

- The forces between particles and elements
- The potential interaction
- The determination of a time scale
- The determination of a length scale
- Definition of constant magnitudes of motion and equilibrium magnitudes
- Continuity equations, balance equations, transfer equations, etc.

3.3 Elaboration of simulation code

The MCS technique has been chosen for this work; knowing its basic algorithm is necessary for elaborating the simulation. This step requires some actions:

- Validation of the model on simple cases
- Simulation calculation on complex phenomena

4. Algorithms and techniques for MCS

The MCS is based on a probabilistic process with a random choice of configurations and samples of the situation of the physical system. The two pedagogical examples most cited in the literature are the integration of a single variable function and Ising's model of spin. In the following subsection, we define the integration of a single variable function. We introduce the Ising model at the end of Section 4.2.2.

4.1 Integration of function of a single variable

Calculation of the definite integral for a function f(x) of a single variable x on domain {a, b} has been proposed (**Figure 1**):

Let:

$$I = \int_a^b f(x)dx \quad (1)$$

Let x_i and y_i be real random numbers (i = 1, 2,..., N), and let H be a real number greater than the f(x) for x belonging to the domain {a, b} (or $x \in \{a, b\}$).

Let r_1 and r_2 be two random numbers belonging to the domain {0, 1} according to a uniform distribution law. Generators (e.g., Ran, RANDOM, RANDUM, or other IMSL mathematical libraries) of random numbers can be used:

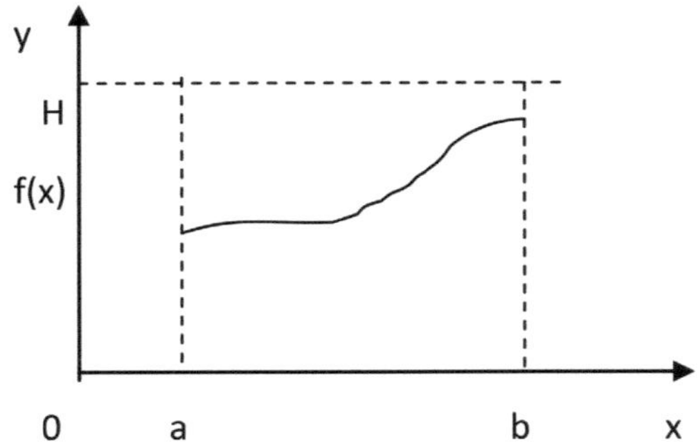

Figure 1.
The integral of a function f(x).

$$x_i = a + r_1(b - a) \text{ and } y_i = 0 + r_2(H - 0) \tag{2}$$

where x_i and y_i are random numbers ($x_i \in \{a, b\}$ and $y_i \in \{0, H\}$).

The Monte Carlo (MC) method is based on a probabilistic process. Let N be the total number of cases chosen (possible cases). It is necessary to count the number of favorable cases (or the number of points below the curve y = f(x)); let $y_i \leq f(x_i)$). The number of favorable cases is N_{fav}. When N → ∞, the value *I* of the integral is [26]:

$$I = \frac{N_{fav}}{N}(b - a)(H - 0.0) = \frac{N_{fav}}{N}(b - a)H \tag{3}$$

An example [26] is the calculation of the value π by calculating the integral *I* on a quarter circle of unit radius (R = 1.0). The pairs of random numbers (x_i, y_i) satisfying the condition: $x_i^2 + y_i^2 \leq 1$. The function f(x) is equal to $\sqrt{1 - x^2}$.

We take a = 0.0, b = 1.0, and H = 1.0.

For different values of N, we show that the numerical solution tends to π = 4*I*.

Although this integral is simple, it shows the strength and simplicity of the method. The technique can be generalized for the integration of multivariate functions.

We note that integration by the MC method is based on:

- The choice of **random configurations** according to a **uniform distribution law**
- Each configuration chosen is either **favorable** or **unfavorable** (the "or" is exclusive).

4.2 Principle of the MCS model

4.2.1 Calculation algorithm (Metropolis algorithm)

For statistical physics problems, the probabilistic choice of configurations is not always deterministic; the favorable and unfavorable cases are not exclusive. According to the Metropolis algorithm [26, 27], the steps of the simulation are:

a. Choice of a simulation cell of adequate shape to the studied phenomena. The size of the simulation cell is related to a scale of length characteristic of the forces and interaction potential of the studied phenomenon. This cell may contain N_{pc} particles (and/or elements).

b. Choice of an initial configuration that responds to some physical and thermodynamic properties. The total or internal energy of the system is E_i.

c. Infinitesimal random displacement of a particle (or element of the system) and calculation of the new internal energy of the system E_f. This displacement is related to the physical magnitudes: time scale and length scale. **The physical system tends toward a minimization of the internal energy of the system** *with* some *fluctuation*. Let $\Delta E = E_f - E_i$ the *fluctuation*.

d. If $\mathbf{\Delta E \leq 0}$; the new configuration is retained (favorable) and the different averages can be obtained; go to step (c).

e. If $\mathbf{\Delta E > 0}$; a random number ε is chosen such that $0 < \varepsilon < 1$. Let the probability P_r equal to: $P_r = \exp.(-\Delta E/k_B T)$ (where k_B is the Boltzmann constant and T is the temperature).

f. If $\varepsilon < P_r$, accept the move and in any case go back to step (c) for a new choice of an infinitesimal displacement (new configuration). Note that if such a trial move is rejected, the old configuration is again counted in the averaging with probability P_r.

Figure 2 shows how to choose between the selected configurations. Let ε be a random number following a uniform law; If $\varepsilon_1 \leq P_r$ the configuration is retained, and if $\varepsilon_2 > P_r$ the configuration is rejected.

Numerical simulation using the MC method is a very important tool for the study of static properties. The basic algorithm is based on probability notions. Understanding of the distribution function and/or interaction potentials is the heart of the calculation.

4.2.2 Thermodynamic quantities at equilibrium

In equilibrium statistical physics, the system has a certain probability that can be in any states. The probability of being in a state μ with energy $H(\mu)$ is given by the Boltzmann distribution $P(\mu)$:

$$P_\mu = \frac{\exp\left(-H(\mu)/k_B T\right)}{Z} \tag{4}$$

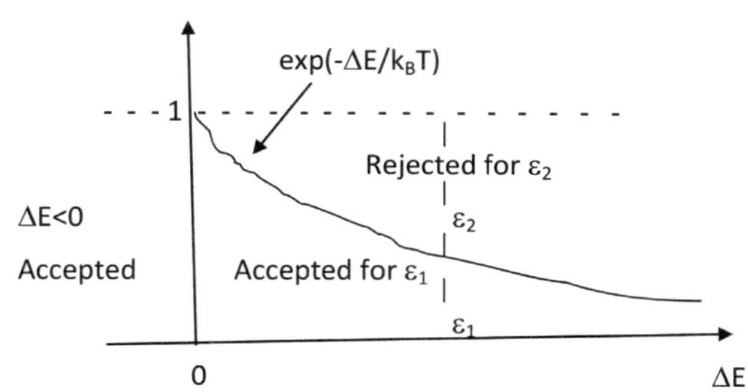

Figure 2.
Configuration choice according to Metropolis scheme.

where T is the absolute temperature and k_B is called Boltzmann's constant. It is conventional to denote the quantity $(k_B T)^{-1}$ by the symbol β. The normalizing factor Z, or partition function, is given by:

$$Z = \sum_{\mu} \exp\left(-H(\mu)/k_B T\right) = \sum_{\mu} \exp\left(-\beta H(\mu)\right) \tag{5}$$

The average of a quantity Q fora system in equilibrium is:

$$<Q> = \sum_{\mu} Q_{\mu} P_{\mu} = \frac{1}{Z} \sum_{\mu} Q_{\mu} \exp\left(-\beta H(\mu)\right) \tag{6}$$

The internal energy U, is given by:

$$U = \frac{1}{Z} \sum_{\mu} H(\mu) \exp\left(-\beta H(\mu)\right) \tag{7}$$

which can be written in terms of a derivative of the partition function:

$$U = \frac{1}{Z}\frac{\partial Z}{\partial \beta} = -\frac{\partial \log Z}{\partial \beta} \tag{8}$$

From thermodynamics we have expressions for the specific heat C, the entropy S, and the Helmholtz free energy F:

$$C = \frac{\partial U}{\partial T} = -k_B \beta^2 \frac{\partial U}{\partial \beta} = -k_B \beta^2 \frac{\partial^2 \log Z}{\partial \beta^2} \tag{9}$$

or

$$C = T\frac{\partial S}{\partial T} = -\beta \frac{\partial S}{\partial \beta} \tag{10}$$

and

$$S = -k_B \beta \frac{\partial \log Z}{\partial \beta} + k_B \log Z \tag{11}$$

and

$$F = U - TS = -k_B \log Z \tag{12}$$

We can calculate other parameters affecting the system.

The Monte Carlo method is an excellent technique for estimating probabilities, and we can take advantage of this property in evaluating the results. The simplest and most popular model of a system of interacting variables in statistical physics is the Ising model. It consists of spins σ_i which are confined to the sites of a lattice and which may have only the values (+1) and (−1). These spins interact with their nearest neighbors on the lattice with interaction constant J; they can interact with an external magnetic field B coupling to the spins. The Hamiltonian H for this model is [26]:

$$H = -J \sum_{i,j} \sigma_i \sigma_j - B \sum_{i} \sigma_i \tag{13}$$

The Ising model has been studied in one and two dimensions to obtain results of thermal properties, phase transition, and magnetic properties [26–28]. For chosen values of J and/or B, different steps may be taken for the calculations (simulation cell, initialization, configurations, boundary conditions, calculation algorithms). For any configuration, each spin takes the two possible directions. The detail of the calculation procedure is not the purpose of this chapter.

4.2.3 MCS module designs

4.2.3.1 Simulation cell and initialization

We give a system of N particles (atoms, molecules, ions or particles) placed in a cell of fixed volume, generally of cubic form. The initial positions may, depending on the case, be distributed randomly according to a certain law (uniform or otherwise) or have a given symmetry. In a fluid, a gas, or a plasma, the particles may have random positions in general; in a solid or surface, with a crystal structure, the particles take ordered positions. The choice of random initial positions allows great freedom on the choice of the number of particles in the cell.

At the first step, the particles are given velocities that are generally selected to have a zero total momentum. If the system is in thermodynamic equilibrium, the initial velocities will be randomly chosen according to a Maxwell-Boltzmann law. In the general case, the velocity distribution is according to the problem dealt with. All other phase properties can be initialized to the particles; the main thing is the conservation of the total quantities of the system.

4.2.3.2 Potentials of interaction

The particles interact with each other according to chosen interaction potentials. Since the interaction potentials are specific for each "numerical experiment," the main part of the work consists in calculating the interaction energies for each proposed configuration.

The choice of interaction potentials is directly related to the mathematical formulation of the problem according to the state of the medium: fluid, gas, plasma, or solid. It can be Lennard-Jones potential, Coulomb potential, Debye potential, Morse potential, Stillinger-Weber potential, Born-Mayer potential, Moliere potential, or others.

4.2.3.3 Boundary conditions

In general, two main boundary conditions are used: periodic boundary conditions (PBC) and minimum image convention (MIC) [29].

To minimize the surface effect, periodic boundary conditions (PBC) [30] are invariably imposed. The simulation cell is reproduced throughout the space to form an infinite mesh. We can simulate the properties of an infinite system. The particles that we follow are in the central cell; if a particle crosses a wall with a certain velocity, its image returns with the same velocity by the opposite wall. Under these conditions, the number of particles in the central cell, and consequently the density, is constant. These conditions also allow the conservation of the energy and the momentum of the system and do not introduce periodic effects (because of the interaction between particles).

According to the hypotheses and according to the geometry of the problem, other boundary conditions are proposed [26]. For example, in order to model thin films, the simulation cells are longitudinal and parallel to the film; one uses PBC in the directions parallel to the film. In the direction normal to the film, free edge boundary conditions can be used. In such cases, it may be appropriate to also include surface fields and surface interactions. In this way, one can study phenomena such as wetting, interface localization-delocalization transitions, surface-induced ordering and disordering, etc.

The core of the program includes calculating the potential energies of particle configuration and particle collisions. The interactions and collisions between particles can be elastic or inelastic; they can be binary or collective. For computation, the interaction energy of a particle with its neighbors is carried out by refocusing a base cell on the particle. This particle only interacts with particles in this region. This is called the "minimal image convention" (MIC) [1].

4.2.3.4 Sampling of random data

Generally, a RANDOM generator of real random numbers r_i belonging to the domain {0, 1} (or $r_i \in \{0, 1\}$ is available. This distribution law is uniform.

To have a real random number x_i belonging to the domain {a, b} (or $x_i \in \{a, b\}$) according to a law of uniform distribution, we have:

$$x_i = a + r_i(b - a) \tag{14}$$

To have a real random number x_i belonging to the domain {a, b} (or $x_i \in \{a,b\}$) according to a formula (or law) of nonuniform distribution f(x), a histogram technique is used. Let N_m be the number of intervals. If the mesh is regular (**Figure 3**):

$$\Delta x = (b - a)/N_m \tag{15}$$

We define:

$$f_i = f(x_i) \text{ for } i = 0, \dots, m \text{ and} : x_i = a + i.\Delta x \tag{16}$$

We define the sequence:

$$S_0 = 0 \text{ and} : S_{i+1} = S_i + \Delta x(f(x_i) + f(x_{i-1}))/2 \tag{17}$$

and the sequence:

$$rx_0 = 0 \text{ et } rx_i = S_i/S_m \tag{18}$$

Hence each real random number r_i belongs to the domain {0, 1} (where $r_i \in \{0, 1\}$) (according to the uniform law); this number belongs to the domain $\{rx_{j-1}, rx_j\}$. It

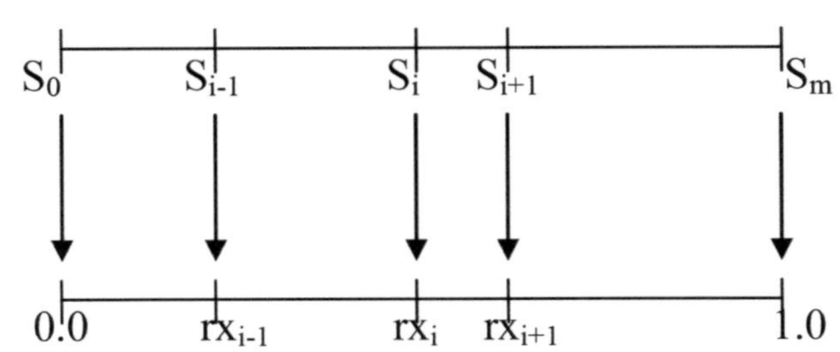

Figure 3.
Random number selection according to f (x) distribution.

corresponds to a random value x_{ran} of the domain $\{x_{j-1}, x_j\}$; this number satisfies the formula (or the law) of nonuniform distribution f(x).

This technique can be generalized for a nonuniform distribution law f(x) with an irregular mesh Δx_i, or with tabular data $f(x_i)$ with $i = 1,..., m$.

The technique can be generalized, too, for a discrete distribution law f(i) with $i = 1,..., m$.

In the literature, the reader can find simple algorithms for the choice of random numbers of some simple functions (Gaussian, etc.).

4.2.3.5 Control of the evolution of the physical system

It is necessary to find some parameters allowing the control of the smooth course of the evolution of the system. We must look for the constants of movement. For example for an isolated system, we have the conservation of the total energy and the quantity of matter.

4.2.3.6 Statistical calculations

By using the numerical simulation, it is possible to calculate many spatiotemporal quantities F(r,t). These quantities can be positions, speeds, kinetic moments, particle energies, concentrations, transport coefficients, etc. It would then be possible to calculate all other quantities related to F(r,t).

For the calculation of the averages, one can note the quantities on the space, on the time or on both. The histogram methods can be used. Static or dynamic distribution functions and spatial or temporal correlation functions can be calculated. It should be noted that the SMC is much more adequate for static properties because of the probabilistic choice of configurations.

Any calculated function or parameter F(r,t) can be used for another application in another calculation program.

4.3 Other large methods of Monte Carlo simulation

In the MCS model discussed extensively in this chapter, it's more about collisions between particles. It's ***particle-particle MCS*** or PP-MCS. In many problems of physics, the general idea is the same, but the applications and proposed models are numerous.

Other MCS models, named ***particle-in-cell MCS*** (PIC-MCS), are based on particle-cell interactions. In these last models, we also use a probabilistic choice of configurations and small variations in the state of the system (following the Metropolis algorithm); the interaction is between the particle with a cell, a mesh, or a drop. The parameters and variables of the cell, although local and instantaneous, are macroscopic. These parameters and variables can be thermodynamic, fluid, or electromagnetic. An example of the model based on PIC-MCS is described by Mattei et al. [31] for simulation of electromagnetic particle-in-cell collision in inductively coupled plasmas. Several works can be found in the literature on this same line of work. Other MCS models using particles may be considered. [32].

For statistical physics problem solving (such as thin film deposition problems), MCS models use experimental, numerical, or theoretical data from other methods and models. Models can be improved to ***hybrid models***. In the hybrid models, connections between two modules can be realized. The first module is MCS; the second module is fluid, electromagnetic, or other. An example of a three-module hybrid model is presented by Mao and Bogaerts [33] to study gas mixtures in PECVD system. The three modules are MCS, fluid, and electromagnetic. The first

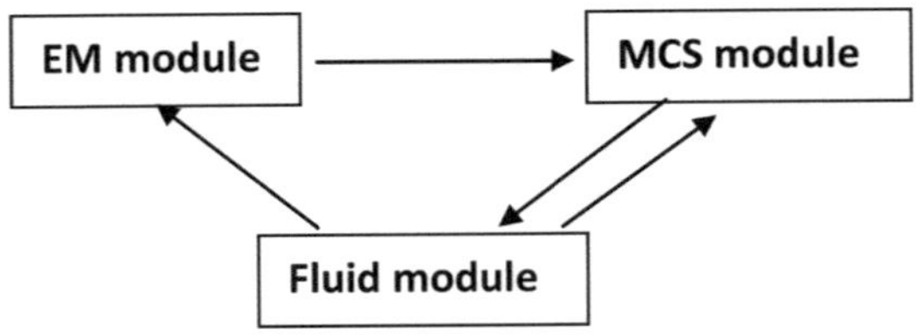

Figure 4.
Schematic of a hybrid model of three modules used to study gas mixtures in the PECVD [33].

module EM calculates the electromagnetic fields by solving Maxwell equations. These fields are used as inputs in the module MCS, where the electron density, electron temperature, electron energy distribution function, and electron impact reaction rates can be computed with a Monte Carlo procedure. Subsequently, the module fluid calculates densities and fluxes of the various plasma species (i.e., heavy particles and electrons) with continuity equations and the electrostatic field with Poisson's equation. This electrostatic field is used as input again in the EM. This cycle is iterated until convergence. The schematic of the hybrid model is given in **Figure 4**.

To solve statistical physics problems with evolutions as a function of time, ***kinetic models of MCS*** (kMCS) are used. Using kMCS, Battaile and Srolovitz [17] described kinetic phenomena of the diffusive motion of a single interstitial atom in a close-packed metal crystal. The motion of the interstitial atom is usually limited to two types: vibration of the atom around the center of the interstitial hole in which it resides and hops to nearest-neighbor interstitial sites. The atom can hop into any of the nearest-neighbor interstitial sites; it executes a random walk. In an MC simulation of this diffusion process, the new position of the interstitial atom is chosen at random from a list of the adjacent interstitial sites.

Other CVD and PECVD works on MCS are presented in Ref.s [15, 34–38]. They show how MCS methods can study properties of gas mixtures and properties of the growth of thin films.

5. Example of application: Monte Carlo simulation of a gas mixture in the PECVD

In this section, we present an example of PP-MCS of collisions and reactions in gas phase of SiH_4/H_2 mixture used in PECVD process. Some paragraphs have been treated in previous works [21, 24].

5.1 Description of the physical phenomenon

We use a MCS to study collisions and chemical reactions in gas phase of SiH_4/H_2 mixture used in the PECVD process. In this phase, important reactions have been identified that contribute to the production and the consumption of hydrogen (H), silylene (SiH_2), and silyl (SiH_3). The hydrogen consumption reactions $SiH_4 + H \rightarrow SiH_3 + H_2$ and $SiH_3 + H \rightarrow SiH_2 + H_2$ are found to play a central role in deciding the distribution of hydrogen [39].The plasma chemistry indicates that H atoms and SiH_3 radicals play an important role in the a-Si:H deposition process [40]. Experimentally, it is generally accepted that SiH_3 radicals dominate a-Si:H and μc-Si film growth from SiH_4 plasmas in the PECVD; it is the key precursor of a-Si:H deposition [41]. The proposed MCS allowed to get the ratio SiH_2/SiH_3 and mean value of densities of species. It provides information on SiH_4 dissociation and on the production of SiH_3, H, SiH_2, and Si_2H_6 and other important parameters.

The plasma in the PECVD reactor is weakly ionized. For our study, the mixture gas contains 22% of SiH_4 and 78% of H_2; the pressure is 100 mtorr, the temperature of the gas ranges from 373 to 723 K, the electron temperature is about 2.5 eV, and the electron density is 3. 10^8 cm^{-3}. The process is considered to be stationary. We take into account electrons and eight neutral species (SiH_4, SiH_3, SiH_2, H, H_2, Si_2H_6, Si_2H_5, SiH). *Reactions* taken into account include seven *electron-neutral* and 14 neutral-*neutral reactions*. **Table 1** shows the 21 reactions and rate constants K_{reac}. At low temperature, the neutrals interact occasionally with each other and move under the effect of thermal agitation; their velocity distribution function is Maxwell-Boltzmann distribution. Electrons have the mean velocity with kinetic energy T_e.

Let K_{reac}^{cons} and K_{reac}^{prod} be the rate constants of the consumption and the production of species A. The chemical reaction for the consumption of A is as:

$$a \cdot A + b \cdot B \xrightarrow{K_{reac}^{cons}} c \cdot C + d \cdot D$$

And chemical reaction for the production of A is as:

$$a' \cdot A' + b' \cdot B' \xrightarrow{K_{reac}^{prod}} c' \cdot A + d' \cdot D'$$

Symbol	Reactions	K_{reac} (cm^3/s)
R1	$SiH_4 + e \rightarrow SiH_3 + H + e$	$k_1 = 3 \times 10^{-11}$ [42]
R2	$SiH_4 + e \rightarrow SiH_2 + 2H + e$	$K_2 = 1.5 \times 10^{-10}$ [42]
R3	$SiH_4 + e \rightarrow SiH + H + H_2 + e$	$K_3 = 9.34 \times 10^{-12}$ [42]
R4	$SiH_4 + e \rightarrow SiH_2 + H_2 + e$	$K_4 = 7.19 \times 10^{-12}$ [42]
R5	$H_2 + e \rightarrow 2H + e$	$K_5 = 4.49 \times 10^{-12}$ [42]
R6	$Si_2H_6 + e \rightarrow SiH_3 + SiH_2 + H + e$	$K_6 = 3.72 \times 10^{-10}$ [42]
R7	$Si_2H_6 + e \rightarrow SiH_4 + SiH_2 + e$	$K_7 = 1.1 \times 10^{10} \times (1.(1./(1. + (0.63 \times P))))$ [43]
R8	$SiH_4 + H \rightarrow SiH_3 + H_2$	$K_8 = 2.8 \times 10^{-11} \times \exp.(-1250/T)$ [44]
R9	$SiH_4 + SiH_2 \rightarrow Si_2H_6$	$K_9 = 1.1 \times 10^{10} \times (1.-(1./(1. + (0.63 \times P))))$ [43]
R10	$SiH_3 + SiH_3 \rightarrow SiH_4 + SiH_2$	$K_{10} = 0.45 \times 1.5 \times 10^{-10}$ [44]
R11	$SiH_4 + Si_2H_5 \rightarrow SiH_3 + Si_2H_6$	$K_{11} = 5 \times 10^{-13}$ [42]
R12	$SiH_3 + H \rightarrow SiH_2 + H_2$	$K_{12} = 2 \times 10^{-11}$ [44]
R13	$SiH_3 + Si_2H_6 \rightarrow SiH_4 + Si_2H_5$	$K_{13} = 4 \times 10^{-10} \times \exp. (-2500/T)$ [44]
R14	$SiH_2 + H \rightarrow SiH + H_2$	$k_{14} = 2 \times 10^{-11}$ [44]
R15	$Si_2H_6 + H \rightarrow Si_2H_5 + H_2$	$K_{15} = 0.66 \times 2.4 \times 10^{-10} \times \exp. (-1250/T)$ [43]
R16	$Si_2H_6 + H \rightarrow SiH_4 + SiH_3$	$K_{16} = 0.34 \times 2.4 \times 10^{-10} \times \exp. (-1250/T)$ [44]
R17	$SiH + H_2 \rightarrow SiH_3$	$K_{17} = 2 \times 10^{-12}$ [43]
R18	$SiH_2 + SiH_3 \rightarrow Si_2H_5$	$K_{18} = 3.77 \times 10^{-13}$ [43]
R19	$SiH_2 + H_2 \rightarrow SiH_4$	$K_{19} = 3 \times 10^{-12} \times (1. + (1./1. + (0.03 \times P)))$ [43]
R20	$2SiH_3 \rightarrow Si_2H_6$	$K_{20} = 0.1 \times 1.5 \times 10^{-10}$ [43]
R21	$SiH_4 + SiH \rightarrow Si_2H_5$	$K_{21} = (1.-(1./(1. + (0.33 \times P)))) \times (6.9 \times 10^{-10})$ [43]

Table 1.
List of gas phase reactions and corresponding rate constants [24].

Rate production and consumption for any species A are taken as:

$$R_A = +\sum_{K^{prod}_{reac}} K^{cons}_{reac(A',\ B')} n^{a'}_{A'} n^{b'}_{B'} - \sum_{K^{cons}_{reac}} K^{cons}_{reac(A,\ B)} n^{a}_{A} n^{b}_{B} \quad (19)$$

5.2 Description of Monte Carlo simulation technique

5.2.1 Simulation cell and phase coordinates

The MCS is based on binary collisions at the microscopic level. Elastic collisions are between all particles, and inelastic collisions (or effective collisions) are those that result in a chemical reaction. A chemical reaction needs a collision involving at least two particles (atoms, ions, electrons, or molecules). According to kinetic theory, gases consist of particles in random motion. These particles are *uniformly distributed* in a cell which has a parallelepiped form of sizes L_x, L_y, and L_z (**Figure 5**). These *particles move in a straight line until they collide with other particles or the walls of their container*. Dimensions and volume of Monte Carlo cell must take into consideration the mean free path of species.

Let n_i be the density of neutral spice *i* (i = 1,..., 8). The first particle *i* is randomly chosen according to a probability of neutral species $Pr_{sp,I}$ (*nonuniform discrete distribution*) given by:

$$\mathrm{Pr}_{\mathrm{sp,\ i}} = \frac{n_i}{\sum_{j=1}^{8} n_j} \quad (20)$$

The chosen particle takes randomly three components of space in cell $\mathbf{r}_i(x_i, y_i, z_i)$ according to the *normal distribution (nonuniform distribution)*. It takes also randomly three components of velocity $\mathbf{v}_i$ (vx_i, vy_i, vz_i) according to Maxwell-Boltzmann distribution.

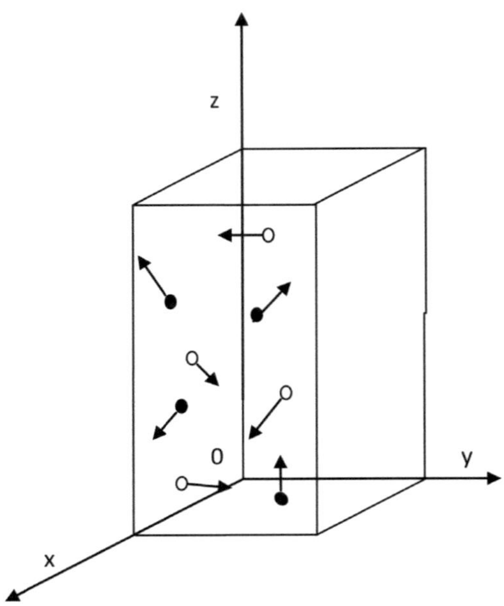

Figure 5.
Form of the simulation cell.

5.2.2 Treatment of elastic and inelastic collisions

Let n_i and n_j be the densities of species *i* and *j* in the gas and V_{ij} the relative velocity between the two species *i* and *j*.

According to the kinetic theory of gases, we have for an incident particle *i* on a target particle j the average collision frequency ν_{ij} as:

$$\upsilon_{ij} = V_{ij} n_j < \sigma_{ij} > \tag{21}$$

where $< s_{ij} >$ is the cross section of the particle *j*.

The mean free path $<\lambda_i>$ of species *i* is:

$$< \lambda_i > = \frac{1}{n_j < \sigma_{ij} >} \tag{22}$$

The time between two collisions τ_{ij} is then:

$$\tau_{ij} = \frac{< \lambda_i >}{V_{ij}} = \frac{1}{\upsilon_{ij}} \tag{23}$$

For chemical effective reactions (inelastic collisions) between two reactive species *i* and *j* giving products *i'* and *j'*, the rate constant reaction verifies [45]:

$$k_{ij} = < \sigma_{ij}(V_{ij}) \cdot V_{ij} > \tag{24}$$

General rules of collision theory are applied:

- The new velocities of the colliding particles are calculated using conservation of energy and momentum for elastic collisions.
- Conservation of total energy as isolated system.
- Movement of the center of mass and relative motion around the center of mass.

The reader can refer to some fundamental physics books that deal with general notions of collisions and corresponding parameters [45–48].

The plasma in the PECVD reactor is weakly ionized. At low temperature, particles interact occasionally with each other and move under the effect of thermal agitation. In reality, only a small fraction of collisions are effective (result in a chemical reaction) [21].

In our MCS, after traveling a random walk given by a Gaussian distribution, the first chosen particle collides with a second particle (molecule, atom, radical, or electron). The last particle *j* is randomly chosen according to a (i-j) collision probability $Pr_{col,j}$ (*nonuniform discrete distribution*) given by:

$$Pr_{col,j} = \frac{\nu_{ij}}{\sum_{k=1}^{9} \nu_{ik}} \tag{25}$$

where ν_{ij} is the neutral-neutral or electron-neutral collisional frequency. The *collision* theory indicates that the *collision* between molecules *can provide* the energy *needed* to *break* the *necessary bonds so* that *new bonds can be formed* [49]. Particles must have sufficient energy to initiate the reaction (activation energy), so the two chosen particles must have kinetic energy equal to or greater than the barrier *energy* (E_a) of a gas phase reaction. The difference between the kinetic energy of the two particles and the activation energy define the kind of collision (effective or not effective).

The activation energy is given by:

$$E_a = -k_B T ln\left(K_{reac}/\nu_{ij}\right) \tag{26}$$

where the pre-exponential factor is assumed to be the collision frequency factor and K_{reac} is the rate constant of the gas phase reaction.

The two colliding particles (e.g., the electron and SiH_4 molecule) can interact by several reactions (R1, R2, R3, and R4 in **Table 1**); we choose randomly one of gas phase reactions occurring according to a, *nonuniform discrete distribution* reaction probability Pr_{reac} (i,j):

$$Pr_{reac}(i,j) = \frac{K_{reac}(i,j)}{\sum K_{reac}(i,j)} \tag{27}$$

where $\sum K_{reac}(i,j)$ is the sum of all rate constants of possible reactions between i and j.

All chemical systems go naturally toward states of minimum Gibbs free energy [21, 24]. A chemical reaction tends to occur in the direction of lower Gibbs free energy. To determine the direction of the reaction that is taking place, we use the old and new values of K_{reac} and the equilibrium constant with reactants and product concentrations. Each set of binary collisions can be related or converted into time. As cited in section (a), **Table 1** gives gas phase reactions and corresponding rate constants used in this MCS.

To continue the simulation, after the elastic collision, particle i takes new values of components velocity and new mean free path; mean free path is taken from a *normal (nonuniform) distribution (Gaussian distribution)*. If the collision is inelastic, we have to take a new particle.

From Metropolis algorithm, the scheme of this MCS is as follows:

a. Choices of particle of spice i with random position, velocity, and mean free path; periodic boundary conditions are used to keep particles in the elementary cell.

b. Choices of random collision with a spice j.

c. Study of collision type (elastic, inelastic). If the collision is elastic the particle i move with a new velocity and mean free path, and we return to step (b). If the collision is inelastic particles i and j give new particles i' and j', according to Metropolis scheme, and we return to step (a) or (b). Periodic boundary conditions are used to keep particles in the elementary cell.

d. At each step, we can note the different statistics.

5.2.3 The choice of simulation parameters

Once the species are selected for the simulation model, an estimate of species densities should be made. Following the model of interaction and collisions between particles (binary, collective, etc.), a first choice of the minimum number N_i of particles of each species is made. A first estimate of the sizes (L_x, L_y, L_z) of the elementary cell is made.

The study of the types of interaction potentials and the calculation of the approximate values of the force ranges, the kinetic energies, the internal energies, and the energies of activation make it possible to correct the minimal numbers N_i of particles and the sizes (L_x, L_y, L_z) of the elementary cell.

Let kp be the number of a species, kp = 1,..., 9. The minimal numbers Qnp(kp) and the sizes (L_x, L_y, L_z) have to be discussed for statistical calculations.

For numerical programming, according to the programming language used and according to the size (or the computational capacity) of the computer, it is necessary to find a judicious choice of the tables of integer or real values and which values would be useful to save all during simulation. Let $N_{col,m}$ be the maximum number of elastic collisions per particle, and let N_{cycle} be the number of cycles to average the simulation calculations.

For this MCS, the numerical chosen values are in **Table 2**.

For radicals (e.g., SiH_3), particle numbers Qnp(k) are very small; we take Qnp (k) = 10. These numbers cannot take value 1 or 0, even if a species k is in trace form in the gas. The value 0 for a species k means that any other species k' does not make a collision with the species k; and the value 1 means that we have no collisions between particles of the same species in the cell.

Qnp1, Qnp5, and Qnp9 are calculated from the volume of cell, the pressure, the temperature, and the total number of particles in the cell (Qnp1 = 0.81187824 * 10^9; Qnp5 = 0.20296956 * 10^9; Qnp9 = 131).

5.2.4 Calculation of statistical properties and some results of the calculations

As we have chosen a stationary regime, we must reach the values and properties at equilibrium. The results of the simulation show this trend. In MCS, averaged values, distribution functions, autocorrelation functions, and correlation functions can be calculated. To ensure rapid convergence of calculations, it would be useful to look for statistically symmetric (or stationary or unsteady) parameters [26, 50].

As an example for our MCS calculation, we have:

- The number of Si_2H_6, SiH, and Si_2H_5 particles reaching the surface is negligible.
- Let $N_{s,i}$ and N_s, H_2 be the densities of a species *i* and H_2 reaching the surface. The ratios $N_{s,i}/N_s$, H_2 are too small (**Table 3**).

Cell dimensions and steps for collisions		Number of species Kp	Initial number of particles in cell	
L_x (m)	4.68 10^{-6}	1	Qnp(SiH_4)	Qnp1
L_y (m)	4.68 10^{-6}	2	Qnp(SiH_3)	10
L_z (m)	20.0 10^{-3}	3	Qnp(SiH_2)	10
		4	Qnp(H)	10
$N_{col,m}$	500	5	Qnp(H_2)	Qnp5
N_{cycle} internal cycle	2000	6	Qnp(Si_2H_6)	10
N_{cycle} external cycle	200,000	7	Qnp(SiH)	10
		8	Qnp(Si_2H_5)	10
		9	Qnp(e)	Qnp9

Table 2.
Used quantities and parameters in calculations for the gas temperature Tg = 520 K.

Type	H_2	SiH_4	H	SiH_3	SiH_2
$N_{s,i}/N_s$, H_2	1	0.23	$1.67\ 10^{-4}$	$8.60\ 10^{-5}$	$9.86\ 10^{-6}$

Table 3.
Ratios $N_{s,i}/N_s$, H_2 of particles reaching the surface compared to H_2.

Type	SiH_4	SiH_3	SiH_2
v, j	$6.695\ 10^{-6}$	$7.965\ 10^{-6}$	$775\ 10^{-6}$

Table 4.
Ratios $N_{s,i}/N_{v,i}$ of particles reaching the surface compared to volume.

- Let $N_{s,i}$ be the density of a species i reaching the surface and $N_{v,i}$ the density of same species i in volume. The ratios $N_{s,i}/N_{v,i}$ are too small (**Table 4**); the surface effect is negligible.

- The reactions begin with the dissociation (consumption) of H_2 and SiH_4 by R5, R1, and R2 reactions.

- The production of SiH_3 is done by R8, and then there is production of SiH_2 by R12.

- The reaction R2: $SiH_4 + e \rightarrow SiH_2 + 2H + e$ plays the central role in SiH_4 dissociation by electron impact [24]. This result is compatible with [39].

- The second important chemical reaction in the SiH_4 dissociation is R1: $SiH_4 + e \rightarrow SiH_3 + H + e$ [24]. This result is compatible with that of Perkins et al. [51] and that of Doyle et al. [52].

6. Conclusions

MCS is a widely used method in statistical physics to study thermodynamic, structural, or phase properties. It is based on random and probabilistic processes. The purpose of this chapter is to present the technique for general use in physics for the study of thin film deposition problems. The technique can be generalized to other fields of science: biology, economics, transportation, and social sciences.

We started by presenting general rules for numerical simulation methods. Metropolis algorithm has been considered as the basic algorithm. After, we presented the different steps for the realization of a MCS code. We chose the particle-particle model MCS (PP-MCS) to explain the different steps and procedures to be applied in the deposition of thin layers by PECVD processes. We have shown that this technique can be generalized to the particle-in-cell MCS (PIC-MCS) case or kinetic MCS (kMCS), as it can be joined with other modules to give hybrid models. It is important to know how to choose random configurations from the laws or probability distributions in the system.

A numerical application is presented for collisions in a SiH_4/H_2 gas mixture in the PECVD process. A preliminary work of determination of the chemical reactions between molecules and radicals is made. A choice of the simulation cell is made, and the definition of the probabilities of the collisions between peers is made. The Metropolis algorithm makes it possible to follow the various elastic and inelastic collisions; it also makes it possible to make the statistics of the interactions with the surface. The results are compatible with [39, 51, 52].

Other questions may be asked to account for molecular ions, surface and volume kinetics, or thin film formation. The techniques and different models of the MCS (PP-MCS, MCS-PIC, kMCS) allow taking care of these questions.

The interconnection of the MCS with other models (MDS, hybrid model, fluid model, electromagnetic model, etc.) would allow answering more questions. The methods can be applied to other specialties than the physical sciences.

Author details

Fethi Khelfaoui* and Oumelkheir Babahani
Physics Department, RPPS Laboratory, Faculty of Mathematics and Matter Sciences, Kasdi Merbah Ouargla University, Algeria

*Address all correspondence to: fethi.khelfaoui@gmail.com; khelfaoui.fe@univ-ouargla.dz

References

[1] Metropolis N, Rosenbluth AW, Rosenbluth MN, Teller AH, Teller E. Equation of state calculations by fast computing machines. The Journal of Chemical Physics. 1953;**21**:1087-1092. DOI: 10.1063/1.1699114

[2] Wood WW, Parker FR. Monte Carlo equation of state of molecules interacting with the Lennard-Jones potential. The Journal of Chemical Physics. 1957;**27**: 720-733. DOI: 10.1063/1.1743822

[3] Bridgman PW. Compressibilities and electrical resistance under pressure, with special reference to intermetallic compounds. Proceedings of the American Academy of Arts and Sciences. 1935;**70**:285-317. DOI: 10.2307/20023138

[4] Michels A, Wijker H, Wijker HK. Isotherms of argon between 0°C and 150°C and pressures up to 2900 atmospheres. Physica. 1949;**15**:627-632. DOI: 10.1016/0031-8914(49)90119-6

[5] Alder BJ, Wainwright TE. Phase transition for a hard sphere system. The Journal of Chemical Physics. 1957;**27**: 1208. DOI: 10.1063/1.1743957

[6] Alder BJ, Wainwright TE. Studies in molecular dynamics. I. General method. The Journal of Chemical Physics. 1959;**31**:459-466. DOI: 10.1063/1.1730376

[7] Verlet L. Computer "experiments" on classical fluids. I. Thermodynamical properties of Lennard-Jones molecules. Physics Review. 1967;**159**:98-103. DOI: 10.1103/PhysRev.159.98

[8] Wong J, Kherani NP, Zukotynski S. Monte Carlo modeling of the dc saddle field plasma: Discharge characteristics of N_2 and SiH_4. Journal of Applied Physics. 2007;**101**:013308-013314. DOI: 10.1063/1.2409566

[9] Matsuda A, Nomoto K, Takeuchi Y, Suzuki A, Yuuki A, Perrin J. Temperature dependence of the sticking and loss probabilities of silyl radicals on hydrogenated amorphous silicon. Surface Science. 1990;**227**:50-56. DOI: 10.1016/0039-6028(90)90390-T

[10] Gorbachev YE, Zetevakhin MA, Krzhizhanovskaya VV, Shveïgert VA. Special features of the growth of hydrogenated amorphous silicon in PECVD reactors. Journal of Technical Physics. 2000;**45**:1032-1041. DOI: 10.1134/1.1307013

[11] Gorbachev YE. Effect of oligomers on the growth of amorphous silicon films in a PECVD reactor. Technical Physics. 2006;**51**:733-739. DOI: 10.1134/S1063784206060089

[12] Gorbachev YE, Zetevakhin MA, Kaganovich ID. Simulation of the growth of hydrogenated amorphous silicon films from an RF discharge plasma. Journal of Technical Physics. 1996;**41**:1247-1258

[13] Valipa MS, Aydil ES, Maroudas D. Atomistic calculation of the SiH_3 surface reactivity during plasma deposition of amorphous silicon thin films. Surface Science. 2004;**572**:L339-L347. DOI: 10.1016/j.susc.2004.08.029

[14] Graves DB, Brault P. Molecular dynamics for low temperature plasma-surface interaction studies. Journal of Physics D. 2009;**42**:1-27. DOI: 10.1088/0022-3727/42/19/194011

[15] Pandey SC, Singh T, Maroudas D. Kinetic Monte Carlo simulations of surface growth during plasma deposition of silicon thin films. The Journal of Chemical Physics. 2009;**131**: 1-12. DOI: 10.1063/1.3152846

[16] Rodgers WJ, May PW, Allan NL, Harvey JN. Three-dimensional kinetic Monte Carlo simulations of diamond chemical vapor deposition. The Journal

of Chemical Physics. 2015;**142**:214707. DOI: 10.1063/1.4921540

[17] Battaile CC, Srolovitz DJ. Kinetic Monte Carlo simulation of chemical vapor deposition. Annual Review of Materials Research. 2002;**32**:297-319. DOI: 10.1146/annurev.matsci.32.012102.110247

[18] YangY G, ZhouX W, Johnson RA, Wadlty HNG. Monte Carlo simulation of hyperthermal physical vapor deposition. Acta Materialia. 2001;**49**: 3321-3332. DOI: 10.1016/S1359-6454(01)00139-2

[19] Chen Z-Y, Zhu Y, Chen S-H, Qiu Z-R, Jiang S-J. The kinetic process of non-smooth substrate thin film growth via parallel Monte Carlo method. Applied Surface Science. 2011;**257**:6102-6106. DOI: 10.1016/j.apsusc.2011.02.004

[20] Babahani O, Khelfaoui F, Meftah MT. Analytical calculation of site and surface reaction probabilities of SiH_x radicals in PECVD process. The European Physical Journal Applied Physics. 2013;**62**:10301-10307. DOI: 10.1051/epjap/2013120345

[21] Babahani O. Simulation numérique par la méthode de Monte Carlo de la déposition de couches minces par procédés CVD [thesis]. Ouargla: Kasdi Merbah Ouargla University; 2013

[22] Kebaili HO, Babahani O, Khelfaoui F. Simulation par la dynamique moléculaire de l'interaction plasma-surface lors de la croissance de couches minces a-Si:H par procédés PECVD. Annales des Sciences et Technologie. 2014;**6**:165-171

[23] Babahani O, Khelfaoui F. Simulation Monte Carlo de réactions chimiques dans le volume d'un réacteur PECVD lors de déposition d'une couche mince a-C:H. Annales des Sciences et Technologie. 2014;**6**:156-164

[24] Babahani O, Hadjadj S, Khelfaoui F, Kebaili HO, Lemkeddem S. Monte Carlo simulation of chemical reactions in plasma enhanced chemical vapor deposition: From microscopic view to macroscopic results. Silicon. 2019;**11**: 1267-1274. DOI: 10.1007/s12633-018-9916-y

[25] Babahani O, Khelfaoui F. Calcul des concentrations de molécules et de radicaux lors de déposition de couches minces a-Si:H par procédés PECVD. Annales des Sciences et Technologie. 2012;**4**:115-120

[26] Landau DP, Binder K. A Guide to Monte Carlo Simulations in Statistical Physics. Cambridge University Press; 2009. DOI: 10.1017/CBO9780511994944

[27] Murthy KPN. An Introduction to Monte Carlo Simulations in Statistical Physics. Tamilnadu, India: Indira Gandhi Centre for Atomic Research; 2003

[28] Gould H, Tobochnik J. An Introduction to Computer Simulation Methods: Applications to Physical Systems, Part 2. Addisson-Wesley Publishing Company; 2006. ISBN-10: 0805377581

[29] Hansen JP, Mc Donald IR. Theory of Simple Liquids. London: Academic Press; 1976. 428 p. ISBN: 97800804 55075

[30] Born M, Von Karman T. Reappraising 1907 Einstein's model of specific heat. Physikalishce Zeitschrift. 1912;**13**:297-309

[31] Mattei S, Nishida K, Onai M, Lettry J, Tran MQ, Hatayama A. A fully-implicit particle-In-cell Monte Carlo collision code for the simulation of inductively coupled plasmas. Journal of Computational Physics. 2017;**350**: 891-906. DOI: 10.1016/j.jcp.2017.09.015

[32] Hockney RW, Eastwood JW. Computer Simulation Using Particles. IOP Publishing Ltd; 1988

[33] Mao M, Bogaerts A. Investigating the plasma chemistry for the synthesis of carbon nanotubes/nanofibers in an inductively coupled plasma enhanced CVD system: Effect of different gas mixtures. Journal of Physics D: Applied Physics. 2010;**43**:205201. DOI: 10.1088/0022-3727/43/20/205201

[34] Battaile CC, Srolovitz DJ. A kinetic Monte Carlo method for the atomic-scale simulation of chemical vapor deposition: Application to diamond. Journal of Applied Physics. 1997;**82**: 6293. DOI: 10.1063/1.366532

[35] Lothar K, Kuhn Frank M, Olaf D. Kinetic Monte Carlo simulations of surface reactions on supported nanoparticles: A novel approach and computer code. The Journal of Chemical Physics. 2015;**143**:044108. DOI: 10.1063/1.4926924

[36] May PW, Harvey JN, Allan NL, Richley JC, Mankelevich Yu A. Simulations of chemical vapor deposition diamond film growth using a kinetic Monte Carlo model and two dimensional models of microwave plasma and hot filament chemical vapor deposition reactors. Journal of Applied Physics. 2010;**108**:114909. DOI: 10.1063/1.3516498

[37] Harris SJ. Mechanism for diamond growth from methyl radicals. Applied Physics Letters. 1990;**56**:2298. DOI: 10.1063/1.102946

[38] May PW, Harvey JN, Allan NL, Richley JC, Mankelevich Yu A. Simulations of chemical vapor deposition diamond film growth using a kinetic Monte Carlo model. Journal of Applied Physics. 2010;**108**:014905. DOI: 10.1063/1.3437647

[39] Aman-ur-Rehman, Kwon HC, Park WT, Lee JK. A study of the role of various reactions on the density distribution of hydrogen, silylene, and silyl in SiH_4/H_2 plasma discharges. Physics of Plasmas. 2011;**18**:093502. DOI: 10.1063/1.3630933

[40] Moravej M, Babayan SE, Nowling GR, Yang X, Hicks RF. Plasma enhanced chemical vapour deposition of hydrogenated amorphous silicon at atmospheric pressure. Science and Technology. 2004;**13**:8-14

[41] Hoefnagels JPM, Barrell Y, Kessels WMM, Van de Sanden MCM. Inflow and shock formation in supersonic, rarefied plasma expansions. Journal of Applied Physics. 2004;**96**: 4094

[42] Gorbachev YE, Zatevakhin MA, Krzhizhanovskaya VV, Shveigert VA. Special features of the growth of hydrogenated amorphous silicon in PECVD reactors. Technical Physics. 2000;**45**:1032-1041. DOI: 10.1134/1.1307013

[43] Perrin J, Leroy O, Bordage MC. Cross-sections, rate constants and transport coefficients in silane plasma chemistry. Contributions to Plasma Physics. 1996;**36**:3-49. DOI: 10.1002/ctpp.2150360102

[44] Amanatides E, Stamou S, Mataras D. Gas phase and surface kinetics in plasma enhanced chemical vapor deposition of microcrystalline silicon: The combined effect of RF power and hydrogen dilution. Journal of Applied Physics. 2001;**90**:5786-5798. DOI: 10.1063/1.1413241

[45] Moison M, Pelletier J. Physique Des Plasmas Collisionnels: Application Aux décharges Haute fréquence. France: EDP Sciences; 2006

[46] Delcroix J-L, Bers A. Physique Des Plasmas 1. Paris: Inter Editions/CNRS Editions; 1994

[47] Atkins PW, de Paula J. Chimie Physique. 4th ed. De Boeck; 2015. 973 p. ISBN-10: 2804166511

[48] Atkins PW. Eléments de Chimie Physique. De Boeck Université; 1998. 512 p. ISBN-10: 2744500100

[49] Moore JT, Hren C, Mikulecky PJ. U Can: Chemistry I for Dummies. Wiley; 2015. 456 p. ISBN: 978-1-119-07940-8

[50] Allen MP, Tildesley DJ. Computer Simulation of Liquids. Oxford: Clarendon Press; 1987

[51] Perkins GGA, Austin ER, Lampe FW. The 147-nm photolysis of monosilane. Journal of the American Chemical Society. 1979;**101**:1109-1115

[52] Doyle JR, Doughty DA, Gallagher A. Silane dissociation products in deposition discharges. Journal of Applied Physics. 1990;**68**:4375

Chapter 6

Application of Local Information Entropy in Cluster Monte Carlo Algorithms

Artur Chrobak, Grzegorz Ziółkowski and Dariusz Chrobak

Abstract

The chapter refers to a modification of the so-called adding probability used in cluster Monte Carlo algorithms. The modification is based on the fact that in real systems, different properties can influence its clusterization. Finally, an additional factor related to property disorder was introduced into the adding probability, which leads to more effective free energy minimization during MC iteration. As a measure of the disorder, we proposed to use a local information entropy. The proposed approach was tested and compared with the classical methods, showing its high efficiency in simulations of multiphase magnetic systems where magnetic anisotropy was used as the property influencing the system clusterization.

Keywords: Monte Carlo simulations, cluster Monte Carlo methods, magnetic simulations, entropy methods, ultra-high coercive alloys

1. Introduction

The problem of simulation magnetization processes of multiphase magnetic materials seems to be important, regarding the tendency for applications of high-efficient permanent magnets with reduced or without rare earth elements. Recently, we reported unique hard magnetic properties of Tb-Fe-B-Nb bulk alloys, i.e., coercive field over 7 T at room temperature, attributed to a specific micro-structure of dendrite-like $Tb_2Fe_{14}B$ grains [1, 2]. In this system, Tb and Fe magnetic moments are coupled antiferromagnetically, which is responsible for relatively low magnetic remanence ($\mu_0 M_r \approx 0.3$ T) and in consequence $|BH|_{max}$ (about 13 kJ/m^3). However, the Fe-Nb-B-Tb bulk alloys can be considered as a material with extremely high resistance to the external magnetic field and can be a source of magnetic anisotropy in powders as well as bulk spring-exchange composites containing magnetically soft and ultra-high coercive phases. For this reason, the ability of simulating of such systems is very useful in the process of examining and designing of spring-exchange composites in the pre-lab phase.

Monte Carlo (MC) algorithms are now widely used to clarify various physical phenomena, as well as to investigate their potential application in modern technology. Among many simulation methods, the Metropolis MC (MMC) approach [3, 4] is especially attractive in statistical physics for the determination of system physical quantities in thermodynamic equilibrium. The MMC algorithm realizes an ergodic stochastic process, ensuring the fulfillment of the detailed balance condition.

One of the bright examples of the application of the MMC algorithm is the Ising model of spins located on the nodes of some lattice. Indeed, using this method one can study a course of magnetic ordering and its dependence of temperature and details of interactions between the spins.

The MMC method utilizes the single-spin-flip procedure to change the spin configuration; however, in many cases (e.g., simulations of magnetization processes) a more effective algorithm is needed. The simplest approach relies on the generation of a cluster of uniformly oriented spins and their subsequent flip to reach new state of the system. The main question is how to determine the cluster and how to establish a rule of its acceptance, simultaneously satisfying the detailed balance condition. Classical approaches, based on the Kasteleyn-Fortuin theorem [5, 6], were proposed by Swendsen and Wang (SW) [7] as well as by Wolff [8] who assumed a specific cluster-building procedure controlled by the so-called adding probability. It is known that the cluster Monte Carlo methods (CMC) are very efficient in the analysis of critical phenomena, e.g., transformation from ferromagnetic to paramagnetic phase [9, 10]. In contrast, their application for studying magnetization processes of systems far below the Curie point produces artificial results, which can be demonstrated for the systems containing magnetically different phases (e.g., hard and soft) as well as geometrical irregularities. The cluster-building algorithms implemented within SW and Wolf approaches are steered by the exchange interactions and the system temperature, but they are not sensitive to other features, potentially affecting the clusterization of spins.

In order to broaden the applications of the CMC methods to simulations of real magnetic composites, we proposed a new method based on some modification of the SW/Wolff adding probability and a particular Metropolis-like algorithm, ensuring the principle of detailed balance [11]. The idea is based on the fact that some kind of regions of the system, characterized by a local disorder of selected system property, constitutes natural barriers for the extension of clusters. In the case of magnetic multiphase composites, spatial distribution of the magnetic anisotropy can be considered as the property affecting the cluster formation.

In the chapter, the disorder-based CMC algorithm is introduced and discussed in a context of classical CMC methods. We show that the new simulation procedure is efficient leading to physically reliable results, especially for multiphase magnetic composites.

2. Local disorder-based CMC method

Let the considered physical system be characterized by a discrete spectrum of microscopic energy states (microstates) labeled by E_α. Furthermore, let the system be in equilibrium with a thermostat having a temperature T. According to basic principles of statistical mechanics, the probability that the system occupies the state α is proportional to the Boltzmann factor: $\exp(-\beta E_\alpha)$, where $\beta = 1/k_B T$, k_B refers to the Boltzmann constants. Then, the equilibrium value of some system quantity (observable) F can be calculated using the following formula [12, 13]:

$$\overline{F} = \frac{1}{Z} \sum_\alpha F_\alpha \exp(-\beta E_\alpha), \qquad (1)$$

where $Z = \sum_\alpha \exp(-\beta E_\alpha)$ is the partition function. The direct use of Eq. (1) is impractical due to a very large number of states that should be taken into account. Indeed, even for small systems as, for example, a two-dimensional 10×10 lattice of spins, we get a total of 2^{100} states—the number that makes the summation occurring in Eq. (1) impossible.

In order to estimate the average $\acute{}F$, a nonuniform sampling of the system states can be applied. If $\{\alpha\}$ denotes a set of indices of M system states selected with the probability p_α, the equilibrium value of the observable F can be modeled [13] by the estimator:

$$F_S = \frac{\sum_{\{\alpha\}} F_\alpha \exp\left(-\beta E_\alpha\right) p_\alpha^{-1}}{\sum_{\{\alpha\}} \exp\left(-\beta E_\alpha\right) p_\alpha^{-1}} = \frac{1}{N} \sum_{\{\alpha\}} F_\alpha, \tag{2}$$

where probabilities p_α were selected to be equal $\exp\left(-\beta E_\alpha\right)/Z$. All we need is a method that generates a set of system states with the Boltzmann probabilities p_α. Because the exact value of the partition function Z is unknown, the generation of the states is usually carried out by the ergodic Markov process. This process produces a proper chain of states under the assumption that transition probability $W_{\alpha\beta}$ (from α to β state) is independent of the states preceding α. Moreover, It is also assumed that the detailed balance condition, $p_\beta W_{\beta\alpha} = p_\alpha W_{\alpha\beta}$, is satisfied when the system is in a state of equilibrium [12–15].

The transition probability $W_{\alpha\beta}$ can be considered as a product of the selection probability $g_{\alpha\beta}$ and the acceptance ratio (probability)$A_{\alpha\beta}$. In general, the selection probabilities can be chosen to a large extent freely, e.g., they can be symmetrical $g_{\alpha\beta} = g_{\beta\alpha}$ [12]. In that case the acceptance probabilities satisfy the equation:

$$A_{\alpha\beta}/A_{\beta\alpha} = \exp\left(-\beta\left(E_\beta - E_\alpha\right)\right) \tag{3}$$

As an example, let us consider Ising model of N interacting spins placed at the nodes of a two-dimensional regular. The energy of the system is, then, given by the formula

$$E = -J \sum_{i \neq j = 1}^{N} s_i s_j \tag{4}$$

where $s_i = \pm 1$ describes the spin state at the ith lattice node and J refers to the exchange integral. In order to determine the physical properties of our magnetic system, the Metropolis algorithm can be employed. It relies on the particular choice of both the selection probability and the acceptance ratio. Having some configuration of spins, the next one is obtained by the flip of a single spin (*single-spin-flip algorithm*) [12, 13]. This procedure results in uniform distribution of the selection probabilities, i.e., each new state participates in simulations with probability $g_{\alpha\beta} = 1/N$. Then, the new spin configuration can be accepted or rejected with an acceptance ratio $A_{\alpha\beta} = \exp\left(-\beta\left(E_\beta - E_\alpha\right)\right)$ (for $E_\beta - E_\alpha > 0$) and $A_{\alpha\beta} = 1$ (for all other cases). Although the Metropolis algorithm can be applied to a variety of physical problems, when applied to magnetic systems, it has disadvantage that relies on a very rapid increase of the correlation time as well as correlation length near the critical point. As a result the system contains domains of the same oriented spins and therefore becomes configurationally frozen. This unexpected behavior (*critical slowing down*) of the Metropolis algorithm is the reason for the difficulties in the generation of statistically independent spin configurations that are needed for the calculation of the estimator F_S.

The solution of the critical slowing down problem was proposed by Swendsen-Wang [7] and later by Wolff [8]. The approach developed by Wolf (*cluster-flipping algorithm*) based on the generation of the uniformly oriented spin cluster and its subsequent flipping [12]. In contrast to single-spin-flip algorithm, this procedure easily destroys domains of correlated spins and allows the system to walk through the configuration space. The Wolff algorithm is recognized to be more effective than the Swendsen-Wang one [16–18]. The selection of a spin cluster starts from randomly chosen spin to which the neighbors occupying the same spin state are added with the probability P_{add}. The cluster grows up until no spin is added to it. It is a great advantage that the Wolff algorithm is a rejection-free one. Indeed, adding probability P_{add} is defined so that the detailed balance condition (with acceptance ratio equal to one) is met:

$$P_{add} = 1 - \exp(-2\beta J) \tag{5}$$

Despite the great achievements, the Wolff model is not able to correctly simulate magnetic phenomena that occur far below the critical point in real magnetic materials, including those that are composed of various magnetic phases as well as those containing geometrical irregularities. To be more precise, one can consider, as an example, remagnetization of the system build of two magnetically hard and soft ferromagnetic spheres coupled by a narrow bridge. Let us assume that in the initial state, the magnetization of the system is collinear with the direction of the external magnetic field and then the magnetic field is switched in the opposite direction. What happens to the system is that the magnetization of the soft sphere will follow the change of the magnetic, and then the similar behavior of the hard sphere is expected. Unfortunately, for systems with strong spin-spin coupling, the two-step behavior of the considered system cannot be modeled using Wolff clusterization algorithm. Indeed, every attempt to build a cluster within the two-sphere magnetic system results in that the hard and soft spheres belong to the same cluster independently on magnetic anisotropy and geometry of the system. So, even if the two-step remagnetization process is energetically preferred, the simulated magnetization curve consists of one step related to the common spin rotation. Taking into account the problems encountered during modeling the remagnetization of magnetically inhomogeneous system, we propose a modification of the Wolff algorithm that relies on an assumption that some regions of the system, characterized by a disorder of selected system property, can serve barriers for an extension of magnetic clusters.

We began from the introduction a distribution of system property K that can refer, for example, magnetic anisotropy or some other properties potentially affecting the clusterization of the system. Let us define a sphere V around a node of the spin lattice—the sphere containing N nodes in total. Furthermore, let the system property be characterized by a discrete and finite set of values: $K_1, K_2, ..., K_{N_K}$. The local distribution of the K system property is defined by the numbers $\{n_i\} = \{n_1, n_2, ..., n_{N_K}\}$, where n_i stands for the number of nodes having the value K_i. The sum overall is n_i equals N. Thus, the particular K-state of the sphere V is defined by the set of numbers $\{n_i\}$. The number of possible realizations of the K-state denoted by $\Omega_{\{n_i\}}$ is given by the expression

$$\Omega_{\{n_i\}} = \frac{N!}{n_1!n_2!...n_{N_K}!} \tag{6}$$

Using the Stirling formula, the previous equation takes the form

$$\ln\left(\Omega_{\{n_i\}}\right) \approx -N\sum_{i=1}^{N_K} p_i \ln\left(p_i\right) \tag{7}$$

where $p_i = N_i/N$ stands for the probability of finding K_i value inside the sphere V. The expression on the right side of Eq. (7) contains the term called *local information entropy* [19]:

$$S^{loc}_{\{n_i\}} = -\sum_{i=1}^{N_K} p_i \ln (p_i) \tag{8}$$

So the number of "microstates" corresponding to the K-state is

$$\Omega_{\{n_i\}} \approx \exp \left(NS^{loc}_{\{n_i\}}\right) \tag{9}$$

The probability of particular local distribution $\{n_i\}$ of the system property K is proportional to $\Omega_{\{n_i\}}$. If the only one value of K dominates its distribution inside the sphere V, e.g., $\{\mathrm{N}, 0, ...0\}$, the local information entropy achieves the lowest value $S^{loc} = 0$. Other local distribution $\{n_i\}$ that involves more than one value of K results in $S^{loc} > 0$.

Now we can introduce the perception of *local disorder* of the K system property and its measure p_K. We will say that the K system property is fully ordered inside the sphere V if all the nodes inside the sphere have the same value of K. Consequently, one can say that the sphere V exhibits some local disorder of K if more values of K are distributed inside the sphere. The measure of the local disorder can be defined by as follows:

$$p_K = \exp \left(-S^{loc}\right) \tag{10}$$

which gives $p_K = 1$ if the case of fully ordered system property ($S^{loc} = 0$). One can see that p_K decreases when local disorder of K system property increases ($S^{loc} > 0$).

We assume that local disorder of K system property decreases the probability of cluster growth and constitutes barriers for cluster expansion. Thus, one could expect nonuniform distribution of adding probability P'_{add} among the system nodes. In order to derive a reasonable formula for P'_{add}, we follow an analogy with derivation of the van der Waals equation. Our "ideal gas" corresponds to the uniform distribution of adding probability given by Wolff algorithm, while "real gas" refers to the case when the distribution of adding probability is affected by local disorder of some system property. In order to still play with Wolf algorithm, an influence of local disorder should be compensated in some way, e.g., by multiplication P'_{add} by p_k^{-1}. Then, assuming that this product satisfies the Wolff's formula $P'_{add} \exp \left(S^{loc}\right) = 1 - \exp (-2\beta J)$, the adding probability that takes into account the impact of local disorder of some system property can be easily obtained:

$$P'_{add} = [1 - \exp (-2\beta J)] \exp \left(-\alpha S^{loc}\right) \tag{11}$$

The above equation is the clue of our method which expresses the decrease of the classical adding probability by the disorder-based factor. A set of property, for which the disorder is determined (by the local information entropy), should be chosen dependently on a specific application. The α parameter expresses some enhancement or weakness of the influence of the entropy on the system clusterization. It should be defined regarding the specific problem (see next paragraphs).

3. Simulation procedure

The main simulation procedure consists of a series of Monte Carlo steps, and it is based on the classical Metropolis algorithm applied to the so-called spin continuous approach. However, the main difference lies in the cluster-building procedure which is executed with a small probability P_{cl}, as shown in **Figure 1**.

First of all, a random node i of the system is chosen, and then it is decided, regarding the probability P_{cl}, whether to analyze the selected node or build a cluster, starting from the node as a seed. In the first case, the algorithm goes to the typical Metropolis procedure and spin continuous method, i.e., the spin direction is randomly modified by angle $\pm\theta$, and then the energy difference ΔE between the new and the old configuration is calculated. The energy of the system is computed in the frame of the 3D Heisenberg model:

$$E = -\sum_{i,j} J_{ij} S_i \cdot S_j - \sum_i K_i (S_i \cdot n_i)^2 - g\mu_B\mu_0 \sum_i H_i \cdot S_i + D \sum_{i,j} \frac{S_i \cdot S_j - 3(S_i \cdot e_{ij})(S_j \cdot e_{ij})}{r_{ij}^3} \quad (12)$$

where J_{ij} is the exchange parameter, S_i is the spin vector on site i, K_i is the anisotropy constant (per site), n_i is the easy magnetization axis, g is the Lande factor, μ_B is the Bohr magneton, μ_0 is the vacuum permeability, H_i is the magnetic field on site i, D is the dipolar constant, e_{ij} is the directional versor between the ith and jth nodes, and r_{ij} is the distance between the ith and jth nodes. The change is accepted with the Metropolis acceptance probability. In the second case, the algorithm is similar; however, it is necessary to find a cluster around the selected node and, if it exists, carry out a coherent rotation of all spins belonging to the cluster. The

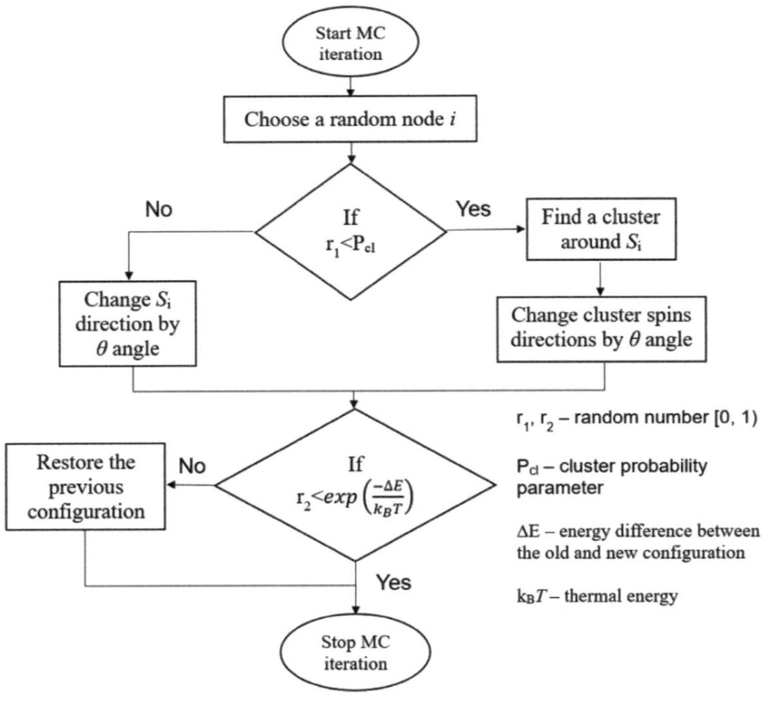

Figure 1.
Schematic diagram of the used algorithm.

procedure of the cluster building is the key and important point. We used the Wolff algorithm but with the modified adding probability P'_{add} expressed by the formula

$$P'_{add} = \left[1 - \exp\left(-\beta E_{coupling}\right)\right] \exp\left(-\alpha S^{loc}\right) \tag{13}$$

where E_{coupling} is the exchange interaction energy between the neighboring spins.

The local information entropy is computed in the defined sphere around each node. In general, the choice of properties (used in the entropy calculation) will depend on the problem being considered; however, for magnetic systems, the natural limit of cluster growth is the change in the value and direction of magnetic anisotropy K. Therefore, an optimal feature is a set of three components $[K_x, K_y, K_z]$, whereby the nonmagnetic nodes do not participate in the entropy calculations. In addition, at the beginning of each cluster-building procedure, the α coefficient is drawn that will weaken ($\alpha < 1$) or strengthen ($\alpha > 1$) the influence of a local property disorder on the system clusterization. Moreover, it is recommended that from time to time (typically about 20% cases), it completely ignores the impact of disorder and builds a cluster based on the standard Wolff method.

The presented algorithm gives some freedom of the cluster building for which the thermodynamic balance is fulfilled. Indeed, even if the cluster rotation slightly disturbs the balance, the remaining single-spin MCM iterations restore it again. The only condition is that the P_{cl} and θ values are relatively low (it can be determined experimentally for cases when the results do not depend on the parameters).

Parameter	Description	Recommendation and notes
θ	The angle at which the direction of the spin or cluster can be changed in a single iteration	Note, it affects the energy changes in a single step. A large θ value will freeze the system, while the small will make it very loose as well as more iterations will be needed to obtain the same change
P_{cl}	Probability of cluster analysis instead of spin in a single iteration	If many independent clusters in the system are expected, then the value of the parameter should be raised to give everyone a chance to be analyzed. However, high values may destroy the thermodynamic equilibrium
S_{range}	The range of local information entropy	The range of local entropy should be selected depending on the geometry of the system. The larger range increases the chance to separation between the magnetic grains and a small common area
N_{iter}	The number of iterations contained in one MC step	Typically, we suggest N_{iter} = 3 N where N is the number of all spins in the system
N_{step}	The number of MC steps used to calculate the average spin of the system $<S_Z>$	We propose N_{step} = 400
α	Modifier of the impact of local information entropy	For $\alpha < 1$ and for $\alpha > 1$, the S_{loc} impact will be depressed and strengthened, respectively. The best approach is to draw an α value before each cluster search
P_{Wolff}	The probability of searching for a cluster based only on the Wolff method	In some cases, you can build a cluster ignoring the impact of local entropy. Typically, we suggest P_{Wolff} = 0.2

Table 1.
A guide of the parameters used in the algorithm.

Finally, one MC step consists of N_{iter} iterations presented in **Figure 1**, and the N_{step} steps are taken to obtain the magnetization of the system $<S_z>$ (the average spin in the external field direction).

The most important parameters of the algorithm, their possible values as well as our recommendations from a practical point of view are summarized in **Table 1**.

The algorithm can be, in some aspects, paralleled [20–23]. The main limitations of the parallelization process are due to three reasons. First of all, each step in the Monte Carlo procedure should be based on the system modified in the previous step. In particular, the decision to accept the new spin direction depends on the current direction of the neighboring spins due to the exchange energy. Consequently, a situation in which different threads are testing a new configuration for the two neighboring spins at the same time should be refused. Similarly, simultaneous analysis of the whole cluster and individual spins inside it (as well as spins interacting with it) is not allowed. The second thing to keep in mind is to ensure that each state of the system can be selected with the same probability. This means that none of the actions can interfere with the probability of choosing a spin for analysis. For example, the spin cannot be temporarily omitted in the draw as well as the analyzed cluster must always be found in the real time and cannot be taken from a fixed database. Finally, it should be taken into account that a change of the spin direction inside a cluster, which is constructed based on the P'_{add} probability, may disrupt the thermodynamic balance of the system. Therefore, from the statistical point of view, after each change of the cluster spins, there should be many iterations analyzing single spins in the cluster and whole system.

Despite all the above restrictions, there are three time-consuming problems in the algorithm which can be parallelized: the main MC loop, the calculation of cluster energy as well as the cluster-building procedure around the chosen spin. Our experience shows that the parallelization of the algorithm accelerates the computation time

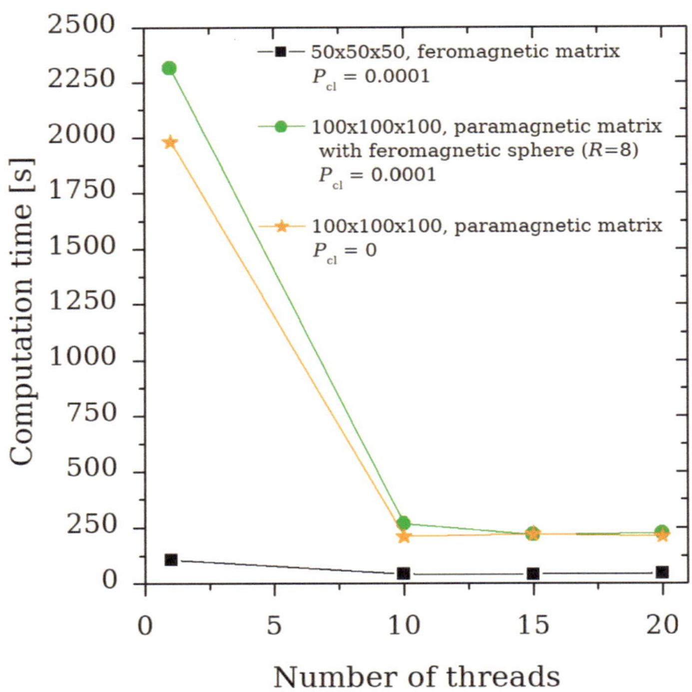

Figure 2.
Comparison of computation time (400 MC steps) for different P_{cl}, system size, and its magnetic properties.

more than 10 times (depending on the probability of cluster analysis and the system size) and maintains the correctness of results. **Figure 2** shows a comparison of computation time (needed for 400 MC steps) for different P_{cl}, system size, and its magnetic properties. On this graph, the independent quantity is a number of threads applied for the simulations (HP ProLiant DL580 G7, 4x Intel Xeon 8C X7560 2.27 GHz).

Generally, this aspect of calculations is very complex. Nevertheless, one can conclude that the parallelization is more effective for the systems with small number of the cluster-building trials.

4. Application of the method to multiphase magnetic systems

In order to show an efficiency of the disorder-based cluster MC algorithm and its comparison with the classical Wolff method, the two systems containing magnetically hard and soft phases were analyzed. The 3D system space consists of $50 \times 50 \times 50$ (1,25,000) nodes; the spins are arranged in shapes of joined spheres with hard and soft magnetic properties. The bonding between the spheres, further called "bridges," is different for the two cases, and it equals 1 or 7 nodes, receptively. **Figure 3** depicts an example of the system with one-bridge coupling between the hard and soft spheres. The parameters of the magnetic phases and simulation procedure are listed in **Table 2**.

The difference between classical and disorder-based approaches lies in the definition of adding probability. It can be demonstrated by the cluster-building

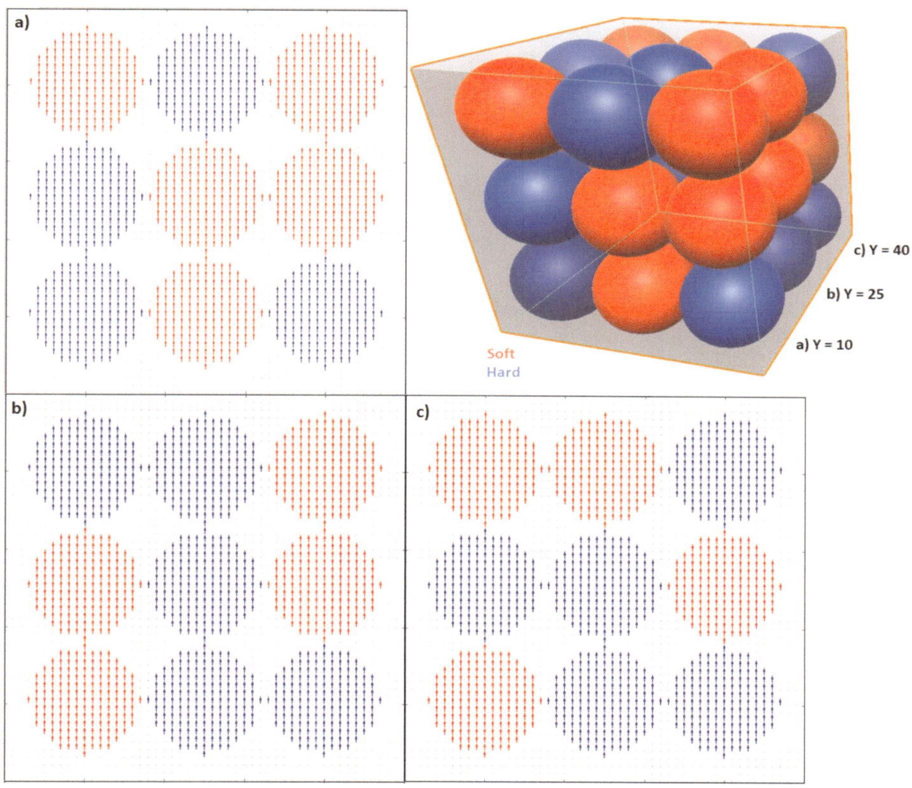

Figure 3.
Example of the system with one-bridge coupling between the hard and soft spheres. The graphs on the right show cross sections (z-x plane) for different y values equal to 10 (a), 25 (b) and 40 (c).

Parameter	Soft phase	Hard phase
Exchange coupling J	1.5e–2 eV	1.5e–2 eV
Anisotropy constant K	0	1e–3 eV
	Simulation procedure	
Dipolar constant D	1.8e–7 eV	
Thermal energy k_BT	1e–4, 1 e–5, 1e–6 eV	
α parameter	Random value from 0 to 25	
Cluster analysis probability P_{cl}	10^{-3}	
Range of the entropy S_{range}	±3 nodes	
Spin change angle θ	π/100	
System size (in one direction) n	50	
Number of iteration in one MC step	$3n^3$ = 3,75,000	
Number of MC steps for magnetization averaging	400	

Table 2.
Parameters of the analyzed systems and simulation procedure.

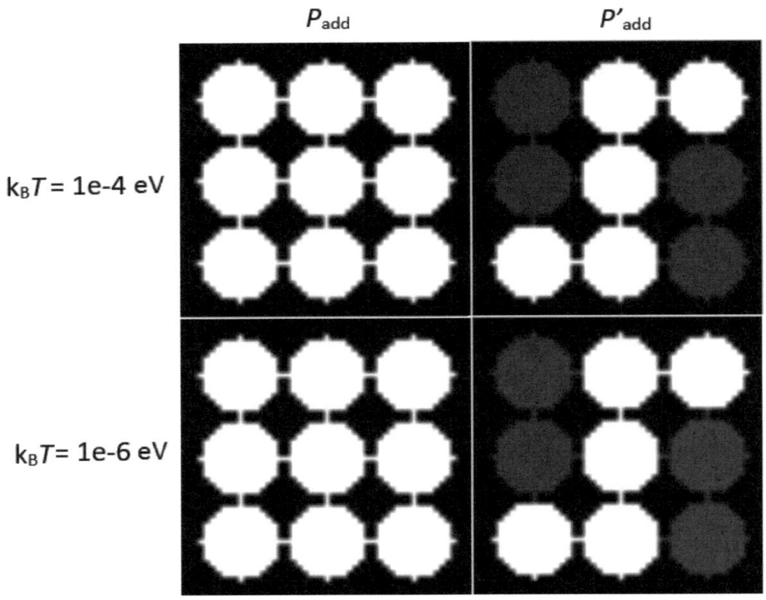

Figure 4.
Comparison of the adding probabilities for the one-bridge system.

successes when the procedure starts from the same cluster "seed." **Figures 4** and **5** show the comparison for the one- and seven-bridge systems, respectively. The cluster seed is placed in the center, and the white color is attributed to 100 cluster-building successes per 100 trials.

As shown, using the classical Wolff algorithm, all spins in the system belong to the same cluster independently on their magnetic properties. This means that during simulations, a possibility of closing the clusters inside the hard or soft phase is not available. The modification of adding probability causes that the cluster-building procedure can distinguish the hard and soft phase with relatively high

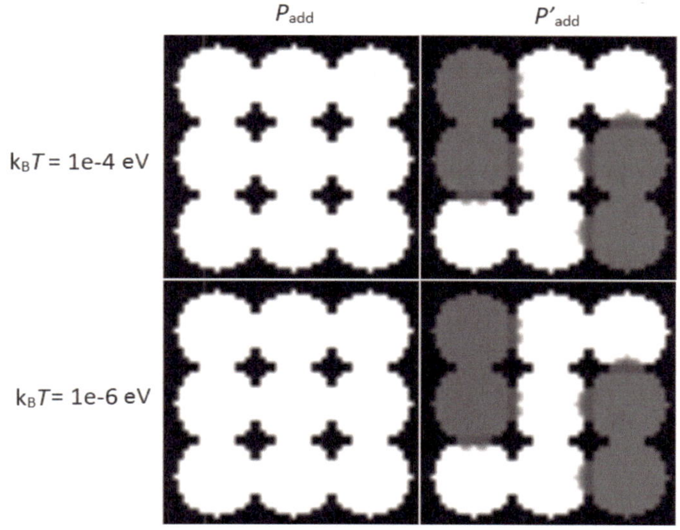

Figure 5.
Comparison of the adding probabilities for the seven-bridge system.

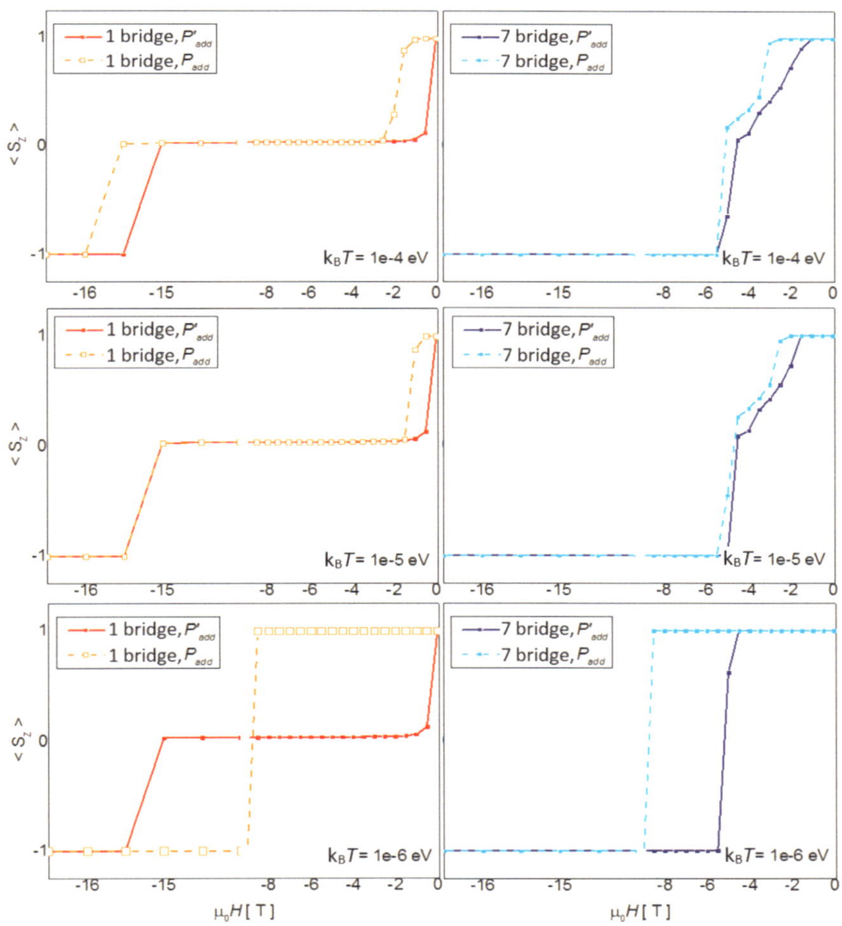

Figure 6.
Reverse magnetization curves simulated using the classical P_{add} and modified P'_{add} adding probability.

probability. However, with lower probability, the cluster contains whole spins in the system (like in the Wolff algorithm) which is related to a random value of the α parameter. The modification of adding probability causes that the configurations necessary for modeling of real magnetization processes are available during MC iterations. In other words, if magnetization processes require separate behavior of the hard and soft phase, the simulation procedure will test such a possibility.

As a final test, the so-called reverse magnetization curves were simulated using the classical as well as modified adding probability. Initially, the system was saturated in the field direction (all spins are directed up), and then the field was switched off. During calculations the field was increased in the opposite direction. Magnetization, determined as average spin value in the field direction, as a function of the external magnetic field for all examined cases is shown in **Figure 6**.

The difference between P_{add} and P'_{add} appeared in all studied examples. Note that for the one-bridge system (relatively low interactions between the hard and

Figure 7.
Spin configurations depicting the reverse magnetization process for the seven-bridge system at $k_B\,T$ = 1e–4 eV. Red and blue colors indicate the soft and hard phase, respectively.

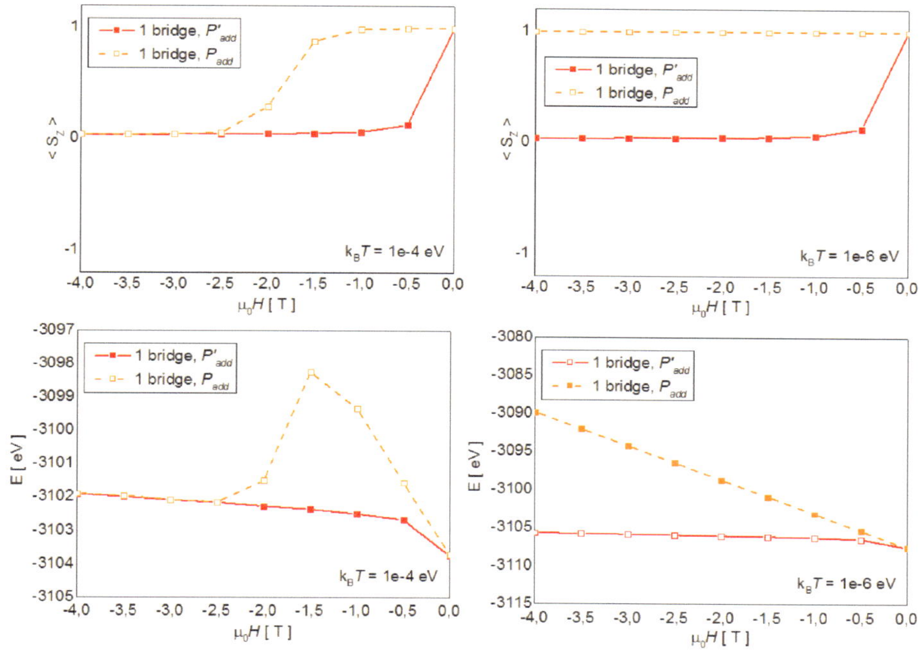

Figure 8.
Reverse magnetization curve and energy of the system in the fields related to the spin flip of the soft phase.

soft phases), the two-step reverse magnetization curve is expected. The first step is attributed to the spin flip of the soft phase, while the second one related to spin flip of the hard phase. For the seven-bridge system, the reverse magnetization is different due to stronger interphase coupling. However, at temperatures k_BT above 1e–6 eV, this process consists of a subsequent change of the "soft" spins and next, coherent flip of the "hard" spins. Such a scenario is fully confirmed by the spin configurations depicting the reverse magnetization process for the seven-bridge system at k_BT = 1e–4 eV (see **Figure** 7).

Regarding the fact that in some cases also for P_{add} the two-step behavior occurs, the main question is which curve is physically correct. For this reason, it is worth to analyze the curves in fields when the soft phase changed spin direction using P'_{add} in the cluster-building procedure. It is known that thermal equilibrium is related to a minimum of the free energy of the system. Comparing the spin configurations for the Wolff and our modified algorithm, one can state that entropy (as a thermodynamic function) is higher for the second one, i.e., applying P'_{add}, which contributes to a decreasing of the free energy. Therefore, this approach is correct for which the energy of the system is lower. **Figure 8** shows a focus of the interesting region as well as the energy of the system for the two tested algorithms. In all cases the application of P'_{add} results in "faster" (in lower fields) minimization of the system energy than the procedure based on the classical adding probability.

It is clear that the introduced modification of adding probability results in more effective finding of the free energy minimum and, therefore, produces physically reliable results which allows modeling multiphase magnetic systems.

5. Conclusions

As it was shown, in some conditions (low temperature and/or strong exchange coupling) the classical CMC algorithm can produce incorrect results in the application of multiphase magnetic systems. The problem lies in the adding probability used in the cluster-building procedures. This problem can be overcome by the proposed modification of P_{add} accompanied by the specific Metropolis-like algorithm. The key point is to recognize a property that influences the system clusterization and, next, introduction of the local information entropy of this property into the adding probability.

In summary, one can conclude that the method proposed for modeling of magnetic systems allows sampling spin configurations practically inaccessible by original Wolff clusterization procedure. An interesting future of our method is the acceleration of the energy minimization process.

Acknowledgements

This work was supported by the National Science Centre in Poland by grant no. 2015/19/B/ST8/02636 (A. Chrobak, G. Ziółkowski). D. Chrobak acknowledges support from the National Science Centre of Poland, grant no. 2016/21/B/ST8/02737.

Author details

Artur Chrobak[1]*, Grzegorz Ziółkowski[1] and Dariusz Chrobak[2]

1 Institute of Physics, University of Silesia in Katowice, Chorzów, Poland

2 Institute of Materials Science, University of Silesia in Katowice, Chorzów, Poland

*Address all correspondence to: artur.chrobak@us.edu.pl

References

[1] Chrobak A, Ziółkowski G, Randrianantoandro N. Magnetic hardening of Fe–Nb–B–Tb type of bulk nanocrystalline alloys. Journal of Alloys and Compounds. 2014;**583**:48-54

[2] Chrobak A, Zółkowski G, Randrianantoandro N, Klimontko J, Chrobak D, Prusik K, et al. Ultra-high coercivity of (Fe86xNbxB14) 0.88Tb0.12 bulk nanocrystalline magnets. Acta Materialia. 2015;**98**: 318-326

[3] Binder K, editor. The Monte Carlo Method in Condensed Matter Physics. 2nd ed. Berlin: Springer; 1995

[4] Metropolis N, Rosenbluth AW, Teller AH, Teller E. Equation of State Calculations by Fast Computing Machines. The Journal of Chemical Physics. 1953;**21**:1087

[5] Fortuin M, Kasteleyn PW. On the random-cluster model: I. Introduction and relation to other models. Physica. 1972;**57**:536

[6] Coniglio A, Klein W. Clusters and Ising critical droplets: A renormalisation group approach. Journal of Physics A. 1980;**13**:2775

[7] Swendsen RH, Wang JS. Nonuniversal critical dynamics in Monte Carlo simulations. Physical Review Letters. 1987;**58**:8688

[8] Wolff U. Collective Monte Carlo Updating for Spin Systems. Physical Review Letters. 1989;**62**:361

[9] Plascak JA, Ferrenberg AM, Landau DP. Cluster hybrid Monte Carlo simulation algorithms. Physical Review E. 2002;**65**:066702-1-066702-8

[10] Ferrenberg AM, Xu J, Landau DP. Pushing the limits of Monte Carlo simulations for the three-dimensional Ising model. Physical Review E. 2018;**97**: 043301-1-043301-12

[11] Chrobak A, Ziółkowski G, Granek K, Chrobak D. Computer Physics Communucation. 2019;**238**:157-164

[12] Binder K. Applications of Monte Carlo methods to statistical physics. Reports on Progress in Physics. 1997;**60**: 487

[13] Newman MEJ, Barkema GT. Monte Carlo Methods in Statistical Physics. New York: Oxford University Press Inc; 2001

[14] Kalos MH, Whitlock P. Monte Carlo Methods I: Basics. New York: Wiley; 1986

[15] Wood WW. Physics of Simple Liquids. Amsterdam: North-Holland; 1968

[16] Coddington PD, Baillie CF. Empirical relations between static and dynamic exponents for Ising model cluster algorithms. Physical Review Letters. 1992;**68**:962

[17] Matz R, Hunter DL, Jan N. The dynamic critical exponent of the three-dimensional Ising model. Journal of Statistical Physics. 1994;**74**:903

[18] Nightingale MP, Blote HWJ. Dynamic Exponent of the Two-Dimensional Ising Model and Monte Carlo Computation of the Subdominant Eigenvalue of the Stochastic Matrix. Physical Review Letters. 1996;**76**:4548

[19] Jaynes ET. Information Theory and Statistical Mechanics. Physics Review. 1957;**106**:620

[20] Rosenthal JS. Parallel computing and Monte Carlo algorithms. Far East Journal of Theoretical Statistics. 2000;**4**: 207-236

[21] Hallekalek P. Proceedings of the 1998 Workshop on Parallel and Distributed Simulation; Vol. 1: pp. 82-89

[22] Khan MO, Kennedy G, Derek YC, Chan J. Computers & Chemistry. 2005; **26**:72-77

[23] Campillo F, Rakotozafy R, Rossi V. Mathematics and Computers in Simulation. 2009;**79**(12):3424-3433

Section 3

Structure

Chapter 7

Utilization of Digital Twins and Other Numerical Relatives for Efficient Monte Carlo Simulation in Structural Analysis

Bernt Johan Leira, Arifian Agusta and Sebastian Thöns

Abstract

Analysis of structures will in general involve large and complex numerical models, which require extensive computation efforts. These models are frequently referred to as digital twins. This analysis becomes particularly cumbersome for cases where a large number of response calculations are repeatedly performed, such as in the case of Monte Carlo simulation. One way of avoiding this will be to introduce simplified numerical models, which are no longer twins but some kind of more distant numerical relative. As an example of such a simplified numerical representation, a so-called response surface model can be applied in order to overcome the excessive computational efforts. Such models are also sometimes referred to as meta-models or cyber-physical models. One possible approach is to use a response surface model based on first- or second-order polynomials as approximating functions, with the function parameters being determined based on multivariate regression analysis techniques. In this chapter, various types of approximate models are first discussed in connection with a simplistic example. The application of response surface techniques is subsequently illustrated for a quite complex physics-based structural model for an offshore jacket structure in combination with Monte Carlo simulation techniques.

Keywords: digital representation, structural analysis, Monte Carlo simulation, response surface techniques, structural integrity management

1. Introduction

Analysis of structures will in general involve large and complex numerical models both with respect to the loading and the structure. This typically implies extensive computational efforts. For cases where a large number of load and response calculations are repeatedly performed this becomes particularly cumbersome, such as in the case of Monte Carlo simulation. In the present paper, application of physics-based response surface methods for the purpose of reducing computation time is illustrated. In Section 2, various types of numerical approximations are first discussed in connection with a very simple structure. In Section 3 a complex offshore jacket structure is analyzed by means of response surface techniques for the loading and a physics-based "digital twin" of the structure.

IntechOpen

2. Numerical representations of physical structures

2.1 The (near to) perfect twin based on multi-physics models

In the present text, the concept of a digital twin is understood in the following sense: A digital twin is a numerical model capable of reproducing the state and behavior of a unique real asset in real time (or faster), with this model also being able to represent the performance of the asset for new and artificially generated conditions (i.e., in connection with extrapolated predictions). As a primary candidate for a digital twin, a complete numerical model based on first principles in terms of multi-physics modeling seems to be most relevant. Such a model will also be able to represent non-linear features of the structural behavior of the asset.

As an example, a relatively simple structure with pronounced non-linear behavior is considered: **Figure 1** shows a structure composed of two truss members. The structure is subjected to a vertical load R.

If the geometry is assumed to be non-deformed, the relationship between the vertical load R and the vertical displacement is obtained as:

$$R = \frac{2EA}{l}(\sin\alpha_0)^2(\cos\alpha_0)r \tag{1}$$

which for small angles can be approximated by

$$R = \frac{2EA}{l}\alpha_0^2 r \tag{2}$$

where α_0 is the slope angle of both truss members.

However, by accounting for changing geometry due to the vertical load, a different relationship between the vertical load, R, and displacement, r, is obtained. By consideration of geometric compatibility, equilibrium conditions and a linear stress-strain relationship, the expression for the load-displacement curve can then be derived as:

$$R = \frac{2EA}{l}\left(\frac{h}{r} - 1\right)\left(\frac{1}{\sqrt{l^2 + (h-r)^2}} - \frac{1}{\sqrt{l^2 + h^2}}\right)r \tag{3}$$

where h is the height of the truss and l is half the horizontal span length. E is the modulus of elasticity for the relevant material and A is the cross-section area of both truss members. The model uncertainty associated with this relationship is presently considered to be negligible, such that it can be assumed to represent a

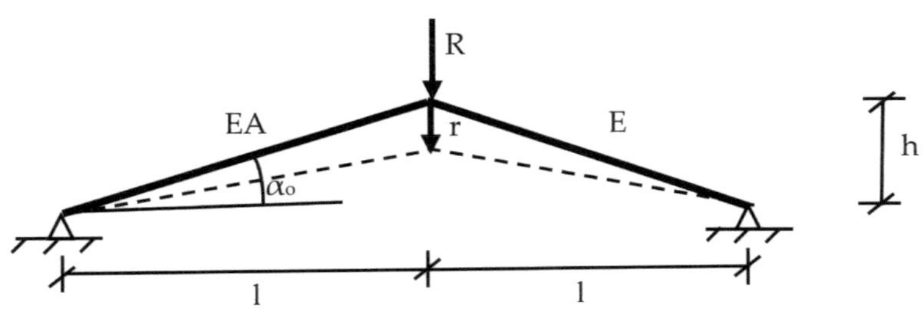

Figure 1.
Truss structure subjected to vertical load R.

"digital twin" of the structure (implying that, e.g., buckling of the members themselves is not relevant due to their non-slender characteristics).

This highly nonlinear expression in Eq. (3) can be closely approximated by a third order polynomial as follows, [1]:

$$R = \frac{2EA}{l}\alpha_0^2\left(1-\frac{r}{h}\right)\left(1-\frac{r}{2h}\right)r \tag{4}$$

By inserting $\alpha_0 = h/l$ (also assuming small angles), this can be written as

$$R = 2EA\cdot\alpha_0^3\left(1-\frac{r}{h}\right)\left(1-\frac{r}{2h}\right)\frac{r}{h} \tag{5}$$

Both of the *R*-*r* (i.e., load and displacement) relationships according to Eqs. (3) and (5) are shown in **Figure 2** for a slope angle of $\alpha_0 = \pi/15$. It is seen that they can barely be distinguished from another. (This implies that the third order representation can also be regarded as a digital twin, although not of the one-egg kind).

Both of the curves are characterized by a very non-linear behavior, where a so-called snap-through occurs when the two truss members are displaced to a completely horizontal position. After snap-through has occurred, a second equilibrium configuration is obtained for which a further increase of the vertical load can take place. However, this second equilibrium configuration will in most cases represent a "failed condition" in the sense that the structure will survive but such that an unwanted large displacement has taken place (which would, e.g., be the case if the structure represents a load-carrying roof structure or an arch system).

Up to around one quarter of the maximum load point, the load-displacement curve is quite close to being linear. Accordingly, if only empirical load-displacement data points for this interval are available, this would typically lead to the assumption that the structural behavior is linear for any load level (unless the physical behavior of the system is taken into consideration). Having available data sets for many different structures of the same type, it is very unlikely that any of the sets contain information about the post-snap interval if all the structures are still in operation.

For structures of the present type in cases where also the stress-strain behavior of the material is nonlinear, numerical solution methods will generally be required in order to compute the load-displacement curve. This will increase the computation time significantly, which will be particularly cumbersome in connection with Monte Carlo simulation procedures where a large number of repeated calculations is typically required (e.g., of the order of millions and upwards). In any case, simplified but "adequate" models need to be introduced.

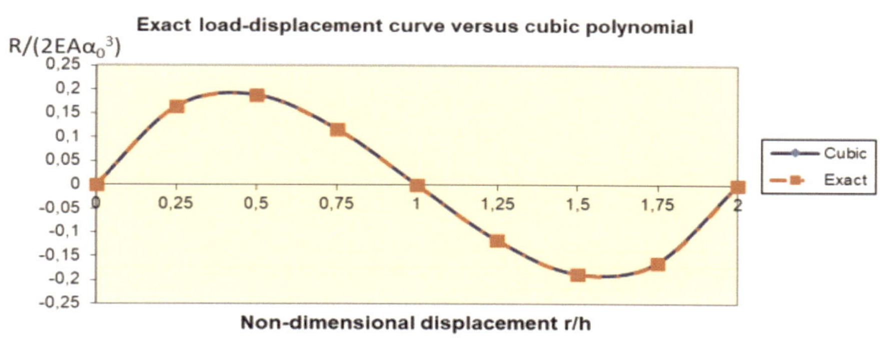

Figure 2.
Load-displacement curves according to Eqs. (3) and (5) $\alpha_0 = \pi/15$.

2.2 More distant numerical relatives based on different kinds of simplified physics-based models

One way of being able to reduce the computation time for even larger and more complex numerical models, is to introduce a simplified representation which is no longer a twin but some more distant numerical relative. As an example, a so-called response surface model can be applied in order to overcome excessive computational efforts. Such models are frequently also referred to as "meta-models" or "cyber-physical" models. One possible approach is to use a response surface representation based, e.g., on first- or second-order polynomials as approximating functions. The parameters of these functions and their weighting coefficients are then determined, e.g., based on minimization of the mean square error. The "control points" for the approximate model are then established based on application of the physics-based model at just these points (i.e., for given input parameter values). By a proper selection of control points, the prediction error associated with the entire range of structural displacement levels can be limited in magnitude.

As examples, we consider approximation of the exact load-displacement relationship with a quadratic and also an alternative quadratic response surface model. For the former, the control points are selected as (0, 0); (0.5, 3/16) and (1.0, 0.0), where 3/16 represents the exact maximum value of the cubic function (but with the location of the maximum point shifted to an abscissa value of 0.5). For the latter, a minimum mean square error approximation within the interval 0.0–1.0. The first of these approximations is compared to the "exact physics-based model" in **Figure 3**.

The error associated with the second order approximations over the range from r/h = 0 to 1 is seen to be acceptable, while for the less interesting range (within the present context) from 1 to 2 it is highly inaccurate and of little use.

2.3 Data-driven simplified models

A numerical representation of the load-displacement relationship based on a data-driven simplified model is next considered. First, it is assumed that 10 data points in the range from r/h = 0 to 0.15 are available, which is mainly in the weakly non-linear regime. These are, e.g., obtained during normal operation of the structure. A measurement noise with a standard deviation of 10% of the measured signal is also introduced. The extrapolated second order approximation (based on regression analysis) is shown in **Figure 4a** together with the data points themselves. It is seen that the maximum value of the load R is significantly underpredicted by this

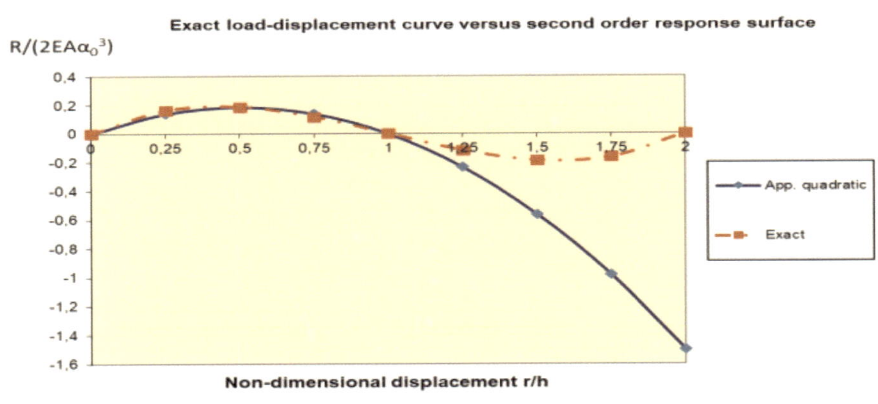

Figure 3.
Comparison of second order response surface with exact relationship.

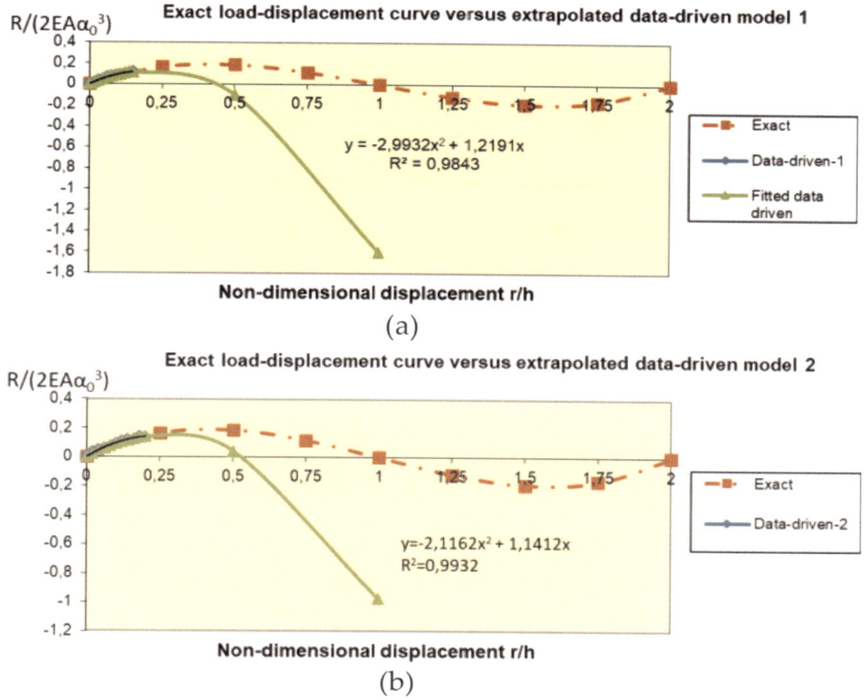

Figure 4.
Measured data points and second order approximations: (a) data range is in the interval from 0 to 0.15 r/h and (b) data range is from 0 to 0.15 r/h.

curve. As a second approximation, the 10 data points (including noise) are next taken to lie in the range from r/h = 0 to 0.2 (i.e., into the slightly more nonlinear regime). The corresponding second order approximation is shown in **Figure 4b**. The maximum load is somewhat closer to the true value, but still a significant underprediction is observed.

These results are intended to illustrate the limitations of extrapolations based on data driven models unless the measurement points are available in the region with "high nonlinearity." For structural systems, such data points are generally scarce as they represent rare events that may even correspond to failure of the structure.

2.4 Comparison of failure probabilities calculated by application of the different numerical models

By introducing a structural failure criterion for the truss in addition to joint statistical models for the inherent random variables, the failure probability corresponding to a given reference period can be computed. Presently, the failure function is expressed in terms of the maximum allowable load (i.e., R_{max}), and the only random variable is the external extreme environmental load (i.e., R_{ex}) which follows a Gumbel distribution with a mean value of 0.9 R_{max} and a coefficient of variation of 10% (i.e., a standard deviation of 0.09 R_{max}). In the present section, a comparison is made between structural failure probabilities, which are obtained by application of the different structural representations that were considered above (**Table 1**).

Not unexpectedly, the accuracy of the physics-based representations is significantly higher than the data-driven models for the present example. While the cubic response surface almost corresponds to the twin representation, the data driven

Numerical representation	Probability of failure
Exact (digital twin)	0.0719
Response surface (physics-based), quadratic	0.0719
Response surface (physics-based), MSE quadratic	0.0671
Data-driven, cubic regression, low loading	1.0000
Data-driven, cubic regression, intermediate loading	0.9102

Table 1.
Failure probabilities corresponding to different numerical representations.

model for the low loading regime could at best be referred to as a more distant relative (e.g., a half-brother or a cousin).

3. Example of a more complex structural analysis by Monte Carlo simulation

In the following, an application of a physics-based digital twin model is illustrated for the analysis and the structural integrity management optimization of a specific jacket structure, also in combination with Monte Carlo simulation techniques. The loading is represented by a response surface with the basic environmental parameters as input. The control points are based on physics-based load models. The structural response is obtained by means of a numerical model, which is able to account for large deformations and plastic behavior. This implies that the load-displacement curve is characterized by a maximum value, which is followed by a rapid decline of load-carrying ability similar to the previous simplified example.

3.1 System modeling and reliability formulation

The failure of a structural system, e.g., offshore jacket platform is often defined as the total collapse of the structure. The collapse event can be modeled as a series system of several parallel subsystems as follows [2]:

$$g_{F_S}(\dots) = \bigcup_{j=1}^{N} \bigcap_{i=1}^{n} \left(g_{F_{ij}}(\dots) \le 0\right) \tag{6}$$

where n is the number of components in the system, N is the number of failure modes, $g_{F_{ij}}(\dots)$ is the limit state function of component i for failure mode j. The system failure probability for systems like offshore jacket platforms can be accurately estimated by considering a single failure mode and expressing the system resistance R and the system load S in terms of base shear [3, 4]. The system resistance R is the ultimate capacity base shear, which is a function of system damage state's matrix **D**. The system load S is the base shear load for a given environmental variable **E**. The probability of system overload failure for a given system damage state **D** is calculated shown in Eq. (7).

$$P\left(F_{S,O}|\mathbf{D}\right) = P[R(\mathbf{D}) - L(\mathbf{E}) \le 0] \tag{7}$$

The performance of structural components in the system deteriorates over time due to, e.g., fatigue damage or corrosion. The system damage state's matrix **D** contains the (fatigue) damage state of each component at time t, i.e.,

$\mathbf{D} = [H_{F_1}(\mathbf{Y}, t), ..H_{F_i}(\mathbf{Y}, t), ..H_{F_n}(\mathbf{Y}, t)]$, where H_{F_i} is an indicator function that equals one if the component i fails (i.e., $g_{F_{ij}}(\mathbf{Y}, t) \leq 0$) and zero if otherwise. $\mathbf{Y}$ is a vector of random variables that influences the fatigue damage (see Chapter 3.2). The total probability theorem is then utilized to calculate the probability of system failure due to both overload and fatigue failures as follows:

$$P(F_S) = \int_{\mathbf{D}} P(F_S|\mathbf{D} = g_{\mathbf{F}}(\mathbf{Y}, t)) f_{\mathbf{Y}}(\mathbf{y}) d\mathbf{y} \tag{8}$$

Following [3], Eq. (8) can be approximated as follows:

$$P(F_S) \approx P\left(F_{S,O}^{intact}\right) + \sum_{i=1}^{n} P(F_i) P(F_{S,O}|F_i) + \sum_{i=1}^{n} \sum_{j=1}^{n-1} P(F_i \cap F_j) P(F_{S,O}|F_i \cap F_j) + \dots \tag{9}$$

where $P\left(F_{S,o}^{\text{intact}}\right)$ is the system failure probability due to overload in the intact condition, $P(F_i)$ is the fatigue failure probability for component i, $P(F_{S,o}|F_i)$ is the conditional system failure probability due to overload after fatigue failure occurs at component i, and $P(F_i \cap F_j)$ is the probability that fatigue failures occurs at components i and j before the overload failure. Eq. (9) is often referred as annual probability of system failure in the context of structural integrity management, where $P(F_i)$ is defined as the probability of failure at component i given survival up until year t [5]. As a first approximation, the annual probability of system failure can be calculated by keeping only the first two terms [5]:

$$P(F_S) \approx P\left(F_{S,O}^{intact}\right) + \sum_{i=1}^{n} P(F_i) P(F_{S,O}|F_i) \tag{10}$$

3.2 Response surface

The system load L is a function of environmental variable vector $\mathbf{E}$. In this work, the wave height H and wave period T are considered as the environmental random variables, i.e., $\mathbf{E} = [H, T]$. The system load L is expressed as the base shear for a given combination of wave height and wave period. The response surface method with quadratic polynomial function is utilized to estimate the system load as follows [6]:

$$L(H, T) = \mathrm{a}_0 + \mathrm{a}_1 H + \mathrm{a}_2 T + \mathrm{a}_3 H_2 + \mathrm{a}_4 T_2 + \mathrm{a}_5 HT \tag{11}$$

where $\mathrm{a}_0 \ldots \mathrm{a}_5$ are the coefficients to be determined. Probabilistic linear regression analysis is employed to obtain the coefficients and the predictive distribution of the system load L. The linear model is written as follows:

$$L = X\beta + \varepsilon \tag{12}$$

where $\boldsymbol{L}$ is a $(1 \times \mathbf{m})$ vector of "responses" (i.e., which here is the load), $\boldsymbol{\beta}$ is a $(1 \times \mathbf{m})$ vector of the regression coefficients (see Eq. (11)), and $\boldsymbol{\varepsilon}$ is the $1 \times \mathbf{m}$ vector containing the error terms. The error is assumed Normal-distributed with zero expected value and variance σ_e^2. $\boldsymbol{X}$ is a $\mathbf{m} \times p$ design matrix which consists of p combinations of individual terms (see Eq. (11)) and m number of samples as follows:

$$X = \begin{bmatrix} 1 & H_1 & T_1 & H_1^2 & T_1^2 & H_1T_1 \\ 1 & H_2 & T_2 & H_2^2 & T_2^2 & H_2T_2 \\ . & & & & & \\ . & & & & & \\ 1 & H_m & T_m & H_m^2 & T_m^2 & H_mT_m. \end{bmatrix} \tag{13}$$

The unconditional predictive distribution is given by the multivariate non-central Students t-distribution i.e., $\tilde{L}|\hat{L} \sim t_{m-p}(E[\tilde{L}|\hat{L}], COV[\tilde{L}|\hat{L}])$ with parameters as given as follows [7]:

$$E[\tilde{L}|\hat{L}] = \tilde{\mathbf{X}}E[\beta] \tag{14}$$

$$COV[\tilde{\mathbf{L}}|\hat{\mathbf{L}}] = \hat{\sigma}_e^2\left(\tilde{\mathbf{X}}\left(\hat{\mathbf{X}}^T\hat{\mathbf{X}}\right)^{-1}\tilde{\mathbf{X}}^T + \mathbf{I}\right) \tag{15}$$

$$E[\boldsymbol{\beta}] = \left(\hat{\mathbf{X}}^T\hat{\mathbf{X}}\right)^{-1}\hat{\mathbf{X}}^T\hat{L} \tag{16}$$

$$\hat{\sigma}_e = \frac{1}{m-r}\left(\hat{\mathbf{L}} - \hat{\mathbf{X}}E[\boldsymbol{\beta}]\right)^T\left(\hat{\mathbf{L}} - \hat{\mathbf{X}}E[\boldsymbol{\beta}]\right) \quad \text{and} \quad r = rank\left(\hat{\mathbf{X}}\right) \tag{17}$$

$\hat{\mathbf{X}}$ and $\hat{\mathbf{L}}$ are matrices that contain the pre-computed load points from, e.g., finite element analysis. $\tilde{\mathbf{L}}$ is a vector of load predictions from regression analysis for given $\tilde{\mathbf{X}}$, which is calculated, e.g., from the samples of wave height and wave period. The predictive distribution of the load, $p(\tilde{\mathbf{L}}|\hat{\mathbf{L}})$, can be seen as a measure of the model uncertainty associated with the response surface.

The wave height is assumed to be Weibull distribution. A special type of a conditional Weibull distribution proposed by Forristal is utilized and written as follows [8, 9]:

$$F_{H|H_s}(h|h_s) = 1 - \exp\left(-2.263\left(\frac{h}{h_s}\right)^{2.126}\right) \tag{18}$$

where h_s is the significant wave height. Probabilistic models for the wave period are less studied compared to wave height. In the present work, the wave period is assumed to follow a Lognormal distribution, which is conditional on wave height, and the parameters are defined as follows:

$$\mu_T(H) = E[\ln T] = b_1 + b_2(0.5H)^{b_3} \tag{19}$$

$$\sigma_T(H) = Std[\ln T] = c_1 + c_2\exp(0.5H \cdot c_3) \tag{20}$$

where b_1; b_2; b_3 and c_1; c_2; c_3 are the coefficients to be determined. Eqs. (19) and (20) ensure that the wave period is dependent on the wave height in order to avoid drawing unrealistic samples of wave height and period (e.g., very large wave heights with very small wave periods).

3.3 Structural fatigue and reliability updating with monitoring and inspection information

Fatigue failure occurs if the crack size exceeds a critical crack size, and this can be modeled by means of a limit state function as follows:

$$g_{F_i}(\mathbf{Y}, t) = \delta_c - \delta(\mathbf{Y}, t) \tag{21}$$

where δ_c is the critical crack size and $\delta(\mathbf{Y},t)$ is the crack size at time t. Here, failure of the structure will occur if this failure function becomes negative. The crack growth is modeled using Paris' Law as follows:

$$d\delta(N_s)/dN_s = \mathrm{C}(\Delta\mathrm{K})^{\mathrm{m}} \tag{22}$$

where m and C are the empirical model parameters, N_s is the number of stress cycles, and ΔK is the stress range intensity factor. For through-thickness cracks on an infinite panel, the solution to Eq. (22) can be written as follows [10]:

$$\delta(\mathbf{Y}, t) = \left(\delta_0^{1-\frac{m}{2}} + \left(1 - \frac{m}{2}\right) C \left(B_{SIF} B_{\Delta S} \Delta S_e \sqrt{\pi}\right)^m \nu t\right)^{\frac{1}{1-\frac{m}{2}}} \tag{23}$$

where δ_0 is the initial crack size, and ν is the annual cycle rate. B_{SIF} and $B_{\Delta S}$ are the model uncertainties of the stress intensity factor and for the stress range calculation, respectively (see e.g., [11]). ΔS_e is the so-called equivalent stress range and calculated as follows:

$$\Delta S_e = \gamma \left[\Gamma\left(1 + \frac{m}{\lambda}\right)\right]^{\frac{1}{m}} \tag{24}$$

$\mathbf{Y}$ is a vector of random variables i.e., $\mathbf{Y} = [\delta_0; C; B_{SIF}; B_{\Delta S}; \ln\gamma; \lambda]$, where γ and λ is the scale and shape parameter of the Weibull distributed stress range. The probability of fatigue failure is calculated as follows:

$$P(F_i(t)) = \int_{g_{Fi}(\mathbf{Y},\, t) \le 0} f_{\mathbf{Y}}(\mathbf{y}) d\mathbf{y} \tag{25}$$

$P(F_i(t))$ is defined as the probability of annual fatigue failure given survival up until year t. Statistical dependencies between fatigue hotspots are modeled using correlation coefficients of the random variables in the $\mathbf{Y}$ vector. There are 6 correlation coefficients: $\rho_{\delta_0}; \rho_C; \rho_{B_{SIF}}; \rho_{B_{\Delta S}}; \rho_\gamma; \rho_\lambda$. The coefficient ρ_{δ_0} represents the statistical dependencies due to the same fabrication process. ρ_C indicates the dependencies due to common material characteristics. ρ_γ and ρ_λ describe the statistical dependencies due to the similar loading patterns. $\rho_{B_{SIF}}$ and $\rho_{B_{\Delta S}}$ depict the dependencies due to common stress intensity factor and stress range calculation.

Probabilistic models that are able to represent inspection activities in a proper way are also required. Information regarding structural performance can be obtained by carrying out inspection or structural monitoring. There are two outcomes of an inspection: no damage indication (I_1) or damage indication (I_2). The objective of inspection modeling is to obtain the marginal probability of indication (and no indication) followed by an update of the probability of system failure. By utilizing detection theory, the probability of an indication can be derived from the noise and signal distributions (see e.g., [9, 12]). Signal and noise characteristics are typically modeled by means of a Normal distribution (see e.g., [9, 13]). The updating of component fatigue failure probability is performed by utilizing Bayes' law. Given no indication after an inspection, the probability of fatigue failure is updated as given in [14].

Furthermore, models for statistical representation of the structural monitoring methods are required. Structural health monitoring (SHM) systems can be installed to monitor specific structural properties such as, e.g., vibration or strain in the structural system. Information from a SHM can be viewed as one of the possible realizations of the model uncertainty (see e.g., [15, 16]), which is associated with the measured property such as, e.g., stress ranges. In the present work, the SHM modeling proposed by [17] is employed, i.e., three different possible SHM outcomes are considered: The outcome Z_1 corresponds to the case where monitoring indicates lower stress ranges than expected and indicates that the monitored component has a high performance. Outcome Z_3 indicates that the monitoring component has a low performance due to higher than expected stress ranges. Outcome Z_2 indicates that the monitored component performs as expected. Calculation of the updated probability of system failure is carried out as described in [14].

3.4 Quantification of the value of SIM strategies

The quantification of the value of SIM strategies builds upon the Bayesian pre-posterior decision analysis framework as formulated by Benjamin and Cornell, [18]. A SIM strategy decision problem can be modeled by a decision tree in pre-posterior form as shown in **Figure 5**. The information space S consists of available information acquirement strategies i (e.g., inspection and monitoring). The outcome space O comprises the possible outcomes of a given information acquirement strategy i. The action space A consists of the possible actions that can be taken such as e.g. repair. The state space θ contains possible states such as, e.g., failure or survival.

The value of SIM strategies is quantified by utilizing the value of information and action (VOIA) analysis (see [19]). A VOIA analysis consists of a base and an enhancement scenario. The base scenario is defined as the scenario without any SHM/inspection and risk-mitigating action such as e.g., repair. There are two states considered in this system state analysis: the (collapse/no collapse) and the component state (failure/no failure). Therefore, the expected cost C_0 in the base scenario is the sum of the expected system $E[C_{FS}]$ and component $E[C_{F,i}]$ failure costs over the service life T_{SL}:

$$C_0 = \left(\sum_{i-1}^{n} E\left[C_{F,i}\right] \right) + E[C_{F_S}] \tag{26}$$

where n is the number of structural components. Procedures for calculation of $E[C_{FS}]$ and $E[C_{F,i}]$ are described in [14]. The failure probabilities, which are required in order to calculate these costs, are computed by means of Monte Carlo simulation.

Two different SIM strategies are analyzed as enhancement scenarios. The first strategy is to perform inspections and repair if required during the service life. The second strategy is to install the SHM system for 1 year at one component and to perform inspections and repair if required. For both strategies, a repair action is performed if the inspection indicates a damage. The expected total cost of the first strategy is calculated as the sum of expected costs of inspection $E[C_i]$, repair $E[C_{R,i}]$, system failure $E[C_{FS}]$, and fatigue failure $E[C_{F,i}]$ costs over the service life as follows:

$$C(S_1, A) = \left(\sum_{i-1}^{N_{IC}} E\left[C_{I,i}\right] + E\left[C_{R,i}\right] \right) + \left(\sum_{i-1}^{n} E\left[C_{F,i}\right] \right) + E[C_{F_S}] \tag{27}$$

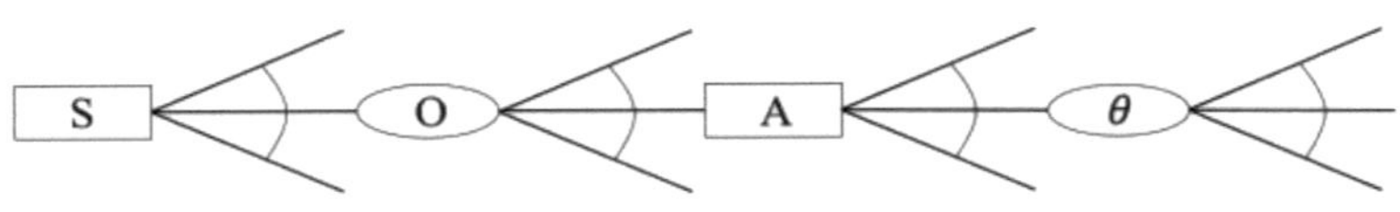

Figure 5.
Illustration of a decision tree with rectangular modeling decision and ellipses for chance nodes.

where N_{IC} is the number of inspected components. $E[C_{FS}]$ and $E[C_{F,i}]$ in Eq. (27) are calculated by considering the updated probability of system and fatigue failure, respectively. $E[C_{R,i}]$ is the expected repair costs over the service with N_{IC} repaired components.

The expected total costs for the second strategy is calculated as follows:

$$C(S_2, A) = E_Z\left[\left(\sum_{i-1}^{N_{IC}} E[C_{I,i}] + E[C_{R,i}]\right) + E[C_{SHM}] + \left(\sum_{i-1}^{n} E[C_{F,i}]\right) + E[C_{F_S}]\right] \tag{28}$$

where $E[C_{SHM}]$ is the expected SHM costs. Further details are given in [14]. The VOIA is then calculated as follows:

$$VOIA = \max_{S,A} C(\mathbf{S}, \mathbf{A}) - C_0 \tag{29}$$

3.5 Case study

A typical deepwater offshore jacket platform with 25 years of service life and located at 190 m waterdepth is utilized in the present work (see **Figure 6a**). The jacket platform has 200 components and each component is subjected to fatigue deterioration. In this study, each component is assumed to have exactly one hotspot for which a trough-thickness crack will result in fatigue failure. The incoming wave direction is taken as 135° and the 100-year significant wave height $H_{S;100y}$ equals to 24.3 m.

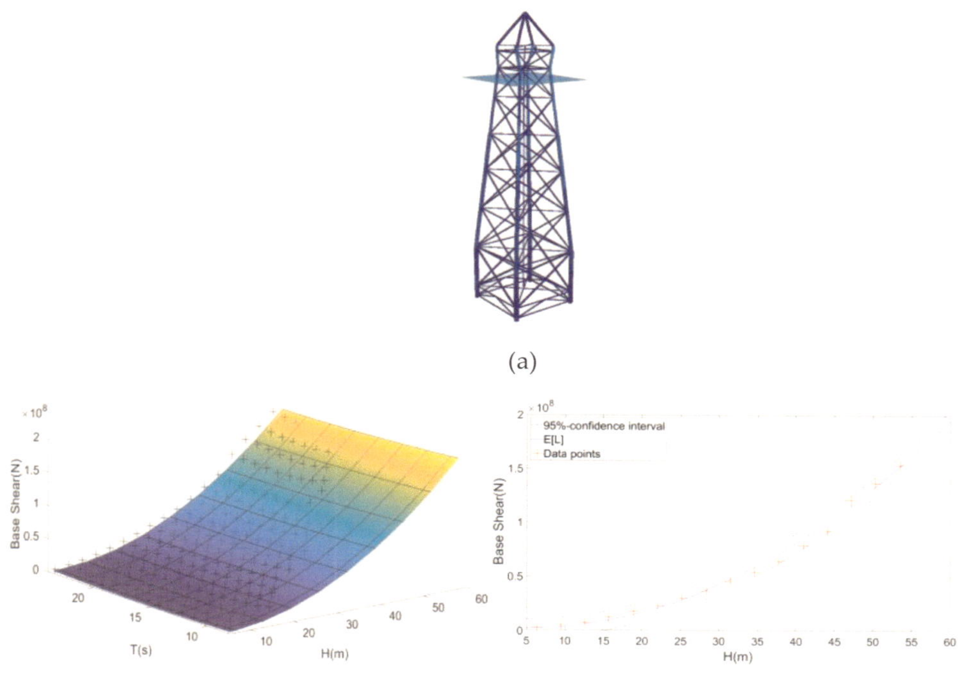

Figure 6.
(a) Deepwater finite element jacket model used in the case study. (b) The response surface of L with the black crosses signify the training data set. (c) The expected value of the load prediction (blue line) with 95%-confidence interval (black lines) for T = 20.8 s.

System failure is defined as the collapse of the jacket platform due to overload and fatigue deterioration. In this example, it is assumed that only single component failure is possible before the overload failure and the probability of system failure is calculated by Eq. (10). The resistance R is the ultimate base shear for given damage state matrix **D** and is calculated by performing pushover analysis with software USFOS [20]. The system load L is approximated by utilizing response surface analysis outlined in Section 3.2 with 248 pre-computed load points. The samples of L are drawn from the predictive distribution for a given H and T. The coefficients in Eq. (19) and (20) are assumed to have the following values (based on a typical North Sea environment): **b** = [1.322; 0.8; 0.242] and **c** = [0.005; 0.09374; 0.32]. The conditional probability of system collapse (see Eq. (7)) is calculated by utilizing Monte Carlo simulation with 10^6 samples. The response surface of the system load L is shown in **Figure 6b** with the coefficient of determination $R^2 = 0.9905$. **Figure 6c** shows the predictive distribution of L for T = 20.8 s.

The system failure probability in intact condition is 5E−6. The conditional system failure probabilities for different damaged components and its associated ultimate base shears are given in **Table 2**. The components in **Table 2** are located on the jacket's legs.

3.5.1 Fatigue model

All components are subjected to fatigue deterioration over the service life with one critical hotspot for each component. The contributions from the fatigue failure probabilities to the system failure are weighted w.r.t. the conditional system failure probabilities. Due to the high number of structural components, only the 10 most critical components with the highest conditional system failure probabilities (see **Table 2**) are presently considered. Fatigue failure contributions from other components are considerably smaller and can hence be neglected. Fatigue failure probability at time t is calculated by application of Monte Carlo simulation. The probability is calculated for a period of 1 year, where survival until year t is given. All fatigue hotspots are modeled with the same probabilistic models, which are shown in **Table 3**. $B_{\Delta S}$ and B_{SIF} are assumed fully correlated between components following [21]. The other random variables are assumed to have a correlation coefficient of 0.8 [21].

Damaged component	Ultimate base shear (N)	$P(F_{S,O}\|D)$
All intact	1.51E+08	5.00E−06
10035	7.05E+07	3.54E−03
10037	7.19E+07	3.16E−03
10038	7.42E+07	2.63E−03
10013	7.98E+07	1.67E−03
10036	8.61E+07	1.01E−03
10039	8.68E+07	9.60E−04
10014	8.71E+07	9.37E−04
10015	8.99E+07	7.55E−04
10016	1.03E+08	2.93E−04
10024	1.06E+08	1.90E−04

Table 2.
Ten highest conditional probabilities of system failure.

Variable	Dimension	Distribution	Expected value	St. deviation
TSL	year	—	25	—
δ_0	mm	Exponential	0.11	—
δ_C	mm	—	8	—
lnC	N and mm	Normal	−29.97	0.5095
m	—	—	3.0	—
B_{SIF}	—	Lognormal	1.0	0.1
$B_{\Delta S}$	—	Lognormal	1.0	0.2
lnγ	N and mm	Normal	2.1	0.22
λ	—	Normal	0.8	0.08
ν	1/year	—	10^7	—

Table 3.
Summary of the random variables for fatigue modeling.

3.5.2 Structural integrity management (SIM)

Two SIM strategies are considered: inspection and repair and inspection with SHM and repair. For the first strategy, inspections are performed at 3 critical components 1 year before the annual system failure probability $P(F_S)$ is estimated to exceed the threshold $P_{th}(F_S)$ (i.e., constant threshold approach). The minimum system failure probability threshold during operation is set equal to 10^{-4} which corresponds to target system failure probability recommended by JCSS [15] for structures with large consequences of failure and large relative cost of safety measure.

In order to simplify the decision analysis, a repair action is performed only if any damage is detected by inspections. This decision rule is practical and VoI-optimal, see [22]. Repaired components are assumed to behave as components with no damage indication. The probability of indication is derived from the noise and signal distributions. The noise S_R is assumed to follow a Normal distribution with zero mean and a standard deviation of 0.5. The signal threshold t_{hs} is calibrated to the probability of false indication (PFI) of 0.01. The signal S is also Normal distributed with the following parameters:

$$\mu_S(t) = 0.8 + 0.1 \cdot \delta(t), \quad \sigma_S(t) = 0.3 - 0.01 \cdot \delta(t) \tag{30}$$

where δ(t) is the crack size at year t.

In the second SIM strategy, a SHM system for stress range monitoring is installed 1 year before the first inspection is performed, with a monitoring duration of 1 year (i.e., up to the time of the inspection itself). SHM performance is modeled as proposed in [17] by utilizing the stress range model uncertainty $B_{\Delta S}$. Two thresholds distinguishing the outcomes Z_1 (low stress ranges), Z_2 (stress ranges as designed) and Z_3 (high stress ranges) are calibrated to target probabilities of $P_1^T(F_i) = 1{\cdot}10^{-4}$ and $P_2^T(F_i) = 1{\cdot}10^{-3}$, respectively. The target reliabilities are selected following [13] for structures with minor consequences of failure with normal and large relative cost of safety measure. The time dependent threshold's calibration is illustrated by **Figure 7**. The measurement uncertainty U is assumed Normal distributed with the expected value of 1.0 and a standard deviation of 0.05. A summary of the probabilistic models is shown in **Table 4**.

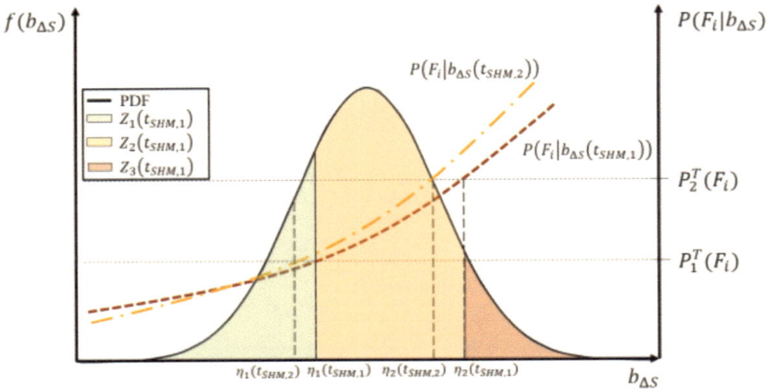

Figure 7.
Illustration of thresholds calibration for two different SHM installation times for SHM modeling. η_1 and η_2 are the thresholds of stress range model uncertainty $B_{\Delta S}$ associated with $P_1^T(F_i)$ and $P_2^T(F_i)$, respectively. The integration of the colored regions results in the probabilities of (Z_1, Z_2, and Z_3), which are modeled as three indication events.

Variable	Dimension	Distribution	Expected value	Std. deviation
S_R	—	Normal	0	0.5
S	—	Normal	$\mu_S(t)$	$\sigma_S(t)$
PFI	—	—	0.01	—
$P_1^T(F_i)$	—	—	$5\cdot10^{-4}$	—
$P_2^T(F_i)$	—	—	$5\cdot10^{-3}$	—
U	—	Normal	1.0	0.05

Table 4.
Summary of the random variables for inspection and SHM modeling.

The costs considered in this case study are consisting of inspection costs C_I, SHM costs C_{SHM}, repair costs C_R, system failure costs C_{FS}, and component failure costs C_{Fi}. SHM costs are further divided into investment costs $C_{Inv}{}^{SHM}$, installation costs $C_{Inst}{}^{SHM}$, and operational costs $C_{op}{}^{SHM}$. The cost model used in this example is shown in **Table 5** based on [23, 24].

3.5.3 Results

The annual component and system failure for t = 1....25 years are shown in **Figure 8**. The system failure probability for the intact condition is $P(F_{S,O}|D = 0) = 5E-6$. The annual system failure probability at the end of service life is 9.5E−5, which is less than the minimum operational threshold, i.e., no SIM implementations are required to achieve the minimum operational requirement. However, the decision-maker may wish to increase the structural reliability above the minimum requirement and presumably enhance the value of SIM. In this work, three different annual system failure probability thresholds are studied: 6E−5, 7E−5, and 8E−5.

For the inspection-only strategy ($S = S_1$), inspections and repairs are performed at three components 1 year before the system failure probability threshold $P_{th}(F_S)$ is predicted to be reached. After each inspection, probabilities of fatigue and system failure are updated. **Figure 9a** shows the annual system failure probability for the inspection-only strategy as a function of time for a specific threshold value.

DOI: http://dx.doi.org/10.5772/intechopen.89144

Type	Cost
C_I	0.001
C_{Inv}^{SHM}	$1.33{\cdot}10^{-4}$/channel
C_{Inst}^{SHM}	$1.33{\cdot}10^{-4}$/channel
C_{op}^{SHM}	$2{\cdot}10^{-4}$/year
C_R	0.01
$C_{F,i}$	1
C_{FS}	100

Table 5.
Cost models used in the case study.

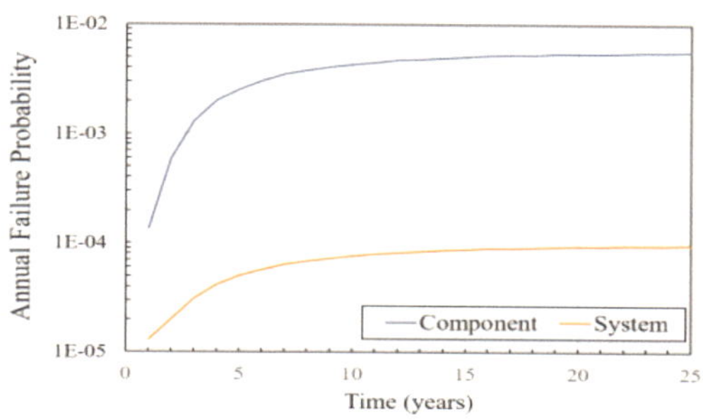

Figure 8.
Annual component and system failure probability over the service life.

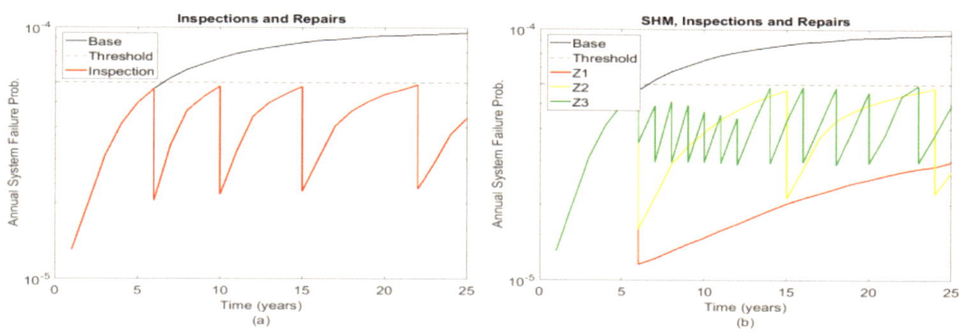

Figure 9.
(a) Annual system failure probability with inspections and repairs for one specific threshold, $P_{th}(FS)$ = 6E−5. (b) Annual system failure probability with SHM, inspections and repairs for one specific threshold, $P_{th}(FS)$ = 6E−5. The inspections and repairs are performed at three components while monitoring is performed at one component.

The first inspection time is at t = 8 years. Increasing the threshold means that the inspections are performed later during the service life. Because of this, the inspection frequency during the service life is decreasing with a higher threshold in exchange of a higher annual system failure probability.

The second SIM strategy ($S = S_2$) is based on installation of a SHM system at one component to monitor stress ranges for 1 year before the first inspection. There are three possible outcomes for monitoring based on the component performance. **Figure 9b** shows the annual system failure probability with monitoring and inspections for a system failure probability threshold of 6E-5. Compared to **Figure 9a,** it is observed that the outcome of monitoring can influence the future inspection

SHM outcome	Annual system failure probability threshold		
	6.00E-05 t_{SHM} = 6 years	7.00E-05 t_{SHM} = 8 years	8.00E-05 t_{SHM} = 11 years
High performance (Z_1)	0.175	0.0991	0.0497
As-expected performance (Z_2)	0.553	0.5036	0.4084
Low performance (Z_3)	0.272	0.3973	0.5419

t_{SHM} is SHM installation time for a given annual system failure probability threshold.

Table 6.
The probability of SHM outcomes for different annual system probability thresholds.

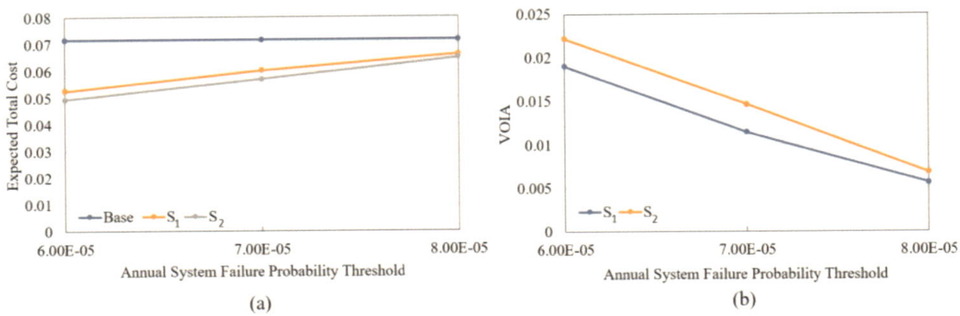

Figure 10.
(a) Expected total costs for base scenario, inspection and repairs strategy (S_1), and SHM, inspections, and repairs (S_3). (b) Value of information and action based on SIM strategies for different annual system failure probability thresholds.

schedule. The SHM installation time differs depending on the thresholds (see **Table 6**). A higher threshold means that the SHM system is installed closer to the end of service life. With increasing annual system failure probability threshold, the probability of obtaining low performance outcome (Z_3) becomes higher.

The values of information and action (VOIA) of the two SIM strategies are shown in **Figure 10**. It is observed that increasing the system failure probability threshold will reduce the value of information and action. With a higher threshold, inspection and monitoring are performed later in the service life, which reduces the benefits due to a higher annual system failure probability during the remaining service life compared to a lower system failure probability threshold. It is also observed that the VOIA of the SIM strategy SHM, inspection and repair (S_2) is higher than the inspection-only strategy (S_1) for all investigated system failure probability thresholds. This shows that information from SHM system can enhance the value of the SIM, i.e., reduce the expected total cost. In this example, the cost of system failure is dominating the expected total cost over the service life.

4. Summary and conclusions

In the present analysis, physics-based numerical models of the load, structural behavior and for the integrity management have been utilized in combination with response surface techniques and Monte Carlo simulation. An application of a physics-based digital twin model is illustrated for the structural and integrity management analysis of a specific jacket structure. The loading is represented by a response surface with the basic environmental parameters as input. The control points are based on physics-based load models. The structural response is obtained by means of a numerical model, which is able to account for large deformations and plastic behavior.

A framework has been developed to plan and to optimize the structural integrity management (SIM) by utilizing the physics-based digital twin model. By extending the concept of the value of information to a value of information and action analysis, the value of inspection and monitoring information and repair actions is quantified. A novel approach of SHM modeling introduced by Agusta and Thöns [17] has been employed in conjunction with inspection modeling based on a probabilistic representation of inspections. The optimal SIM strategy leading to the least expected costs and structural risks is associated to the lowest annual system failure probability threshold. It is further demonstrated that structural systems with a high reliability requirement will benefit more from a SHM system implementation.

It is believed that for the present type of analysis, which involves large structural deformations and structural failure behavior, data-driven models will not be adequate due to an insufficient amount of relevant data. Clearly, this belief is also based on the assumption that the model uncertainties associated with the physics-based numerical models can be adequately controlled. This can be achieved by collecting data from laboratory (destructive) testing and full-scale measurements including failure records. In this way, data-calibrated and physics-based numerical models can be developed, rather than relying on data-driven models based on conditions corresponding to normal operation of the structures.

Acknowledgements

The authors acknowledge the funding received from the Center for Oil and Gas-DTU/Danish Hydrocarbon Research and Technology Center (DHRTC). The authors are also grateful to Professor Jørgen Amdahl for his support regarding the Finite element analysis with USFOS.

Conflict of interest

There is no conflict of interest.

Author details

Bernt Johan Leira[1*], Arifian Agusta[2] and Sebastian Thöns[2,3]

1 Department of Marine Technology, NTNU, Trondheim, Norway

2 Department of Civil Engineering, DTU, Lyngby, Denmark

3 Department for Safety of Structures, BAM Federal Institute for Materials Research and Testing, Berlin, Germany

*Address all correspondence to: bernt.leira@ntnu.no

References

[1] Krenk S, Høgsberg J. Statics and Mechanics of Structures. Dordrecht: Springer; 2013

[2] Madsen HO, Krenk S, Lind NC. Methods of Structural Safety. Mineola, NY: Dover Publications; 2006

[3] Moan T. Reliability-based management of inspection, maintenance and repair of offshore structures. Structure and Infrastructure Engineering. 2005;**1**(1):33-62

[4] Wu Y, Moan T. A structural system reliability analysis of jacket using an improved truss model. In: Proceedings of the 5th ICOSSAR. San Francisco: ASCE; 1989. pp. 887-894

[5] HSE. Target Levels for Reliability-Based Assessment of Offshore Structures during Design and Operation. London: Offshore Technology Rep; 2002

[6] Bucher C, Bourgund U. A fast and efficient response surface approach for structural reliability problems. Structural Safety. 1990;**7**:57-66

[7] Thöns S, Faber M, Rücker W. Support structure reliability of offshore wind turbines utilizing an adaptive response surface method. In: Proceedings of the 29th OMAE; ASME. 2010. pp. 407-416

[8] Forristal G. On the statistical distribution of wave heights in a storm. Journal of Geophysical Research. 1978; **83**(C5):2353-2358

[9] Gandossi L, Annis C. Probability of Detection Curves: Statistical Best-Practices. Luxembourg: Publications Office of the European Union; 2010

[10] Ditlevsen O, Madsen HO. Structural Reliability Method. Chichester: John Wiley and Sons Ltd.; 1996

[11] Folsø R, Otto S, Parmentier G. Reliability-based calibration of fatigue design guidelines for ship structures. Marine Structures. 2002;**15**(6):627-651

[12] Kay SM. Fundamentals of Statistical Signal Processing: Detection Theory. New Jersey: Prentice Hall; 1998

[13] Schoefs F, Clément A, Nouy A. Assessment of roc curves for inspection of random fields. Structural Safety. 2009;**31**(5):409-419

[14] Agusta A, Leira BJ, Thöns S. Value of information-based structural integrity management. Journal of Structural Integrity and Maintenance. 2019

[15] JCSS. Probabilistic Model Code. JCSS Joint Committe on Structural Safety; 2006

[16] Thöns S. On the value of monitoring information for the structural integrity and risk management. Computer-Aided Civil and Infrastructure Engineering. 2018;**33**(1):79-94. DOI: 10.1111/mice.12332

[17] Agusta A, Thöns S. Structural monitoring and inspection modeling for structural system updating. In: Proceedings of the 6th International Symposium on Life-Cycle Civil Engineering IALCCE. CRC Press; 2018

[18] Benjamin JR, Cornell CA. Probability, Statistics and Decision for Civil Engineers. New York: McGraw-Hill; 1970. ISBN: 070045496

[19] Thöns S, Kapoor M. Value of information and value of decisions. In: Proceedings of the 13th International Conference on Applications of Statistics and Probability in Civil Engineering. CRC; 2019

[20] Søreide TH, Amdahl J, Holmås T, Hellan Ø. USFOS—A computer

program for progressive collapse analysis of steel offshore structures. In: Theory Manual (Report STF71 F88038); 1993. Retrieved from: http://www.usfos.no/manuals/usfos/theory/documents/Usfos_Theory_Manual.pdf

[21] Schneider R, Thöns S, Rücker W, Straub D. Effect of different inspection strategies on the reliability of Daniels systems subjected to fatigue. In: Safety, Reliability, Risk and Life-Cycle Performance of Structures and Infrastructures. Proceedings of the 11th International Conference on Structural Safety and Reliability, ICOSSAR 2013. CRC Press/Balkema; 2013. pp. 2637-2644

[22] Agusta A, Thöns S, Leira B. Value of information-based inspection planning for offshore structures. In: Proceedings of the 36th OMAE, ASME; 2017

[23] Thöns S, Faber M, Rücker W. Optimal design of monitoring systems for risk reduction and operation benefits. SRESA's International Journal of Life Cycle Reliability and Safety Engineering. 2014;**3**:1-10

[24] Thöns S, Schneider R, Faber M. Quantification of the value of structural health monitoring information for fatigue deteriorating structural systems. In: Proceedings of 12th International Conference on Applications of Statistics and Probability in Civil Engineering. CRC Press; 2015